WITHDRAWN

ADVANCES IN
SERIALS MANAGEMENT

Volume 1 • 1986

ADVANCES IN
SERIALS MANAGEMENT

A Research Annual

Editors: **MARCIA TUTTLE**
Head, Serials Department
University of North Carolina
Chapel Hill

JEAN G. COOK
Head, Serials Department
Iowa State University Library

VOLUME 1 · 1986

 JAI PRESS INC.

Greenwich, Connecticut   *London, England*

CONTENTS

LIST OF CONTRIBUTORS

Ruth C. Carter

Assistant Director for Technical
    Services
University of Pittsburgh Libraries

Jean G. Cook

Head, Serials Department
Iowa State University Libraries

Jan Derthick

Serials Acquisitions Librarian
University of New Mexico
    Library

Joline R. Ezzell

Head, Serials Department
Duke University Library

Mary Ellen L. Jacob

Vice President for Library
    Planning at OCLC

Barbara B. Moran

School of Library Science
University of North Carolina at
    Chapel Hill

Ann Okerson

Head, Library Serials Division
Simon Fraser University
British Columbia

Marcia Tuttle

Head, Serials Department
University of North Carolina at
    Chapel Hill

PREFACE

The significance of the serial as a form of communication has increased in the 1980s, not only in scientific disciplines, but also in the social sciences, the humanities, and nonscholarly fields such as hobbies and personal computing. In light of the growing recognition of the place of serials in today's research and leisure environment, it is appropriate that an annual publication be devoted to librarians' work with these materials.

The purpose of *Advances in Serials Management* is to monitor and publicize trends in acquiring, processing, and making available library materials issued in serials format. The editors' objectives are to survey and document the past, to present today's issues, and to take a speculative look into the future of our profession. The scope of this series is the serials publishing and distribution industry and the library functions that would comprise a completely integrated serials department. The editors intend to publish substantial articles that enable serials librarians to understand what is happening in our professional world—what we need to know, what changes are occurring (or should occur), what we need to do to prepare for the future. We expect to publish the work of new serials librarians as well as that of persons known in the profession. A further objective is to present occasional articles by serials librarians, publishers, and vendors working outside the United States.

In this first volume we offer an important research study of criteria used in vendor selection by serials acquisitions librarians at Association of Research Libraries member institutions. The study investigates the impact of and opportunities provided by changes in the economy and in automation. On the occasion of the tenth anniversary of the CONSER Project, the OCLC officer responsible for CONSER reflects on the relationship of the bibliographic utility to this ambitious and highly successful cooperative endeavor. Three articles on the topic of organization for library serials management review the trends of the last fifty years and examine today's fluid situation, with the opportunities provided by automation of library functions. The final article studies the broad topic of serial prices including price indexes, serials publishing, marketing devices, and librarians' responses to a tightening economic situation.

The final section of the book is an annotated bibliography of recent literature on serials management, an update of the bibliography in Marcia Tuttle's *Introduction to Serials Management* (JAI Press, 1983). The quantity of publications on serials and serials librarianship documents the growing recognition of serials as a means of communication. Where the original bibliography contained 649 entries of primary and secondary works covering generally 12–15 years, this supplement lists 625 works, entirely secondary.

The editors welcome your comments and recommendations about this first volume of *Advances in Serials Management*. They will give thoughtful consideration to presenting in future volumes articles on topics that readers suggest.

Marcia Tuttle
Jean G. Cook
Series Editors

SERIAL AGENT SELECTION IN ARL LIBRARIES

Jan Derthick and Barbara B. Moran

A survey conducted by Katz and Gellatly in 1975 showed that 95 percent of American libraries use subscription agents to assist with serials acquisitions. According to Katz and Gellatly, librarians use these agents because:

> Instead of entering orders with hundreds or even thousands of individual publishers, the library uses one agent. This means a single order, a single invoice, a single payment, and a single source of most, if not all, periodicals. Furthermore, the agent renews subscriptions, offers a variety of purchasing plans, handles claims for missing or slow material, and proportionately offers a number of other services.[1]

Not all librarians are enthusiastic about agencies, but most prefer to use them in acquiring the majority of their serials. To date there has been little information available to help librarians select a subscription agent. Often serials librarians ask each other: What agencies do you employ? Are you satisfied with your agencies? Why or why not? Librarians have

Advances in Serials Management, Volume 1, pages 1–42.
Copyright © 1986 by JAI Press Inc.
All rights of reproduction in any form reserved.
ISBN: 0-89232-568-2

provided one another with anecdotal evidence about the strengths and weaknesses of various agents, but there has been a lack of objective information available on the topic.

This study provides information concerning the use of serials agents by the university members of the Association of Research Libraries (ARL). The research focuses on the criteria used by these libraries in choosing subscription agents. But before discussing the agent selection criteria, some general background on the topic will be helpful to understand the present relationship among libraries, subscription agencies, and publishers.

A serial is a publication issued in successive parts and intended to continue indefinitely. As opposed to a monograph order, a subscription to a serial involves a long term commitment that continues until a decision is made to cancel the subscription or until the title itself ceases publication. Serial orders are problematic in that serials involve sporadic changes in title, publisher, price, scope, numbering, frequency, and format; serials merge or split and sometimes are suspended, reinstated or ceased. Serials are also problematic because of their seemingly ever-increasing number and cost. "The number of titles [being published] increases annually and prices have been rising . . . with percentage increases in recent years that are far greater than the increases in the general cost of living."[2] The percentage of libraries' materials budgets allocated to serials increases each year; "70–75%, and sometimes as high as 85–90% of library materials budgets are spent on serials."[3] Though this continuing and troublesome nature of serials affects the work of most library staff members—whether they select, acquire, catalog, bind or assist the public—the serial acquisitions personnel are the most involved with these complicated publications.

The role of the Serial Acquisitions unit is to "order and process what collection development librarians select."[4] Librarians acquire serials either directly from the publisher or, when feasible, through one or more serial subscription agencies. A serial subscription agent is "a person or company that acts as liaison between the library or subscriber and the publisher."[5] It is a commercial service organization which assumes the clerical burden of dealing with multiple publishers, enabling the library to deal with fewer invoices, payments, and sources. An agency can help a library cut costs by functioning as a single source through which orders and invoices are processed. In the case of foreign serials, agents minimize the number of invoices a library receives in foreign currencies and free the library from language problems associated with invoices and correspondence concerning new orders, renewals, and claims. This "consolidation permits the library to process the fewest number of invoices and to deal with only one agency."[6]

Although most serial acquisitions librarians agree that subscription agents save staff time and money and provide valuable services otherwise unattainable, there is not total agreement on this point. In 1982, Huibert Paul, Serials Librarian at the University of Oregon, wrote a controversial article in which he voiced doubts about the use of subscription agents and stated that he no longer believed agents either free libraries from dealing with the clerical burden of paper work or provide libraries with cost effective services.[7] Although Paul's article contains some valuable information (e.g., the historical development which explains the present-day conflict between agents and publishers) and still excites discussion among serial librarians, agents, and publishers, not all of his criticisms hold true at the present time.

Since the publication of Paul's article, agents have expanded and improved the quality of services available to customers. Libraries complained about the receipt of many supplemental invoices (i.e., bills covering price increases), billing for a single title or for relatively few publications. Agents now provide libraries with the option of receiving supplemental invoices either monthly, quarterly, or annually. If the agent supplies accurate information, it is not necessary nor is it required that renewal lists (i.e., printouts documenting expiration dates for every title received from an agency) be used. Systematic claiming (reviewing check-in cards to identify lapses in subscriptions and standing orders) of the entire serials file does not, in the experience of some serials librarians, produce more claims than those generated by gaps in receipt. In fact, Central Serials Record (CSR, often referred to as the "Kardex") "drawer claiming" is a task often impossible to perform because of high staff turnover or understaffing in a serials department. In addition, experienced agents now provide information concerning title changes, cessations, and delays in publication and are beginning to use AACR2 entries more frequently. For those "obscure entries" which continue to appear on invoices from agents and publishers alike, it does not take a "professional librarian's time to decipher them,"[8] as Paul suggests; the staff in the CSR Division who deal with these titles daily are usually extremely competent and well-equipped to handle any cryptic invoices which come their way. Finally, careful automation produces fewer invoicing errors and provides a wider variety of services available to libraries. Because of improvements in service, subscription agencies appear more attractive than ever to most librarians. Although Paul represents a minority opinion in his beliefs that subscription agents are not "worth their keep,"[9] and that "the future of the subscription agent appears to be in doubt,"[10] nevertheless, his comments demonstrate that there is not universal acceptance among librarians of the utility of such agencies.

Formerly, the main impetus for librarians to place serial orders through agents was to take advantage of the discounts and the three fundamental services offered: placing orders with the publishers, handling claims for issues not received, and renewing subscriptions and standing orders. The agents were able to provide these services free of charge and sometimes gave libraries discounts because of the large commissions received from the publishers.

Beginning in the early 1960s, "some major publishers began a trend of the total elimination or drastic reduction of commissions allowed to subscription agencies."[11] The costs of publishing and distributing serials increased. Publishers could no longer afford to furnish agents with the same generous discounts. "At the same time, new concepts in office machinery reduced invoicing costs"[12] to a point where publishers no longer needed or even valued the assistance provided by the agents. This attitude continues to exist and is reflected in some of the larger publishers' practices of providing significant savings to libraries if materials are ordered direct instead of through an agent and in some publishers' policies of not accepting standing orders through agents.

> If they felt that they would save money by having agents service their subscriptions, publishers would certainly have continued to woo the middlemen with discounts [and] . . . refuse[d] to accept orders directly from libraries. . . . On the contrary, many American publishers now try to entice librarians to by-pass the agent.[13]

Publisher commissions had been the revenue for agencies, and their loss forced these organizations into the unpopular task of applying service charges to their customers' invoices in order to maintain an adequate operating margin. Librarians, faced at the same time with cutbacks in their materials budgets and the rising costs of serial publications, became outraged. Because librarians found themselves in the position of paying for services formerly received free of charge, they began to re-evaluate the benefits of using agents and resisted service charges by transferring many of their orders to publishers or demanding more service for their money.

Agents, in an attempt to retain customers, could select one of three courses:

1. Remain low-priced and continue providing only minimum essential services.
2. Remain low-priced and try to keep pace with new service demands.
3. Satisfy additional library requirements and develop new service features, while charging a service fee adequate for providing a reasonable profit.

> Those choosing the first course either went out of business due to financial strains and an inadequate variety of services, or limited their existence to servicing the most simple library market. Those electing to follow the second alternative simply could not realize enough profit to survive, and have disappeared as business entities. The agencies that chose the third course have grown in strength and capabilities.[14]

The agents in this third category succeeded by focusing on further development of their internal computer systems to accommodate the demands for services from the library community. These companies rein-vested their profits so as to provide automated serials management reports, online serials check-in and claiming systems, online bibliographic files, and computer printed renewal lists for their clients. Small companies which could not compete in the development of automated systems either merged, went bankrupt, or ceased their businesses altogether. Hence, over the past 10 to 15 years, companies have been forced to broaden their services in response to the needs of the competitive market.

> In all areas of the library market place, agencies now offer more and varied services, some of which are a direct result of their own efforts to improve efficiency through automation, others as a response to service needs expressed by librarians.[15]

All of the factors discussed above contributed to the rapid growth of some agencies and the demise of others and were influential in the growing trend for libraries to use fewer agents. The automated services available also provided a strong incentive for libraries to use fewer agents than they had in the past. For example, automated systems have the capacity to generate management and claim reports. It is to a library's advantage to receive these types of reports, describing the current serials collection, from a single source. Furthermore, some large agents are attempting to specialize in everything; they are willing to accept both subscriptions and standing orders in all formats and languages and are even supplying back issue and out-of-print orders. Despite the institution of service fees, some companies attract customers by offering them proportionally lower service charges on larger accounts. Finally, there is the pragmatic consideration that there is less confusion and more convenience in using only a few (often, only one) agents. Those who believe in this school of thought maintain that "splitting the list tends to lessen some of the advantages of using an agent."[16]

Many other librarians argue against the single-agent philosophy, saying that it is poor business practice to commit all titles to one agency which may prove to be less enthusiastic once it receives that business. In addition, these librarians believe that competition improves the quality of service, and that there is not a single agent capable of handling all types of serials. They feel it is better to split their titles among agencies giving to each what it does best.

Often it is not possible or even wise to order every title through an agent, and, in those cases, a library orders direct. As mentioned earlier, librarians usually order directly from the publisher if the publisher will not accept standing orders through an agency. Another instance when it is more advantageous for a library to order direct is when the publisher provides libraries with discounts significant enough to make it more cost effective to deal directly with the publisher than with an agent. In addition,

libraries often order highly-priced serials direct if the agent is charging
for services at a fixed percentage of the subscription rate. Other types of
serials that are often ordered through publishers are local publications,
membership publications, literary magazines, and mass circulation titles
available at discounts when multiple-year subscriptions can be placed.

Nonetheless, most librarians utilize subscription agencies for the bulk
of their serial orders. Once serial acquisitions librarians decide to employ
the services of agents, how do they decide which agents to use in acquiring
titles for the libraries' collections when so many sources supply the same
products? Some possible factors considered by serial acquisitions librarians
include the size and the subject matter of the library's serials collection;
the geographic location of the library; adherence to an established library
policy regarding agent selection; the type of serial; the language and country of origin of publication; the number of serial titles handled by an agency;
the subject area of service; the service charges; the agent's reputation,
experience, and performance; and the specialized services offered by an
agent. Librarians learn through experience, through conversations with
agents and their customers, and through evaluations of agents' services,
but, in the end, each library must develop its own criteria for choosing
agents.

Since "the choosing of a subscription agent is not an exact science,"[17]
a study examining the important factors in the agent selection process is
of considerable significance to both libraries and agents. It is the intent
of this research to provide librarians with information to improve and to
assist in the agent selection process. The data that have been gathered
here on the use of serials agents in academic ARL libraries can be useful
to librarians in all types of libraries.

In addition, this study furnishes useful data for agents concerning the
factors librarians consider when choosing an agent. Subscription agents
are eager to listen to what librarians want in an agency; librarians embody
a high percentage of agents' customers, and member institutions of ARL,
the largest libraries in the United States and Canada, are among their
largest accounts. As a result, these libraries are in a position to influence
how agencies develop future services.

Librarians cannot be passive consumers of the services offered by library
vendors. As Cargill writes:

> Vendors have created a supermarket of services from which we can choose. We
> must familiarize ourselves with these services, utilize the ones that have merit, and
> make suggestions for improvement in the ones that don't. Our developing technology
> makes it possible to offer more and better services. As library consumers, we're in
> a position to demand and help design the services to meet our requirements. Librarians
> should not be naive or reticent about making a thorough investigation of the many
> service options. Simply talking won't do. Discuss the services with other librarians

[who manage compatible collections]. If they've utilized some of the services in their library operations, get them to share their experiences. Compare notes. Share and publish service evaluations.

We have a wide range of service options in the marketplace from which to choose. By making our wishes known we can influence vendors to tailor their services to meet our requirements. Examine carefully before exercising your right of choice.[18]

This study provides information that can help librarians become more knowledgeable about the use of agents in the serial acquisition process in libraries.

LITERATURE REVIEW

Before describing the study and its findings, it is useful to review the existing literature on the topic of serial agents. The literature pertinent to this study falls into three major areas: (1) guidelines in the agent selection process; (2) the past and present relationships among libraries, agents, and publishers; and (3) the future role of the subscription agency and its implications on serial acquisitions departments.

Those who write about the agency selection process tend to affirm that the use of an agent, despite service charges, provides a cost effective means of acquiring serial literature. Most of these individuals are librarians who use, or have used, subscription agencies and who are not seeking to promote one agency over another, but instead are looking for means to improve the agent selection process.

In 1973, the Resources and Technical Services Division of the American Library Association published the second in their "Acquisitions Guidelines" series, *Guidelines for Handling Library Orders for Serials and Periodicals.*[19] It was intended to serve as a general guide for librarians, agents, and publishers, with its purpose being to facilitate understanding and communication and to improve relations and service. Part I is a brief discussion about when it is best to order through agents and when it is wise to order from publishers. The first recommendation for ordering through an agent is to consult *International Subscription Agents.*[20] This directory, now in its 5th edition, is based on data collected from questionnaires returned by agents. It is arranged alphabetically by agent, and each entry includes valuable information, such as countries covered, types of materials supplied, services offered, and special notes. There are many cross references and a geographical index useful for libraries selecting agents by country of a publication's origin. Nancy Buckeye, editor of the 4th edition of the directory, discusses its production and identifies developing trends in subscription work in her article "Librarians and Vendors: The Fourth Edition of International Subscription Agents."[21]

Alan Singleton's work, *The Role of Subscription Agents,*[22] provides, in addition to information about the number and size of major British agents, operating procedures of both agents and publishers in the areas of timing of payments, invoicing, service charges, foreign currencies and exchange rates, claims, agents' information and marketing services, and new technology. The pros and cons of using agents to acquire serials are also discussed in a separate chapter.

Guide to Magazine and Serial Agents[23] by William Katz and Peter Gellatly discusses relationships between agencies and libraries and provides helpful information to the librarian concerning agency selection. The last section of this book, "Directories for Analyzing and Locating Serial Agents and Services" contains a checklist for librarians to use when comparing services and procedures of agencies, an agency survey summary, a library survey summary, and a subscription agents' directory with a geographic index. Katz and Gellatly's survey reveals that of 850 libraries throughout the United States, approximately 95 percent use subscription agents, and it identifies points to consider when selecting agents. The book, published in 1975, needs to be updated to account for the changes in agencies' services.

Four articles focus on the process of selecting a subscription agent. Harry Kuntz's article, "Serial Agents: Selection and Evaluation,"[24] provides a checklist of essential points to consider when librarians are comparing costs and services offered by various agents. The list does not include extensive elaboration on each point, but rather serves as a useful overview of factors to consider in the serial agent selection process. Kuntz also discusses the controversial issue of whether to employ a single or multiple agents. Doris New describes the process of transferring serial orders formerly received through a variety of sources to one major serials agent in her article "Serials Agency Conversion in an Academic Library."[25] She provides a list of guidelines developed by one academic library to follow when determining whether orders should be placed directly with publishers or through agents. In addition, she offers some suggestions and a vendor evaluation form for libraries which are considering undertaking a similar project. Sheila Intner "[e]xplores the controversy about the value of using subscription agents as found in the library literature in view of the special needs of sci-tech libraries for serials/periodicals and current problems in their acquisitions"[26] in "Choosing and Using Subscription Agents in Sci-Tech Libraries: Theory and Practice."[27] She provides results of an informal study which investigated the practices and priorities in using agents to acquire serials in ten science and technology libraries in the United States. Margaret O'Connor discusses the aspects of orders, claims, renewals and invoicing in her article "Factors Influencing the Choice of an Agent."[28] These four authors, Kuntz, New,

Intner, and O'Connor, have all investigated aspects of the serial agent selection process, and the information provided in their articles has been particularly relevant to the present research.

Ron Coplen's "Subscription Agents: To Use or Not to Use"[29] describes a methodology for determining internal cost of the services agents provide, using a basic time and motion principle in order to document that agents, despite their service charges, save libraries staff time and money. Though his formula has been criticized as being superficial,[30] the information gathered from the survey furnishes serial acquisitions librarians with criteria to consider in the agent selection process.

Marcia Tuttle raises the question 'Subscription Agent or Not?' in her book *Introduction to Serials Management*.[31] She discusses many factors affecting serial agent selection: service charges, services rendered, personal contacts with agencies, specialties of agencies, and situations when it is best to order direct. Andrew Osborn's *Serial Publications*[32] devotes some space to a discussion of the utility of subscription agents. He borrows quotes from a wide array of sources to discuss the pros and cons of ordering serials direct from publishers and through agents. Other works written about serial acquisitions procedures include Stephen Ford's *The Acquisition of Library Materials*,[33] R. Baker's "Acquisition Methods,"[34] and William Huff's "The Acquisition of Serial Publications"[35] and "Serial Subscription Agencies."[36]

Both librarians and representatives of subscription agencies publish material concerning their respective viewpoints on the relations between libraries, agencies, and publishers. Librarians complain about agents' service charges, supplemental invoices, inaccurate invoices, slow or no response to claims and other correspondence, and slow processing of new orders. Agencies, on the other hand, have a few complaints of their own. They accuse libraries of submitting claims that are premature, too old, or unnecessary; of remitting incomplete information on new orders; and of accusing agents unjustly for the service charges which serve as a major source of agency income.

In addition to methods of choosing an agent, both Katherine Smith and Judith A. Nientimp in their respective articles, "Serial Agents/Serial Librarians"[37] and "The Librarian . . . and the Subscription Agent,"[38] discuss the library's relationship with its agents and furnish librarians with further insight into methods of evaluating and maintaining a relationship with their agents. Stanley R. Greenfield writes in a joint article with Nientimp[39] about this relationship from an agent's perspective. He describes the steps involved in placing subscription orders, focuses upon the various problems which may arise from orders, and relates how librarians can help the agency perform its basic functions, which will thereby improve relations. Other spokesmen for serial subscription agents include

Frank Clasquin,[40] Wayne Thyden,[41] John B. Merriman,[42] and Albert Prior,[43] all of whom represent large subscription agencies. They provide further insight into the agents' operating procedures, defend the position of the large agency and its need to apply service charges to its customers, and uniformly promote the idea that agents save libraries time and money, enabling them to pursue "more meaningful and pertinent endeavors."[44]

Most of the literature relevant to this study includes sections discussing the future role of subscription agencies and the implications that this future will have for libraries. Three individuals who write about this topic are Huibert Paul, Marcia Tuttle, and Jennifer Cargill. As mentioned earlier, Paul writes in "Are Subscription Agents Worth Their Keep?"[45] that he no longer believes agents save libraries any labor or money, but rather cost libraries money. Because of the evidence that publishers are becoming less inclined to cooperate with libraries, he sees an uncertain future for the subscription agent. Tuttle and Cargill, on the other hand, in their respective articles, "Can Subscription Agents Survive?"[46] and "Vendor Services Supermarket: The New Consumerism,"[47] are optimistic about the future of the large subscription agencies. They foresee the development of a wider variety of services and indicate that these services will be shaped by librarians. Tuttle concludes by saying

> [T]he future role of the subscription agent is whatever the customer wants it to be. . . . It is up to librarians to talk to vendor representatives and managers, to ask them questions, to let them know what we do, what we need, and what we are planning.[48]

DESIGN OF THE STUDY

In 1970, William Huff published the results of a study conducted on the acquisition of serial publications in ARL libraries. He reported that all libraries participating in his study used subscription agents to acquire a large proportion of their current serials, but the number of agents and the percentage of orders submitted to agents varied.[49] The purposes of this current study are to investigate the present-day attitudes of these same libraries about the services of subscription agencies and to discover the current criteria upon which libraries base their selection of agents. In order to collect information regarding the criteria librarians consider significant in the agent selection process, a questionnaire was designed and administered to librarians involved in serial acquisition in all of the university member institutions of the Association of Research Libraries.

Research Questions

The primary focus of this study was to investigate the following research question: What criteria do academic members of ARL institutions consider important in the serial agent selection process? Other research questions this study explored were: What percentage of the libraries' total materials budget is allocated to serials? What automated serial acquisitions systems, if any, do these libraries use or plan to use in the future? Where in the library organization do serial acquisition functions occur? How many serial agents are used? Which serial agents are used and what proportion of orders are assigned to these agents? Why are foreign agents, if any, employed? What proportion of orders are received direct? What proportion of orders are placed through agents? What are the advantages and disadvantages of using a serial agent?

Population

The population for this study included all 104 university ARL member institutions both in the United States and Canada. Non-university members of ARL were omitted. ARL members were identified by consulting the current edition of *ARL Statistics* (1982/83).[50] The addresses and names of appropriate individuals to receive the questionnaire were determined by using *American Library Directory* (37th edition).[51] The selection of the individual in each library to whom the questionnaire was sent was based upon the position each held, as indicated in the *American Library Directory*. The following list represents the order in which positions were chosen, with the ones thought to be most closely associated with the agent selection process ranked first:

1. Serials Acquisitions Librarian
2. Serials Department Head
3. Acquisitions Department Head
4. Technical Services Head
5. Director

Hence, if the *American Library Directory* listed a Serials Acquisitions Librarian position, then the survey was addressed and mailed to that individual. If not, then the survey was sent to the person listed as holding the next position. For example, if the first three positions were nonexistent in a library, according to this reference source, then the person holding position number four (i.e., Head of Technical Services) was selected as being the recipient of the questionnaire.

Data Gathering

Criteria influencing the selection of an agent were identified from the literature on this subject, from verbal contacts with experts in the field of serial agent assignment, and from personal working experience in serials librarianship. A preliminary survey was distributed to five full-time professional and para-professional employees working at different academic libraries in North Carolina. Their suggestions were considered and incorporated in the final version of the questionnaire; these responses contributed to the success of this study.

The final version of the questionnaire (Appendix) consisted of five sections. The first section contained questions about the university and the library. The second part dealt with the specific serial agents employed. The third section involved the criteria considered when selecting specific serial agents. The most difficult part of the survey for the respondents to complete was the fourth in which statistics about the serials collection were investigated. It was difficult because most libraries did not have this type of data readily available. In the pre-test survey the fourth section had followed the first, but because individuals participating in the pre-test found these questions hard to answer, this section was shifted nearer to the end, so that the recipients of the survey would not be confronted by complicated questions near the beginning and possibly decide not to respond. The last section included several open-ended questions regarding the advantages and disadvantages of using an agent and future changes in agent selection policies. In this section, participants were invited to record any additional comments.

The survey was mailed to the 104 ARL librarians on March 15th, 1985. The mailout package was assembled in a fashion recommended by Dillman[52] and included the coded questionnaire, two cover letters, a list of definitions of terms used in the survey, and a self-addressed stamped envelope. Once the initial response rate had reached its peak (approximately 50 percent) and fallen off, a follow-up mailout package was assembled, including the same items as in the first mailing except for new cover letters. The follow-up mailing was sent on April 19th, 1985, to all subjects who had not yet responded. As a consequence of the two mailings, 83 questionnaires were received, resulting in an overall return rate of 80 percent.

Data Analysis

The responses were coded and entered into a mainframe computer using the Statistical Analysis System (SAS), a packaged computer system. Most of the data gathered were either nominal or ordinal, therefore, only descriptive statistics were used to analyze the data in this study. Measures of central tendency—the mean and the mode—and frequency distributions were used to describe the findings.

RESULTS

Eighty percent of the questionnaires (83 out of 104) were returned; three returns were received unanswered. These three respondents did not complete the questionnaire because they felt the information asked for was confidential, or they were too busy with other projects to fill in the survey. Hence the response rate of usable questionnaires was 77 percent. This high response rate to the questionnaire reflects both the need for and the strong interest in research on serial agent selection criteria. The interest in the topic was also demonstrated by the large numbers of respondents who enclosed extra sheets of paper on which they made additional comments concerning the agent selection process.

In the following section the results of the survey are discussed question by question. The discussion covers each of the five parts of the survey but is arranged in a slightly different order than the survey. Part IV of the questionnaire, "The Serials Collection," is discussed after Part I, "The University and Library."

Part I. University and Library

The first section of the survey gathered information about the participating libraries and their parent institutions. Each of the libraries in the study was classified by geographic location. The nine U.S. geographical areas selected were based upon census divisions of the United States.[53] The 11 Canadian libraries were all assigned to one geographical category. It was gratifying that all but one of the Canadian members of ARL responded to the survey. The geographical spread of the responses can be seen in Table 1.

Type of Institution

Seventy percent of the ARL libraries that responded are affiliated with public institutions, and 30 percent are private. The return rates for public and private institutions are comparable. Table 2 provides data on the response rate of these libraries according to type of institution.

Table 1.   Geographical Distribution of Population

Geographic Area	Total Number	Responses	Percent
1. New England	8	5	6.250
2. Middle Atlantic	14	11	13.750
3. South Atlantic	17	14	17.500
4. East North Central	15	10	12.500
5. East South Central	4	4	5.000
6. West North Central	7	5	6.250
7. West South Central	8	6	7.500
8. Mountains	7	5	6.250
9. Pacific	13	10	12.500
10. Canada	11	10	12.500

Budget

In general, the amount of funds from libraries' materials budgets being allocated to serials continues to increase each year due to the constant proliferation of new serial publications, the explosive rise in their cost, and the increased role they play in all disciplines. The respondents were asked what percentage of their library's total budget is allocated to serials. As illustrated in Figure 1, the libraries studied devote a large percentage of their budgets to serials. Only 16.5 percent (N = 13) spend less than 50 percent of their materials budgets on serials. Three of the responding libraries devote over 75 percent of their materials budgets to serials. The majority of these institutions (N = 63) spend between 50 and 75 percent of their materials budgets on this type of material.

Automation

In the early 1960s, when libraries were beginning to automate, it was felt that serials acquisitions, a regular and repetitive procedure, was a logical place to start. Unfortunately, system designers did not understand serials; the high incidence of exception to the rule made automation of serials receipt too difficult for existing technology. Thus, most data processors turned to cataloging and other library functions.[54]

As technology has become more advanced, there has been a strong desire to automate serial acquisition functions in libraries. The next group

Table 2.   Type of Institution

Institution	Total Number	Responses	Percent
1. Public	72	56	70
2. Private	32	24	30

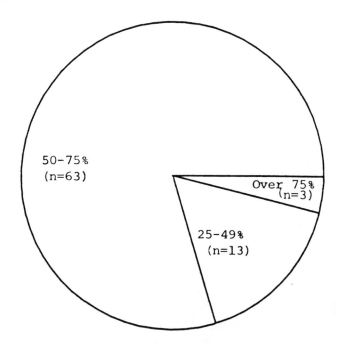

Figure 1.   Percentage of total materials budget
               allocated to serials.

of questions in the survey asked about the use of automated serial acquisitions systems. Of the participating libraries, 46 percent have already
implemented automated systems to assist with their serial acquisition operations. Table 3 lists the systems and the frequency with which they are
used by these libraries.

Of the libraries that responded to this survey, 54 percent are not currently automated in their serial acquisitions procedures, but 93 percent
of this group plan to use automated facilities in the future. Table 4 lists
the systems these libraries are considering.

Organization

In 1935, J. Harris Gable published an article in *Library Journal*[55] ad-
vocating the formation of a separate serials department within libraries.
Soon after Gable's article appeared, libraries began to centralize serial
related activities into one department. With the advent of automation, the
trend is being reversed in some libraries "toward a reintegration of serial
functions into other library departments."[56] Administrators supporting this
viewpoint believe it is better to organize departments by function rather
than by form.[57] The survey participants were asked about the organiza-

Table 3.   Automated Systems Being Used

Systems	Frequency
In house	14
Faxon	9
NOTIS	3
OCLC	3
RLIN	3
INNOVACQ	2
ORION	2
BATAB	1
BLIS	1
Davex	1
MARVEL	1
Nonesuch	1
Perline	1
WLN	1

tional placement of the serial acquisition process in their libraries. In the academic institutions participating in the study, there appears to be an even split on this issue. Exactly half of the libraries place the serial acquisitions operations in a separate Serials Department, 45 percent in the Acquisitions Department, and five percent in another department.

Orders

Throughout the literature, one finds recommendations for placing new serial orders. The *ALA Guidelines* advise that

> Subscriptions should begin with the first issue of the calendar year or, where this is not appropriate, with the first issue of the current (or next) volume. . . . Orders should be placed with sufficient lead-in time, generally three months before the date of publication of the first issue required.[58]

Stanley R. Greenfield, writing from the agent's perspective, says:

> Orders should be placed early enough to allow the agent plenty of lead time in beginning the subscription. Publishers usually require from six to eight weeks to begin the subscription and some processing time for the agency should be added to that.[59]

When asked, "During what time of the year does your library *begin* placing new serial orders?" an overwhelming percentage (85 percent) indicated they placed orders all year round. Table 5 depicts the dispersion of responses to this question concerning the time of year new orders are submitted.

Table 4. Automated Systems Being Considered

Systems	Frequency
Perline	10
GEAC	9
INNOVACQ	9
Faxon	8
BLIS	5
NOTIS	5
Adlib	2
Inhouse	2
OCLC	2
Carlyle	1
Dataphase	1
RLIN	1
SAILS	1
VTLS	1
WLN	1

Assuming that the libraries falling into the "year round" category will not accept incomplete volumes, it is not clear whether they are following the recommendations in the literature on new orders. For example, are they placing a new order for a serial in June 1986, to begin with the first issue of the current volume (in this case, January 1986), or are they submitting an order for this title in June 1986 to begin with first issue of the next volume (i.e., January 1987)? This is unclear, but it is still interesting to note that in the majority of academic ARL institutions, serial acquisition operations are not performed on a seasonal basis as is implied by these recommendations.

Part II.   Serials Collection

This section of the survey asked the respondents for specific information on their serials collections. In the questionnaire, this group of questions appeared as the fourth section for reasons mentioned earlier. However,

Table 5. Time of Year Respondents Submit New Orders

Time of Year	Responses	Percent
1. Winter	1	1.250
2. Spring	2	2.500
3. Summer	3	3.750
4. Fall	6	7.500
5. Year Round	68	85.000

for discussion purposes, it seems more appropriate that the results of Part IV's questions follow those of Part I, where questions about the university and the library were investigated.

Current serial orders were divided into two groups: "free" (i.e., exchanges or gifts) and paid; these groups were subdivided by two categories according to type of serial: periodical and non-periodical. A periodical was defined as a serial intended to appear at least twice a year on a regular basis. A non-periodical serial was described as a serial published on an annual or irregular basis. The first question in this section of the survey asked the respondents for the total number of active serial orders being received in various categories. The mean number of current serials received in academic ARL institutions can be seen in Table 6.

Participants were then asked to provide statistics concerning the sources of paid periodical subscriptions. The mean proportion of paid periodical subscriptions received direct from the publisher in responding academic ARL institutions was 24 percent; agents supplied the remaining 76 percent of these orders.

The next questions asked participants to give a further breakdown concerning the paid periodical subscriptions received through agents. The mean proportion of paid periodical subscriptions received through domestic agents in academic ARL institutions was 68 percent; foreign agents supplied the other 32 percent of these orders.

The fourth set of questions concerned the proportion of paid non-periodical standing orders received from publishers and through agents. The mean proportion of paid non-periodical standing orders received direct from the publisher in the participating institutions was 36 percent; agents supplied the remaining 64 percent of these orders. It is apparent that libraries order more standing orders than subscriptions directly from the publisher. This finding may indicate that librarians are not as satisfied with the agents servicing standing orders as they are with those specializing in subscriptions, or, that subscriptions are more successful through agents than are standing orders. On the other hand, this finding may not reflect the quality of agents' services, but rather the fact that librarians are taking

Table 6. Mean Number of Current Serials Received

Type of Serial	Responses	Mean
Periodicals		
a. Free	60	1624.62
b. Paid	70	8713.98
Non-Periodicals		
a. Free	64	1179.20
b. Paid	69	4932.23

advantage of publishers' practices of offering significant discounts to libraries if they bypass agencies with their standing orders. It also may be that libraries are placing orders for expensive standing order titles with publishers in order to avoid the agency service charges when these charges are based on a fixed percentage of the standing order rate.

The last series of questions asked respondents to provide data regarding the percentages of paid non-periodical standing orders received through both domestic and foreign agents. The mean proportion of paid non-periodical standing orders received through domestic agencies was reported as being approximately 60 percent; foreign agencies supplied the other 40 percent of these orders. These results show that the responding ARL libraries use foreign agencies more often to acquire foreign non-periodicals than to acquire foreign periodicals.

Part III.   Serial Agents

Number of Agents

The total number of serial agents that the responding academic members of ARL institutions use varies from one to 60 but, on the average, each library employs the services of approximately 17 agents in acquiring serials.

In Huff's 1970 study, he reported that of the 49 libraries studied, 98 percent used more than one agent, 41 percent used two agents, and only eight percent used more than seven agents.[60] The present study discovered that of the 74 libraries responding to this question, 99 percent used more than one agent, three percent used two agents, and *over* 69 percent used more than seven agents. When compared to the findings from Huff's study, these results appear to contradict the perception held by many that there is a growing trend for libraries to use fewer agents.

More, Fewer, or Same Number of Agents?

When asked if they would like to use more, fewer, or the same number of agencies, only nine percent indicated they would like to use more, whereas 44 percent said they would prefer to use fewer, and almost 47 percent reported they were satisfied with the current number of agents being utilized. The mean number of agents used by libraries wanting to use fewer agents was 19, the mean number of agents used by libraries wishing to employ the same number of agents was 16, and the mean number in those libraries desiring to utilize more agents was eight. In general, the libraries using the fewest agents wanted to use more, libraries employing the most agents wanted to use fewer, and those using a number close to the overall mean (17) were satisfied with the quantity of agents used.

Libraries reported they wanted to use more agents because they wanted to experiment in seeking better services, they wanted to spread their business among several agents so that the competition would maintain and, perhaps, even improve the quality of service, and that they wanted to find more "reliable subscription agent[s]" in developing countries.

Of the libraries indicating they did not want to change the quantity of agents used, most indicated their reason for this was satisfaction with the service: "fit[s] our needs"; "happy with the balance"; "good variety"; "good comparison of services." Only one participant responded with skepticism: it was "too much work to change" the number of agents used. One response received sums up well the reasons libraries use the number and variety of agents they do:

> Different vendors often excel in different areas. We have also found it not to be a good idea to have everything with one vendor as takeovers/sellouts do occur . . . and this can cause not merely headaches, but large losses of library money as well.

For libraries wanting to employ the services of fewer agents, most indicated that their main reasons for this were to simplify procedures, standardize routines, and consolidate workflow (e.g., fewer invoices or one source claiming). Other reasons mentioned were: to receive "possibly a lower service charge," "to take advantage of automation," and "to phase out poor performance agents." Another comment was, "The fewer hands we must deal with the happier we are!"

The replies to this question do indicate that many respondents would prefer to use the services of fewer agents. Respondents who wish to deal with fewer agents will likely find that automation can help them achieve this objective. When libraries which are not currently using automated serials control systems begin to install automated facilities (particularly if they purchase agent produced systems), the number of agents used will likely decrease. If a library uses an agent's serial control system, it is to the library's advantage to place as many orders with that agency as is feasible in order to take advantage of the automated services offered, such as management and claim reports. For example, one of the leading domestic periodical agencies will not only generate claim reports for every current serial the library receives but will actually initiate the claims to the publishers for those titles it supplies to the library. Thus, when most libraries have fully automated their serials acquisition process, it is likely that libraries will use fewer but larger agencies just as Huff predicted in 1970.

Domestic Agents

The next questions asked the respondents about the domestic serial agents used by their libraries. In this study domestic serials were defined as those originating in either Canada or the United States. The number of domestic serial agents the respondents reported varies from one to 12 but, on the average, each library employs the services of approximately four domestic agents in acquiring serials for their libraries. Over 25 domestic agents were reported as being used by these libraries, but only 10 were listed 5 times or more when libraries were asked to record major domestic agents. Figure 2 depicts these 10 agents and the percentage of libraries reporting their use.

Figure 3 shows the percentage of orders academic ARL institutions

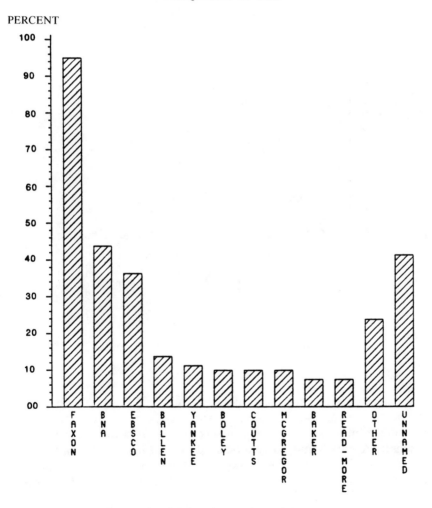

Figure 2. Major domestic serial agents

PERCENT   PERCENT OF TOTAL ORDERS

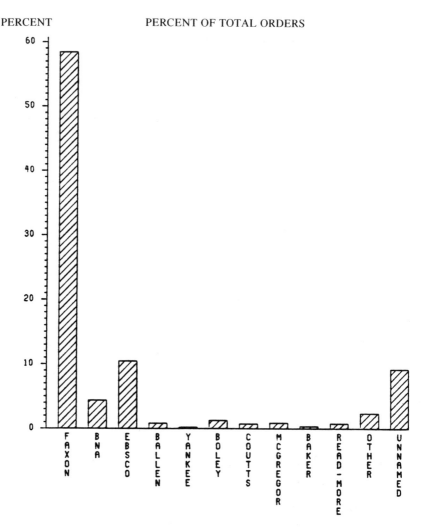

Figure 3.   Major domestic serial agents

reported assigning to their major domestic agents. Whereas Figure 2 shows the percentage of libraries using a particular agent, Figure 3 reflects just how much business these major agents receive from these libraries. For example, Agents X and Y might be used by the same number of libraries, but Agent X might receive a mean of 35 percent of the total domestic orders whereas Agent Y might be supplying 60 percent of the total domestic orders for this population.

Foreign Agents

Only two of the libraries participating in this study do not use foreign agents. The remaining libraries (97.5 percent) combined use more than 50 foreign agents to acquire serials published outside Canada and the United States. However, only 12 agents were listed five times or more when libraries were asked to record major foreign agents. Figure 4 depicts these 12 agents and the percentage of libraries reporting their use.

Figure 5 shows the percentage of foreign titles academic ARL institutions reported assigning to their major foreign agents. As in Figure 2, Figure 4 shows the percentage of libraries using a particular agent, whereas Figure

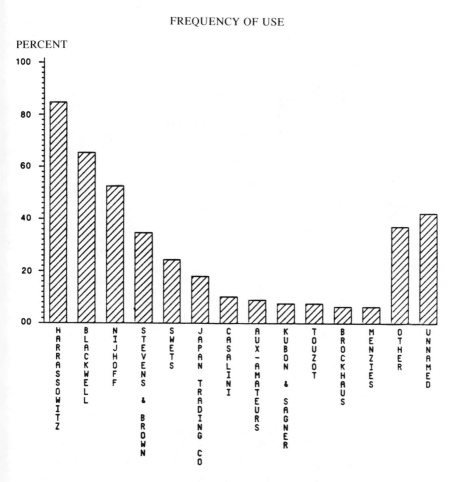

Figure 4. Major foreign serial agents

PERCENT   PERCENT OF TOTAL ORDERS

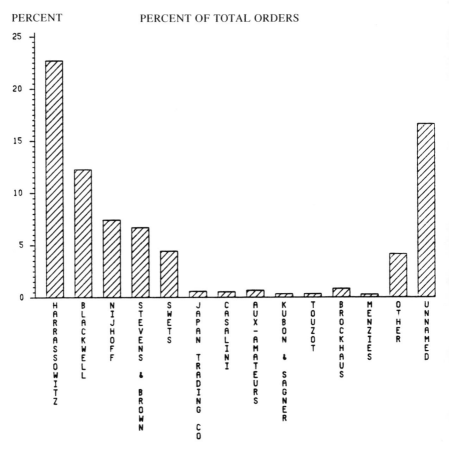

Figure 5.   Major foreign serial agents

5, like Figure 3, reflects exactly how much business these major agents receive from these libraries. In other words, the percentage of libraries using specific foreign agents can be seen in Figure 4, but the degree to which these agents are used is depicted in Figure 5.

An explanation is necessary regarding the two categories "OTHER" and "UNNAMED" in Figures 2–5. If an agent was not reported by at least five participating libraries, then it was *not* considered to be a major agent. The agent and the percentage of orders submitted to that agent were placed in the "OTHER" category. If the percentage of total orders reported by a library did not add up to 100 percent (e.g., 79 percent), then the remaining percentage (e.g., 21 percent) was assigned to the category "UNNAMED" to account for agents not reported. For those libraries not reporting all sources used for 100 percent of their orders, it is possible that some of these orders, assigned to the "UNNAMED" category, were actually submitted to one of the agents identified by other libraries as a high use agent. If this were the case, then different rankings, or even different agents, than the ones presented in Figures 2–5 could occur.

The results would have been more conclusive if the questions concerning the specific agents used and the percentage of orders assigned to these agents had been asked in a closed-ended manner. However, this would have required identification of the top 22 agents used by these libraries *prior* to designing and administering the survey, and this information was not available. Now that the major agents have been identified, the validity of these results could be tested in a future study on the major agents used by, and the amount of business received from, academic ARL institutions.

As libraries become more automated, the ability to provide more accurate data increases. With automated facilities, libraries will be able to calculate exact percentages of orders placed with specific agents rather than providing rough estimates or no estimates at all. Despite all the unknowns, since this survey asked libraries to list "major" agents, the results show clearly that Faxon and Harrassowitz dominate the domestic and foreign fields, respectively, in academic ARL institutions.

Why Not Foreign Agents?

Of the two libraries that do not use foreign agents, one replied that the two domestic agents it used handled its needs satisfactorily. The other library used only one domestic agent and replied that it preferred to place foreign serial orders with foreign publishers. The respondent from this second library said that when their totally integrated online system is completed, it "will eventually eliminate the use of any agent."

The serials acquisition methods within these two libraries do not follow the acquisition practices found in other academic ARL institutions. Most ARL libraries own large foreign language collections and rely heavily upon the services of foreign agents in acquiring foreign serial titles. Foreign agents specialize in knowing their country's (or countries') publishing industry and can communicate better with the individual publishers than can most domestic agencies or libraries when problems arise.

Preference of Source for Foreign Serial Orders

The last question in this section asked about the criteria used in placing foreign serial orders. Though the *country* of a serial's origin was reported as being an important selection criterion for foreign orders (31 percent), most libraries (51 percent) prefer to place foreign serial orders with agents who specialize in particular *areas/regions* in the world (i.e., one agent for all European publications; one agent for all African publications; etc.).

This choice could stem from either the fact that librarians believe there are few good agents in developing countries servicing serials published within their own nations or the fact that librarians prefer to use fewer agents in order to simplify acquisition procedures.

Part IV.   Selection Criteria

The heart of the study, the selection criteria, occurs in Part III of the questionnaire, and the results are provided in Figure 6. A variation of the semantic differential rating scale was employed to measure the degree of

LEVEL OF IMPORTANCE IN SELECTING A SERIAL AGENT

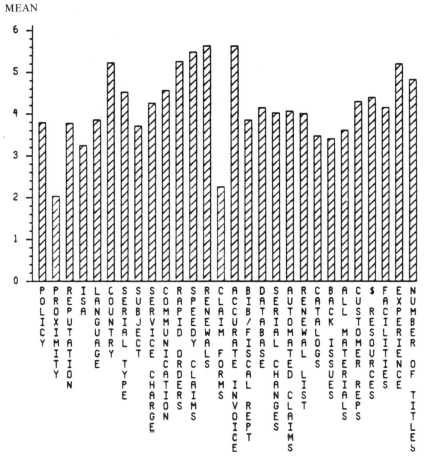

Figure 6.   Selection criteria

importance each criterion has in the serial agent selection process. These scales typically allot an odd number of spaces (either five or seven) for participants to record one of the positions on each continuum between the most positive ("very important") and the most negative ("not important") terms. To prevent participants from responding with a middle-of-the-road approach, an even number (6) of spaces was employed. The criteria presented in this section had been identified as having some influence on the selection of agents through the literature, through conversations with professional and para-professional serials acquisition staff, and through one of the authors' (Derthick's) own working experience with serials.

All 28 criteria appear to influence the agent selection process to some degree, but 6 were identified by the respondents in this study as being the most significant factors in academic ARL institutions:

1. prompt renewals
2. accurate invoices
3. speedy claims
4. rapid placement of orders
5. country of serial's origin
6. agent experience

The two criteria which appear to have the least influence on the selection process are proximity of an agent to the library and the provision of claim forms.

Thus, despite the growing number of customized automated services subscription agencies have been able to offer their customers over the last decade (i.e., management reports, customized invoices, claim reports, etc.), the three fundamental functions of an agency reported by Stanley Greenfield in 1972—"accurate, prompt placement of new orders; speedy and vigorous attention to claims and adjustments; and timely renewal of expiring subscriptions"[61]—remain some of the most influential selection criteria. However, automation has enabled agencies to provide these traditional services much more efficiently than ever before and is a determining factor in the continued growth of some agencies and the decline of others.

Part V.   Conclusion

The last section of the questionnaire included several unstructured questions allowing participants to express their opinions concerning the primary advantages of using serial agents, the major causes for dissatisfaction with serial agents, and changes in libraries' policies regarding the serial agent selection process which might occur in the future. Respondents were also invited to elaborate upon issues in the survey and/or to include any additional comments concerning the serial agent selection process which were not covered in the questionnaire. Since responses were unstructured, statistical tests were not used to analyze them. Instead responses were grouped into general categories.

Advantages of Using an Agent

By far, most respondents indicated that the primary advantage of using a serial agent was economy for the library. These participants believed that agents provided libraries with cost effective services resulting in a significant saving in staff time and in check writing costs. The following responses summarize the feelings of many of the respondents.

> Significant staff time is saved through their providing such services as publisher correspondence, consolidation of invoices, of renewals, [and] of claims. In general, we happily pay them to do our dirty work.

> Agents do much of the clerical work which we could not handle in our area because of the volume of business—agents really enhance our record keeping.

Automatic renewals, consolidated invoicing with common expiration dates, and prepayment to publishers (though this is becoming less common) are all services agents can offer libraries which result in a reduction of clerical work, fewer accounts to be maintained, and a "greater certainty of non-interruption of subscriptions [and standing orders]." Though some librarians said that agents eliminate staff positions, most respondents believed that agents enabled librarians to perform their work more efficiently and allowed staff to perform more challenging tasks.

The claiming service provided by agents was viewed as being the second major advantage of using a serial agent. Claiming could be placed in the first category, but enough participants listed this service as a distinct category to warrant separate treatment. Though "[c]laiming is frequently the most irritating aspect of the relationship between agents and librarians,"[62] the ability to centralize claims through agents was viewed by many respondents as being a major advantage of using a serial agent. Not only does the use of an agent simplify the claiming process, but at least one of the leading domestic subscription agencies provides libraries with automated claim reports which help libraries identify lapsed subscriptions and/or issues needing to be claimed. In addition, if a library purchases this particular agent's automated serials control system, it will initiate claims to the publishers for the library for those titles the agent supplies.

An agent's expertise and clout with publishers was considered to be the third most important benefit of using a serial agent. Respondents believed that they were able to derive "more effective response[s] from publishers via [an] agent"—particularly when foreign titles were involved. "Agents [sic] staff can specialize in publisher relationships" and "[t]hey are often able to track down and deal with elusive publishers/titles."

Customized services provided by agents were viewed as being the next major advantage of using an agent. Such services included "management information and status reports," "consolidated shipments," "invoicing & shipping . . . tailored to our needs," and "personal attention provided by agents' reps (i.e., representatives) assigned to account."

An agent's ability to provide the most up-to-date information through means of a large database was considered by respondents to be the fifth most important benefit of using a serial agent. Agents whose services are automated can offer customers the most current publication and bibliographic information (i.e., changes in title, price, publisher address, frequency, publication status, etc.) on serial titles. "Dealers with computers can track orders and payments better." Also, some of the larger serial agencies provide "online [ordering and] billing or tape invoices for renewals [and new orders]."

The final advantage of using an agent, reported by a few libraries, was the agent's ability to "offer . . . [a] variety of purchase plans, includ[ing] multiple year subscriptions." This service, however, is not unique to agents. All subscribers (both individuals and institutions) can get discounts on multiple year subscriptions through publishers, particularly for fulfillment center titles (i.e., mass circulation titles—for example, *National Geographic*, or *U.S. News & World Report*). Librarians also implied in their statements about discounts that the use of an agent provided libraries with price reductions to serials ordered or renewed on an annual basis. As mentioned previously, agencies formerly received commissions from publishers, and often they passed a portion of this income to their customers in the form of a discount. But the days of publishers' commissions have almost vanished, and, thus, so have the agencies' discounts to libraries; instead, service charges have been implemented. However, these charges should not be viewed in a negative light by librarians since they serve as a major source of income for agencies and make it possible for them to expand and to develop new services for their customers.

Dissatisfaction with Serial Agents

The second question in this last section of the survey asked participants to list some of the major causes for their libraries' dissatisfaction with serial agents. The most common reply was unresponsiveness or slow response to new orders, claims, renewals, and correspondence concerning address changes, adjustments to orders and invoices, multiple subscriptions, cancellations, etc. One example cited was:

Unresponsiveness (e.g., failure to answer/acknowledge repeated claims or to respond adequately to correspondence, particularly letters about specific problems)
. . . not starting orders in timely manner . . . failure to corr[espond about] multi-copy
order problems.

The next two areas—invoicing/shipment problems and poor agent/library
relationships—received an equal number of responses when participants
were asked about the major disadvantages of using serial agents. Respondents complained that agents' invoices were physically difficult to
interpret and process (i.e., "cryptic invoices w[ith]o[ut] order [numbers]/
sufficient identifying info[rmation]") and that often agents were not able
to satisfy local invoicing requirements (i.e., provide library fund codes,
etc.). Participants also said that agents sometimes required payment too
far in advance, billed without regard to publishing patterns, and sent invoices for slow, cancelled, ceased, duplicate or wrong publications. Agents
who do not establish good relationships with publishers and who do not
inquire about possible price increases for serials tend to send invoices to
their customers that do not reflect the current pricing structures. This
often results in a large number of supplemental invoices. However, only
one respondent complained about added-on charges. This might reflect
that agents are improving this aspect of their service through the assistance
of online databases which enable them to communicate more efficiently
with publishers as well as with their customers.

Many librarians reported poor relationships with their agents, and they
viewed this problem as one which was caused by the agents rather than
themselves. Respondents believed that the rapid growth of some agents
and the transition to automation have caused a deterioration in personalized attention. Though most academic ARL institutions appreciate the
customized automated services provided by some agencies, one respondent described the automated printouts as "idiotic computer generated reports." Others were less critical, but felt that these automated stock responses caused difficulties in effective communication. Others complained
of the "erratic quality of customer service staff" or the failure to provide
a local representative. Another common criticism of agents was the agents'
"failure to deliver advertised services"; "Big promises—of any kind—
that are not kept"; "Unfilled promises re: services." Other comments
included the provision of inaccurate or incomplete bibliographic and pricing
information. Although order entries in agents' catalogs and online databases do not always conform to AACR2 standards, some agents are taking
steps to adjust their records to agree with libraries' forms of entries.

The fourth cause for dissatisfaction with serial agents in these libraries
was service charges which respondents described as being "excessive,"
"high," and "exceptional." Libraries need to monitor the agents' service
charges and to be aware of how these charges are calculated in order to

prevent agencies from taking advantage of libraries. Sometimes it *is* more cost effective to order expensive titles direct if agents charge for services at a fixed percentage of the subscription rate. However, as mentioned before, librarians should not be too critical of reasonable service charges since they do provide agents with a major source of their income and are necessary to keep them from going bankrupt or from merging with other companies as has been the fate of so many agencies over the last 15 years. In addition, service charges have also allowed agents to invest in the development of new services for their customers.

The last disadvantage of serial agents from the viewpoint of the survey participants was the inability of agents to supply all types of material (e.g., newspapers, non-periodicals, back issues, serials from Third World countries, "difficult to obtain" publications, and materials furnished via memberships or by societies and institutions). This may be an unfair criticism, for it would be impractical for agents to specialize in all types of material for all types of customers. For example, a periodical subscription agency is typically not set up to handle standing order material; this type of material is usually best handled by a book jobber. And sometimes, publishers of membership material or of society and institutional publications do not make their publications available through agencies. Hence, this "disadvantage" does not seem to be a justifiable reason for libraries to be dissatisfied with serial agents.

Changes in Library Policy

The third question in the final section of the survey asked respondents if they could foresee any changes in their libraries' policies with regard to serial agent selection. An overwhelming number of participants identified the reduction in the current number of agents used as the primary change for the future. Many respondents said they wanted to decrease the number of direct orders and to consolidate as many orders as possible with a few agents. The type of agent which appears attractive to most of these libraries is one with a sophisticated online system capable of "ordering, searching, claiming, [checking-in, generating management reports], etc." with "interface capability with [libraries'] microcomputers," as well as one which provides "the *basic and constant* criterion of competence in service."

Another change that some respondents indicated might occur in their libraries was not necessarily a reduction in the number of agents, but a complete or partial transfer of orders from one agency to another. Respondents predicted this action will happen because libraries want to be able to take advantage of better service and lower service charges, to consolidate types of serials with agents who specialize in these materials (e.g., submitting non-periodical orders with a standing order agent), and, in the case of foreign serials, to place these titles with domestic agents who have established offices in foreign countries or with agents who are able to offer their customers consolidation programs. Consolidation programs are practices devised by European agents to benefit their North American customers; the agents purchase the journals at a domestic rate from the publishers and then ship the issues in batches to their Canadian, American, and Mexican customers. This service prevents North American customers from having to pay the inflated subscription prices—often, higher than the regular overseas rate—set by some foreign, in particular United Kingdom publishers. Consolidation programs are used "as a means of avoiding paying inflated overseas prices by concealing the ultimate destination of the journal."[63]

Only a few participants predicted that their libraries will transfer some titles from agents to publishers. One respondent said "[w]e expect to undertake a study of the cost of procuring 'bill later titles' on a direct basis rather than through a domestic agency because of increased cost and handling charges." Only one library mentioned that it will be able to eliminate the use of any agent once their totally integrated online system is completed.

Additional Comments

Twelve participants took the opportunity to elaborate upon the serial agent selection process in their libraries or in other settings where they have worked. Most of these comments concerned issues already covered elsewhere in this article, but one respondent, who formerly worked for an agent, held a different perspective than most and offered the following information:

> Having once worked for a vendor, it is important to keep in mind that the agent is only as good as the people it hires to do the work. Agents are now tending to hire more librarians as customer representatives and office managers to insure better quality service.
>
> It is also important to distinguish what is the fault of an agent from a publisher's error when evaluating agents. The fact that the publisher's staff can not read an order or renewal correctly certainly is *not* the fault of the agent.

The agents' ability to respond to individual libraries' needs was a frequent comment in this last open-ended section. Respondents said they selected agents who could handle their special requests; this usually meant an agent who could offer automated services such as computer printed payment labels, management and claim reports, and machine readable invoicing. Other factors mentioned which influence the choice of agents are the agents' "visibility in the library field (attendance at conferences; articles in lib[rary] lit[erature] which mention the agent's name, etc.)," personalized attention from customer representatives, the geographic location of the agent, the type of serial, the source of blanket order and/or approval plans, the "existence of state regulations & bid systems," and the current supplier for titles that a library already receives that are produced by large publishers (i.e., "it is advisable to place all titles of a given pub[lisher] w[ith the] same agent").

CONCLUSION

There are unique factors within each library which influence the serial agent selection process, but this study reveals some of the most important selection criteria that are common in academic ARL institutions. These libraries tend to choose agents on the basis of reliable service. An agent's ability to respond promptly to customers' claims, renewals, new orders, and queries and to provide accurate invoices appear to be the most important qualities these libraries seek in an agent. The technological revolution has enabled agencies to improve the quality and efficiency of these services as well as to expand and develop new services (e.g., management reports and data, customized invoicing, and claim reports) for their customers. Agencies not able to invest in computerized services have not been successful; they cannot compete with those who have developed sophisticated automated systems and are, thus, unable to maintain their existing accounts or to attract new customers.

The number of agencies is dwindling. The competition among agencies is intense, and there is a fear among some librarians that the continued demise of agencies will result in "a reduction in the variety of services available, less competition between the leading firms, and an increase in service charges."[64] Others believe that this competition enhances the quality and variety of services and makes agencies eager to comply with individual libraries' needs. If the present trend continues, the number of agencies will steadily decline while the number of serials continues to proliferate, stimulating the growth and success of the few agents who survive.

The results of this study show no signs that the use of agents is waning as was predicted by Huff in 1970.[65] At that time he saw a trend emerging in ARL libraries to order more titles direct. Currently, these libraries generally believe that agents provide them with a cost effective means of acquiring serials, and they have no plans to cease using agents' services. They are (or anticipate) transferring many of their direct orders to agents and are consolidating their agent orders with fewer agents. Libraries are depending more and more on the services agents provide.

The purpose of this study was not to promote one agency over another, but to provide libraries, as well as agents, with useful information concerning the serial agent selection process within a single population: academic ARL institutions. This study has been able to provide some badly needed information on the criteria used in selecting serial agents and on the specific agents used most frequently in these libraries.

More information is needed though, and it would be useful to conduct further research on this topic. In order to test the validity of the results regarding the specific agents these libraries used and the percentage of orders assigned to these agents, a follow-up survey would be necessary. In the current study, it was impossible to investigate these topics with structured questions since there had been no previous study which identified the major domestic and foreign agents used by this population. Hence, open-ended questions were used to gather data. Now, by using the results of this study, a follow-up survey can be conducted. Table 7 illustrates one method that could be used, asking the same questions as in this survey (Part II, questions 4 and 6), but in a close-ended manner. Participants would be asked to circle whether or not they employ the services of one of the agents identified by the libraries in this current study as a high use agent. If the response is "yes", then the survey participant would circle the number approximating the percentage of orders submitted to that agency. Other related research topics which should be

Table 7. Survey Design to Determine the Frequency of Use and the Proportion of Business ARL Institutions Submit to Major Serial Agents

Agents	Use?						*Percent of Orders Placed*					
1. Faxon	Yes	No	05	10	15	20	25	30	35	40	45	50
			55	60	65	70	75	80	85	90	95	100
2. BNA	Yes	No	05	10	15	20	25	30	35	40	45	50
			55	60	65	70	75	80	85	90	95	100
3. Ebsco	Yes	No	05	10	15	20	25	30	35	40	45	50
			55	60	65	70	75	80	85	90	95	100
.												
.												
22. Menzies	Yes	No	05	10	15	20	25	30	35	40	45	50
			55	60	65	70	75	80	85	90	95	100

pursued are the exact proportion of the libraries' materials budgets being allocated to serials, the automated serials control systems being considered and installed in these institutions, additional criteria these libraries consider when choosing serial agents, and selection criteria which *agents* believe libraries consider are the most significant in their choice of serial agents.

The acquisitions of serials is a challenging and exciting field. Librarians need to be aware that they are in a position to influence the success or failure of serial agents and the development of future services provided by agents. Agents depend heavily upon library business and, thus, are eager to listen to what criteria librarians seek in a serial agent. ARL libraries with their large serials budgets are particularly powerful and can be very instrumental in facilitating more cooperative relationships between libraries and agents in the future.

APPENDIX

A Study of Serial Agent Selection Among the University Members of the Association of Research Libraries

Jan Derthick
School of Library Science
University of North Carolina
Chapel Hill, NC 27514
USA

I. The first questions concern the university and the library in which your serial acquisitions functions occur.

1. Is this school: (please circle)
   a) Public
   b) Private

2. What percent of your library's total materials budget is allocated to serials? (please circle)
   a) Above 75%
   b) 50–74%
   c) 25–49%
   d) 0–24%

3. Does your library use any automated (commercial or in-house) serial acquisitions systems? (please circle)
   a) Yes ————   b) No ————

If yes, please list   If no, do you plan to purchase or
which one(s)   develop your own system in the
used: future? (please circle)

1) Yes
2) No

If yes, please list which system(s)
you are considering:

4. Where does serial acquisitions occur in your library's organization? (please circle)
   a) In the Serials Department
   b) In the Acquisitions Department
   c) Other (please specify) _____

5. During what time of the year does your library *begin* placing new serial orders?
   (please circle)
   a) Winter (December–February)
   b) Spring (March–May)
   c) Summer (June–August)
   d) Fall (September–November)
   e) Place orders year round

II. This area deals with the specific serial agents your library uses.

   1. How many serial agents does your library use? _____

   2. Would you like to use: (please circle)
      a) More
      b) Fewer
      c) Same number
      Why?

   3. How many of the serial agents used by your library are domestic? _____

   4. Please list major domestic agents used, ranked by volume of business, with the
      heaviest used being first:

AGENT NAME	% OF TOTAL DOMESTIC AGENT ORDERS

   5. Does your library use any foreign serial agents? (please circle)
      a) Yes
      b) No

6. If you circled "Yes" in question number 5 above, please list major foreign agents used, ranked by volume of business, with the heaviest used being first.

AGENT NAME	% OF TOTAL FOREIGN AGENT ORDERS

7. If you circled "No" in question number 5 above, please indicate below the degree of importance each criterion has in this decision.

not
important ____ ____ ____ ____ ____ ____ important; ____ applicable
      language problems with agent
not   very   not
important ____ ____ ____ ____ ____ ____ important; ____ applicable
      geographical distance from agent
not   very   not
important ____ ____ ____ ____ ____ ____ important; ____ applicable
      domestic agents handle our needs
not   very   not
important ____ ____ ____ ____ ____ ____ important; ____ applicable
      shipping delays
OTHER:

8. Does your library prefer to place foreign serial orders with (please select only 1):

   a) individual agents in each country   ____
   b) agents who specialize in particular areas/regions in the world (i.e., one vendor for all European publications; one vendor for all African publications; etc.)

                                      ____
   c) domestic agents   ____
   d) foreign publishers   ____
   e) domestic distributors for foreign publishers   ____
   f) domestic agents for English language foreign publications; foreign agents for non-English language publications   ____
   g) none of the above; our library does not order foreign titles   ____
   h) other (please specify) _____

III. This next section involves the criteria your library uses in selecting specific serial agents.
Please indicate the degree of importance of the following criteria when selecting a serial agent (domestic *OR* foreign):

not   very   not
important ____ ____ ____ ____ ____ ____ important; ____ applicable
      library policy/tradition

not important ___ ___ ___ ___ ___ ___ very important; ___ not applicable
proximity of agent to your library

not important ___ ___ ___ ___ ___ ___ very important; ___ not applicable
agent reputation among ARL members

not important ___ ___ ___ ___ ___ ___ very important; ___ not applicable
favorable reports in *International Subscription Agents*

not important ___ ___ ___ ___ ___ ___ very important; ___ not applicable
language of publication

not important ___ ___ ___ ___ ___ ___ very important; ___ not applicable
country of serial's origin

not important ___ ___ ___ ___ ___ ___ very important; ___ not applicable
serial type (i.e., periodical; non-periodical)

not important ___ ___ ___ ___ ___ ___ very important; ___ not applicable
subject specialty of agent

not important ___ ___ ___ ___ ___ ___ very important; ___ not applicable
agent percent service charge

not important ___ ___ ___ ___ ___ ___ very important; ___ not applicable
communication services provided by agent (i.e., 800 number; accepts collect calls)

not important ___ ___ ___ ___ ___ ___ very important; ___ not applicable
rapid placement of orders

not important ___ ___ ___ ___ ___ ___ very important; ___ not applicable
speedy handling of claims

not important ___ ___ ___ ___ ___ ___ very important; ___ not applicable
prompt attention to renewals

not important ___ ___ ___ ___ ___ ___ very important; ___ not applicable
claim forms supplied by agent

not important ___ ___ ___ ___ ___ ___ very important; ___ not applicable
accurate invoice

not important ___ ___ ___ ___ ___ ___ very important; ___ not applicable
customized bibliographic and fiscal reports

not important ___ ___ ___ ___ ___ ___ very important; ___ not applicable
access to large serials database

not important ___ ___ ___ ___ ___ ___ very important; ___ not applicable
customized reports of serial changes

not   very   not
important _____ _____ _____ _____ _____ _____ important; _____ applicable
automated claims services

not   very   not
important _____ _____ _____ _____ _____ _____ important; _____ applicable
renewal list provided by agent

not   very   not
important _____ _____ _____ _____ _____ _____ important; _____ applicable
catalogs/printed material

not   very   not
important _____ _____ _____ _____ _____ _____ important; _____ applicable
ability to supply back issues

not   very   not
important _____ _____ _____ _____ _____ _____ important; _____ applicable
ability to supply all types of material (i.e., periodical, non-
periodical, film,.)

not   very   not
important _____ _____ _____ _____ _____ _____ important; _____ applicable
discussions with customer service representatives

not   very   not
important _____ _____ _____ _____ _____ _____ important; _____ applicable
financial resources of agent

not   very   not
important _____ _____ _____ _____ _____ _____ important; _____ applicable
agent facilities (i.e., branch offices, computer)

not   very   not
important _____ _____ _____ _____ _____ _____ important; _____ applicable
agent experience

not   very   not
important _____ _____ _____ _____ _____ _____ important; _____ applicable
number of titles agent handles

IV. The next group of questions is specifically about the serials collection. If statistics
for the following series of questions are not maintained in your library, please
estimate figures to the best of your ability.

1. What is the total number of active serial orders (please include duplicates,
microforms, and newpapers; exclude sets) in your library?
   a) "Free" serials (i.e., gifts, exchanges, etc.):
      1. Periodicals _____ approximate number of titles.
      2. Non-periodicals _____ approximate number of titles.
   b) Paid serials:
      1. Periodicals _____ approximate number of titles.
      2. Non-periodicals _____ approximate number of titles.

2. What proportion of your paid periodical subscriptions do you receive:
   a) direct from the publisher _____ approximate percent.
   b) through an agent _____ approximate percent.

3. What proportion of your paid periodical subscriptions received through agents
are:
   a) supplied by domestic agents _____ approximate percent.
   b) supplied by foreign agents _____ approximate percent.

4. What proportion of your paid non-periodical standing orders do you receive:
  a) direct from the publisher _____ approximate percent.
  b) through an agent _____ approximate percent.

5. What proportions of your paid non-periodical standing orders received through agents are:
  a) supplied by domestic agents _____ approximate percent.
  b) supplied by foreign agents _____ approximate percent.

V. Conclusion

1. What do you view as the primary advantages of using a serial agent?

2. What are the major causes for your library's dissatisfaction with serial agents?

3. Do you foresee any change in your library's policy with regard to serial agent selection? (please elaborate)

4. In this survey, I have tried to cover the major factors which influence agent selection. If there are any additional comments you wish to make about serial agent selection, please use extra sheets of paper for this purpose.

NOTES AND REFERENCES

1.   William A. Katz and Peter Gellatly, *Guide to Magazine and Serial Agents* (New York: R.R. Bowker Company, 1975), 33.
2.   Stephen Ford, *The Acquisition of Library Materials* (Chicago: American Library Association, 1973), 115.
3.   Marion C. Szigethy, "A Course in Serials Librarianship at Columbia University," *Serials Librarian* 2 (1978): 388.
4.   Marcia Tuttle, "Serials Control" (Chapel Hill, N.C., 1985), 4.
5.   Katz and Gellatly, *Guide to Magazine*, 7.
6.   Marcia Tuttle, *Introduction to Serials Management*, Foundations in Library and Information Science, 11 (Greenwich, CT: JAI Press, 1983), 81.
7.   Huibert Paul, "Are Subscription Agents Worth Their Keep?" *Serials Librarian* 7 (Fall 1982): 31–41.
8.   Ibid., 35.
9.   Ibid., 31.
10.   Ibid., 40.
11.   Wayne Thyden, "Subscription Agency Size: Threat or Benefit?" *Serials Librarian* 7 (Spring 1983): 30.
12.   Katherine Smith, "Serial Agents/Serial Librarians," *Library Resources & Technical Services* 14 (1970): 5.
13.   Paul, "Are Subscription Agents," 32.

14. Thyden, "Subscription Agency Size," 31.

15. Jennifer Cargill, "Vendor Services Supermarket: The New Consumerism," *Wilson Library Bulletin* 57 (1983): 395.

16. Harry Kuntz, "Serial Agents: Selection and Evaluation," *Serials Librarian* 2 (1977): 143.

17. William H. Huff, "Serials Subscription Agencies," *Library Trends* 24 (1976): 684.

18. Jennifer Cargill, "The Vendor Services Supermarket: The New Consumerism," in *Serials and Microforms: Patron-Oriented Management;* Proceedings of the Second Annual Serials Conference and Eighth Annual Microforms Conference, ed. Nancy Jean Melin (Westport, CT: Meckler Publishing, 1982), 108.

19. American Library Association. Resources and Technical Services Division. Resources Section. Bookdealer/Library Relations Committee, *Guidelines for Handling Library Orders for Serials and Periodicals,* Acquisitions Guidelines, 2 (Chicago: American Library Association, 1974).

20. Wayne R. Perryman and Lenore Wilkas, eds., *International Subscription Agents,* 5th ed. (Chicago: American Library Association, 1986).

21. Nancy Buckeye, "Librarians and Vendors: The Fourth Edition of *International Subscription Agents,*" *Serials Librarian* 2 (1978): 391–99.

22. Alan Singleton, *The Role of Subscription Agents,* Occasional Papers—BLRD report, 5621 (Leicester, England: University of Leicester and Primary Communications Research Centre, 1981).

23. Katz and Gellatly, *Guide to Magazine.*

24. Kuntz, "Serial Agents," 139–50.

25. Doris E. New, "Serials Agency Conversion in an Academic Library," *Serials Librarian* 2 (1978): 277–85.

26. Sheila S. Intner, "Choosing and Using Subscription Agents in Sci-Tech Libraries: Theory and Practice," *Science & Technology Libraries* 4 (Fall 1983): 31.

27. Ibid., 31–42.

28. Margaret O'Connor, "Factors Influencing the Choice of an Agent," in *Profiling a Periodicals Collection,* ed. Phillip Watson (Melbourne, Aust.: Footscray Institute of Technology, 1979), 129–35.

29. Ron Coplen, "Subscription Agents: To Use or Not to Use," *Special Libraries* 70 (1979): 519–26.

30. Paul, "Are Subscription Agents," 39.

31. Tuttle, *Introduction,* 77–84.

32. Andrew D. Osborn, *Serial Publications,* 3rd ed. (Chicago: American Library Association, 1980), 105–11.

33. Ford, *Acquisition,* 115–29.

34. R. Baker, "Acquisition Methods," in *Serials Librarianship,* ed. Ross Bourne (London: Library Association, 1980), 13–22.

35. William H. Huff, "The Acquisition of Serial Publications," *Library Trends* 18 (1970): 294–317.

36. Huff, "Serial Subscription Agencies," 683–709.

37. Smith, "Serials Agents," 5–18.

38. Judith A. Nientimp and Stanley R. Greenfield, "The Librarian . . . and the Subscription Agent," *Special Libraries* 63 (1972): 292–304.

39. Ibid.

40. F.F. Clasquin, "The Subscription Agency: A Vested Maturity," *Serials Librarian* 4 (1980): 301–05.

41. Thyden, "Subscription Agency Size," 29–34.

42. J.B. Merriman, "The Work of a Periodicals Agent," unpublished manuscript, n.d.;

John B. Merriman, "A Subscription Agent's View," in *Learned Journals: Pricing and Buying Round* (Letchworth, England: Epsilon Press, 1985), 27–32.

43. Albert Prior, "How Serials Agents Can Help Libraries Cut Costs," in *Financing Serials from the Producer to the User,* ed. David P. Woodworth, Proceedings of the UK Serials Group Conference, 2 (Loughborough, England: UK Serials Group, 1979), 44–55.

44. Thyden, "Subscription Agency Size," 32.

45. Paul, "Are Subscription Agents," 31–41.

46. Marcia Tuttle, "Can Subscription Agents Survive?" *Canadian Library Journal* 42 (1985): 259–64.

47. Cargill, "Vendor Services," 97–109.

48. Tuttle, "Can Subscription Agents," 264.

49. Huff, "Acquisition of Serial," 306.

50. Association of Research Libraries, *ARL Statistics 1982/83* (Washington, D.C.: Association of Research Libraries, 1984), 9A.

51. *American Library Directory,* 37th ed., 2 vols. (New York and London: R.R. Bowker Company, 1984).

52. Don A. Dillman, *Mail and Telephone Surveys* (New York: John Wiley & Sons, 1978), 179–81.

53. U.S. Department of Commerce, *1980 Census of Population,* vol. 1: *Characteristics of the Population* (Washington, D.C.: U.S. Government Printing Office, 1981), 1–7.

54. Tuttle, "Serials Control," 17.

55. J. Harris Gable, "The New Serials Department," *Library Journal* 60 (1935): 867–71.

56. Jo Ann Hanson, "Trends in Serials Management," *Serials Librarian* 8 (Summer 1984): 7.

57. Michael Gorman, "The Future of Serials Control and Its Administrative Implications for Libraries," in *Serials Automation for Acquisition and Inventory Control,* ed. William Gray Potter and Arlene Farber Sirkin, Proceedings of a Conference held Sept. 4–5, 1980, in Milwaukee and sponsored by the Library and Information Technology Association (Chicago: American Library Association, 1981), 120–33.

58. American Library Association, *Guidelines,* 3.

59. Nientimp and Greenfield, "Librarian . . . Subscription Agent," 295–96.

60. Huff, "Acquisition of Serial," 306.

61. Nientimp and Greenfield, "Librarian . . . Subscription Agent," 293.

62. Smith, "Serial Agents," 14.

63. Merriman, "A Subscription Agent's View," 30.

64. Thyden, "Subscription Agency Size," 29.

65. Huff, "Acquisition of Serial," 306.

CONSER:

THE ROLE OF OCLC

M. E. L. Jacob

INTRODUCTION

The CONSER (CONversion of SERials) Project is a cooperative effort undertaken by the library community to build a machine-readable database of quality serials cataloging information. The Library of Congress and the National Library of Canada distribute machine-readable CONSER records as part of their MARC distribution system. Bibliographic data for serial titles are entered by one of the twenty participating libraries. These records, key titles and International Standard Serial Numbers (ISSN) are assigned or verified by the National Serials Data Program (NSDP) or ISDS/ Canada, ensuring an authoritative database. CONSER participants adopted the following goal and objectives for the project.

Advances in Serials Management, Volume 1, pages 43–52.
Copyright © 1986 by JAI Press Inc.
All rights of reproduction in any form reserved.
ISBN: 0-89232-568-2

Goal

To continue to enlarge and improve a core database of bibliographic information about serials titles available for use on the international, national, regional, and local levels.

Objectives

1. Provide a reliable and authoritative serials database to meet the needs of library patrons, other users of information, and the developing national and international bibliographic networks.
2. Assist the national libraries of both Canada and the United States in the establishment and maintenance of a machine-readable serials database.
3. Support the interface of national serials database activities with the programs of international serials systems—including the participation of NSDP and ISDS/Canada in the International Serials Data System.
4. Support local, regional, national, and international serial union list activities.
5. Ensure the use of nationally and internationally accepted standards, rules, and conventions for building and maintaining serials bibliographic records.
6. Identify deficiencies in the database, such as subject, language, and retrospective coverage, and implement appropriate remedies.

HISTORY

Formal impetus for CONSER came from the Ad Hoc Discussion Group on Serials Data Bases which met at the 1973 American Library Association Conference in Las Vegas. Earlier discussions on serials databases by the Ontario University Libraries' Cooperative System and the National Library of Canada were incorporated into the Ad Hoc Discussion Group's agenda. The group's main concern was the confusion and duplication of effort associated with activities related to the creation of machine-readable serials databases. The Association of Research Libraries (ARL) expressed interest in the discussion and encouraged the group to seek viable solutions to these problems.

The Council on Library Resources (CLR) became the project sponsor with the Library of Congress (LC) and the National Library of Canada (NLC) as authentication (or final reviewing) centers. CLR, as funding agent, negotiated a contract with OCLC, Inc., to provide the facilities for creating and maintaining a machine-readable serials database. Contracts were signed in December 1974 and participant input began in the fall of 1975. CLR provided project management support through the term of the contract.

Upon expiration of its original contract in November 1977, OCLC announced continued sponsorship and support of CONSER and assumed managerial responsibility. OCLC is a facilitator for participant decisions on policy and international issues. CLR has continued as an active participant in the CONSER Advisory Group and in the CONSER participants' meetings.

CONSER is a landmark project in the history of librarianship. OCLC's role has changed significantly from a passive systems operator to an active participant. Currently OCLC has the equivalent of two full-time staff devoted to CONSER and CONSER related activities.

PROJECT CONSTRAINTS

The initial project was constrained by a number of factors including money and resources available, the ability of participants to achieve consensus and the capabilities of the host system. Achieving a consensus was no easy task and it was not until 1979 that all participants finally agreed to use the second edition of the Anglo-American Cataloguing Rules (AACR2) and successive entry.

The OCLC system was the only system available at the time offering the functions required to support the system, but even it did not have all those needed by the project. Neither a field locking mechanism nor a means of creating detailed serial holdings existed. Locking was to prevent participants from changing fields validated by LC or NLC. The lack of a field locking mechanism in the end proved to be a positive rather than a negative influence.

Initially the Library of Congress (LC) and the National Library of Canada (NLC) did not want participants to have the ability to modify records once worked on by the national centers. Ideally this would have been done on a field basis since the NSDP and ISDS offices verified only certain portions of the record. It would have allowed participants the ability to modify certain portions of the record. Unfortunately the OCLC system could lock the entire record, but not selective portions of it.

CONSER authorizations allowed participants to modify all serial records except those acted on by LC or NLC. Progressively, LC relaxed its restrictions on record modifications and first allowed participants to modify records created or acted on by NSDP with the proviso that certain fields not be changed. This gentlemen's agreement worked sufficiently well for LC to move to self-authentication in 1984.

Each institution is trained to prepare name authority records to LC standards and to create a bibliographic record acceptable to LC. Once the staff is trained, LC spot checks each person's work to ensure a continued adherence to LC standards. With self-authentication, work is done once and used by all participants including LC. Full authentication by only the national centers proved impractical, particularly as more libraries joined the project.

Originally the project was to include serials holdings. A holdings format was not approved until 1985 when the National Information Standards Organization (NISO) accepted the draft for Z39.44, Serials Holdings Statement. OCLC had earlier implemented the 1979 NISO Z39 summary level holding format. Participants have entered bibliographic data and their holdings symbols. No detail holdings have been recorded for the project. The U.S. Newspaper Program described below has used the union listing component of the OCLC serials control system to enter holdings information. This issue was raised again as part of the review of CONSER recently completed by Jeff Heynen and Julia Blixrud and discussed below.

OTHER PROJECTS

Two major projects, the U.S. Newspaper Program (USNP) funded by the National Endowment for the Humanities (NEH) and the Abstracting and Indexing Coverage Project sponsored by ARL and the National Federation of Abstracting and Information Services (NFAIS), have both built on the CONSER database. Both are using existing records as well as adding new records.

United States Newspaper Program

Historians, archivists, and librarians have long been concerned about the preservation of and access to U.S. newspapers. In 1972 the American Council of Learned Societies addressed those concerns by recommending that NEH sponsor a program to organize, preserve, and make available U.S. newspapers. The following year the Organization of American Historians (OAH) approached NEH with a proposal to study ways to best achieve that goal.

After several years of study, the OAH recommended that NEH support planning for a national program of newspaper access and record automation. NEH subsequently funded a pilot project to determine the feasibility of such a program. Advisory panels were convened to consider the future direction of a national program and to recommend standards, guidelines, manuals, and procedures. Under the auspices of LC, preparation of the *Newspaper Cataloging Manual* began.

In 1981 NEH appointed a program officer to initiate a national program of newspaper projects consisting of national repositories and state projects. These repositories have collections that are national in scope. State and territorial projects accept the responsibility to survey, inventory, and catalog newspaper collections within their respective states or territories. NEH provides funding for both repositories and state projects.

CONSER participants agreed in 1981 to incorporate newspaper records as part of the CONSER database. The next year, LC began entering its newspaper records, and in early 1983 six national repositories started projects sponsored by NEH to catalog and enter their records. The first state and territorial projects joined the effort the next year. Participants enter their bibliographic and holding records into OCLC's Online Union Catalog and serials control system. Bibliographic records are self-authenticated by participants and distributed as part of LC's MARC Serial Distribution Service.

The Library of Congress and NEH jointly administer the USNP. NEH provides grants management, LC provides technical management, and OCLC, through CONSER, provides the facilities for the bibliographic phase of the program.

USNP national repositories are American Antiquarian Society, Center for Research Libraries, Kansas State Historical Society, LC, New York Historical Society, New York Public Library, Rutgers University, State Historical Society of Wisconsin, and Western Reserve Historical Society. State projects underway or completed are Alabama, Hawaii, Indiana, Iowa, Kansas, Kentucky, Mississippi, Montana, Nevada, New Jersey, New York, Pennsylvania, Texas, U.S. Virgin Islands, Utah, and West Virginia.

Abstracting and Indexing Coverage Project

This cooperative project enriched the CONSER database by adding information on title coverage by abstracting and indexing (A&I) services. This project links A&I services' citations and library catalog entries, enabling researchers to learn where serials of interest are indexed, and facilitating access to high demand serials (i.e., those that are indexed). The project will also improve related operations in the participating A&I services and in the many libraries that use CONSER bibliographic records.

The goals for the project include:

1. To ensure that the CONSER database contains records for *all* serials titles covered by a selected core group of the most widely used A&I Services in the U.S. and Canada.
2. To add to those records information describing where each serial is indexed or abstracted.

3. To provide to the participating A&I Services standardized biblio-
    graphic data (e.g., ISSN, key titles, library entries) for each serial
    title they cover, enabling them to cite the serials they index in
    standardized library form.
4. To develop the capability to produce machine-readable serials lists
    for use by participating A&I services.
5. To keep the A&I information in the CONSER database up to date.

The project offers an opportunity for increased cooperation by the library
and information service communities. Representatives from five major
institutions or organizations—LC, NLC, OCLC, NFAIS, and ARL—developed the project, supported by a planning grant from the Council on
Library Resources. The five institutions have also pledged in kind con-
tributions totaling over a half-million dollars. Chemical Abstracts Service
(CAS) has also made a significant contribution by adding A&I coverage
information for its complete list of 12,820 serials.

The National Endowment for the Humanities, the Council on Library
Resources, the H.W. Wilson Foundation, and the Xerox Foundation have
contributed project funds. These will allow for complete processing of a
substantial core group of A&I Services, covering over 100,000 serials titles
(approximately 55,500 unique serials).

As of January 1986, 85 abstracting and indexing services (representing
136 indexes and abstracts) were participating in the A&I project. Over
100,000 citation notes (field 510) were added to the CONSER database
in 1984. The project was largely completed in late summer 1985, although
some follow up and additions are still being made. Ongoing maintenance
of the A&I information will be handled by NSDP and NLC.

A capsule history of the CONSER project and its current status are
given in the CONSER brochure published by OCLC[1] and ongoing information is contained in the CONSER newsletter available free from OCLC.[2]

CONSER OPERATIONS

Having described CONSER's history and related projects, the remainder
of this paper will consider the managerial, financial, and quality control
aspects of the project. These functions are shared by the national centers,
OCLC, and the participants.

Management

Technical management of standards and procedures is handled by LC
and NLC. OCLC is responsible for continued system operations, provision

to LC and NLC of CONSER records, organization of meetings, and management of CONSER statistics. As the host system OCLC is also responsible for continued quality control and support.

LC and NLC are the arbiters of serials cataloging policies and standards. OCLC provides a vehicle for implementing and supporting those policies and standards. LC produced the *MARC Serial Editing Guide* and the *CONSER Editing Guide*. OCLC provides extensive documentation on its system and in particular the serials format. OCLC has to respond to its user community on the application of CONSER guidelines to the OCLC Online Union Catalog and serves as an interpreter to and intermediary for its membership. It explains, for example, what partial level records are, why NSDP does what it does to records, why "Do Not Use" notes have been added to records, and what self-authentication means.

Each participant has established its own operating procedures and managerial structure. Meetings of participants and operational staff are held periodically to consider policy and procedural issues and to resolve problems.

The participant and operational staff meetings, the *CONSER Editing Guide*, the national centers' authentication and monitoring, and OCLC's quality control activities ensure consistency.

Financial Support

Financial support for CONSER comes from the participants, from OCLC, and from CLR. Each participant has made a significant contribution to the project by supporting staff time, original cataloging input, authority creation, and record upgrading. OCLC makes no system use charges to CONSER participants. OCLC also pays air travel expenses for participants to CONSER meetings and workshops. Participants contribute living expenses and staff salaries. CLR has continued to fund special projects and to assist the NLC with telecommunication charges.

Quality Control

The cooperative work of CONSER participants has been critical in improving the quality, as well as the coverage, of the serials records in the OCLC Online Union Catalog. Through use of nationally accepted and mutually developed standards, CONSER participants have created high quality cataloging records for serials. As noted above, the OCLC system and procedures imposed certain constraints on OCLC participants. Records could not normally be modified once another participant had attached its holdings symbol to the record. Procedures were changed to allow

CONSER participants to modify records created by other participants, but not those acted upon by the national centers.

The original CONSER procedures required paper surrogates to be sent to the national centers requesting modifications to records and for all new records added. This was done because not all titles in the CONSER database were held by LC or readily available to LC staff.

For serials, in particular, this procedure was extremely time-consuming and expensive. CONSER members are more effective at improving the quality of serials records because the serial publication is available for consultation, the CONSER participant can review the entire record for accuracy and completeness, and CONSER participants follow fully defined standards and conventions for maintaining serials bibliographic records.

Since the beginning of CONSER, OCLC has had arrangements with CONSER participants for processing reports of duplicate records for serials. CONSER participants, when they identify a duplicate record, add a note to the record to be deleted and report the record to Online Data Quality Control Section (ODQCS) at OCLC, for deletion. Prior to September 1983, OCLC staff deleted more than 15,000 serial records. In September 1984, the merge holdings feature was installed in the OCLC online system, thereby greatly expanding OCLC's capability to delete duplicate records; since then, another 15,000 serials records have been deleted.

In addition to deleting duplicate records reported by CONSER participants, OCLC staff deleted more than 20,000 non-serial duplicate records in 1984. OCLC deleted approximately 40,000 such records in 1985.

In addition to its work with CONSER, OCLC has maintained a long-term commitment to improving the quality of records in the Online Union Catalog. Between 1980 and 1984, OCLC staff modified over 600,000 bibliographic records based on reports from OCLC participants.

With the adoption of AACR2, OCLC converted more than 3,700,000 headings in bibliographic records to AACR2 form to assist users in making the transition. This monumental conversion was accomplished by matching headings in bibliographic records with the LC name authority file and by manipulating certain pattern forms of headings. Access to AACR2 headings greatly improved users' ability to adopt AACR2 on schedule.

The CONSER Project, in part, served as a model for OCLC's Enhance Project. The Enhance capability allows selected users to improve the quality of records input by other OCLC users. The capability is limited to a particular format (e.g., books, scores, etc.) for each user. The goals of Enhance are similar to the goals of CONSER: To provide a cost-effective mechanism for authorized users to add or make corrections to data in bibliographic records; to improve the usefulness and quality of cataloging; to reduce the number of requests forwarded to OCLC to modify records; and, to decrease the time lag between detection and correction of errors. In 1984, 24 users were authorized and trained to use Enhance; by January 1986 this number was expanded to 69.

With the advent of the Linked Systems Project OCLC CONSER participants who are also in LC's Name Authority Cooperation Project (NACO) will be able to access LC files from their OCLC terminals and to create name authority entries transferred at least daily to LC. Starting in 1986 the NACO link will improve self-authentication, the process of creating quality records. Work for the national centers and for OCLC will move from correction and review to review and contribution.

FUTURE

In 1979 the CONSER participants broadened the membership of the Advisory Group and asked representatives of the National Library of Australia, the British Library, and the International Federation of Library Associations to participate. The British Library was asked to consider full participation, but declined because it believed it would be unable to support the added workload.

The four English speaking national libraries—LC, NLC, the British Library and the National Library of Australia—cooperate in a number of ways. Cooperating in CONSER would improve the coverage of the data base and equalize the work load. Presently LC covers all non-Canadian titles.

CONSER has succeeded because of the dedication and cooperation of its member libraries and their willingness to devise, not the perfect system, but a workable system. CONSER libraries have created collectively a database of almost 600,000 records in less than 10 years. While grant support was provided to establish the project, it has operated without grant assistance for seven years—a remarkable achievement for a cooperative venture without formal agreements.

The future is cloudy at present. New serials continue to be published and added to the file by participants. Several institutions have ceased active participation. At least one has never become an active participant or contributed one record to CONSER. A few were inactive for a while, but have again become active participants. A number of new, active participants have joined and are contributing significantly to the growth of the CONSER database.

The USNP and the A&I Project have added new records and new life to CONSER. The self-authentication process has enabled LC to make more records available to the library community. The Linked Systems Project (mentioned earlier and described in the Linked Systems Project brochure),[3] while focusing on name authority entries, will enable the self-authentication process to work more smoothly. CONSER-NACO participants will have direct access to LC files as LC will also have to OCLC files. Time delays in distribution of data should be significantly reduced.

Currently, LC has initiated an independent review of CONSER and what its future should be. The report was reviewed at the February 1986 meetings of CONSER Advisory Group and Participants. Discussions are summarized in a recent *CONSER Newsletter*.[4] The topic will also appear on the agenda for the Fall 1986 meeting. The full report is available from LC.[5]

I remain optimistic about CONSER and its viability. The need for cooperation still remains. While a significant database now exists, it must be maintained, and we have yet to deal with retrospective serial publications.

CONSER has provided both data and a model for other serial projects. It is a significant achievement in the bibliographic control of serial publications.

NOTES AND REFERENCES

1.   OCLC. CONSER: Conversion of Serials (brochure), April, 1985. Dublin, Ohio.

2.   OCLC. CONSER: Conversion of Serials (newsletter), edited by M. E. Jacob, vol. 1, 1979. Dublin, Ohio. Published irregularly. Available free from OCLC, Dublin, Ohio.

3.   Linked System Project (brochure), 1985. Available free from the Library of Congress, OCLC, RLG, and WLN.

4.   OCLC. CONSER: CONversion of SERials (newsletter), edited by M.E. Jacob, No. 11, August 1986.

5.   "The CONSER Project: Recommendations for the Future." Report of a Study Conducted for the Library of Congress by Jeffrey Heynen and Julia Blixrud. Network Planning Paper Number 14. 1986.

SERIALS' PLACE ON THE ORGANIZATIONAL CHART:
A HISTORICAL PERSPECTIVE

Jean G. Cook

On January 5, 1665, the *Journal des scavans* appeared in France. Three centuries later librarians are still debating the proper organizational structure for controlling this periodical and the hundreds of thousands of its near and distant serial relatives. It is the capricious nature and ongoing character of serials that provoke and intrigue their caretakers. A librarian can neatly package a monograph for users, but no amount of tying down can keep a serial from popping out with a new title, a stray cumulative index, and an unexpected growth spurt.

While librarians have examined and deplored the problems of acquiring and maintaining serials, they have always recognized their value. Library staff and patrons have echoed the sentiments of this 1831 columnist.

> This is the golden age of periodicals. Nothing can be done without them. Sects and parties, benevolent societies, and ingenious individuals, all have their periodi-

Advances in Serials Management, Volume 1, pages 53–66.
Copyright © 1986 by JAI Press Inc.
All rights of reproduction in any form reserved.
ISBN: 0-89232-568-2

cals. . . . Every man, and every party, that seeks to establish a new theory, or to
break down an old one, commences operations, like a board of war, by founding a
magazine. . . . For my own part, I have no quarrel with the makers of these amusing
works, on account of their number: the more the merrier.[1]

Although the proceedings of the first session of the 1876 Conference of
Librarians lack the carefree tone of the above commentary, the support
for another type of serial, the annual report of organizations, is unequi-
vocal.

If railway companies and hospitals, and colleges, and penitentiaries, and benevolent
institutions of every sort—to say nothing of historical societies and library companies—
keep publishing their annual reports for another century as they publish them now,
may it not require the most active labor of the best librarian in America to collect,
to preserve, to bind, to arrange, and catalogue them all? Yet few books are more
instructive as to special matters; few more often wanted by a large class of readers.[2]

Both of the statements are equally positive concerning the essential role
of serials. However, the earlier author knows only the joy of perusing the
many available periodicals; it is the librarians who are aware of the costs
and efforts involved in providing access to continuing publications. Regardless of a serial's regularity and consistency, problems arise for the
library. The *Journal des scavans* (after 1816 *Journal des savants*) has had
only one title change and only one period of suspension in over 300 years.
Yet, the very fact that it and its 1665–1861 cumulative index are both
historical firsts make a complete set highly desirable and very rare. Libraries determined to obtain full runs must resort to microfilm and reprint
editions and the additional bibliographic and equipment costs these entail.
   But regardless of budgets and travail Ralph Munn trumpeted in the October 1929 issue of *Wilson Bulletin:* "Save the magazines—let the books
burn!" In defending this attitude he noted, first, that most books can be
duplicated or else replaced by later editions, but a periodical issue becomes
a rare item within a year of its publication. Second, "reference librarians
grow gray searching for facts which never found their way into any book
. . . magazines fail them less frequently."[3] Finally, Munn clinched his
argument that librarians considered magazines their prize possession with
the incontrovertible proof.

Through a system of interlibrary loans a library can usually borrow a needed book
from some other city, but requests for magazine files are not encouraged. Stocks,
bonds, and precious jewels may be entrusted to the mails, but not a bound magazine!
Libraries are also beginning to limit the use of magazines within their own buildings. . . . Library assistants are being urged to look first in books and to use the
magazines as a last resort. All of this is, of course, to the end that these files may
be preserved for future generations.[4]

Strong but less flamboyant reasons for the importance of serials were given by Paul Bixler. He believed the use of serials by faculty and students in the science disciplines was an accepted fact. Bixler's concern was documenting the need for scholarly journals by humanists and social scientists.

> The reading of the results of recent scholarship in these fields is as necessary for instruction and research as is familiarity with recent advances in chemistry or physics. A teacher in the social sciences has put the case emphatically. Most of his colleagues, he said, have the intellectual humility to admit that their "sciences" are still seeking to establish first principles. They cannot honestly use authoritarian texts. They are dependent on the results of new investigations into theory and evidence which are only available through the journals.[5]

Bixler further contended that journals as general reading materials broadened the perspective of students beyond their major areas of study.

At the same time librarians were expressing this dependency upon serials, they were becoming apprehensive about their growth rate and the effect on library budgets. Yet articles appearing before 1925 offered no solution to the serials dilemma. The authors limited themselves to descriptions of the procedures followed in their own institutions or discussions of a specific serials concern. Perhaps these writers shared the frustration expressed 55 years later by Michael Gorman. "Imagine being the family planning advisor to a rabbit warren—you now have a faint idea of the difficulties faced by serials librarians."[6]

This hand-wringing indecisiveness ended with the checking for the *Union List of Serials* and its subsequent publication. It was as if the handling of serials had suddenly been declared a respectable occupation. Gertrude Wulfekoetter in 1930 acknowledged this change in status and recognized the need to develop an organizational structure that could cope with this wealth of material.

> During the last few years there has certainly been a growing sense of importance of periodicals in library work. The appearance of the *Union List of Serials*, without which none of us could now exist, has brought this fact to our attention more vividly. The larger part played by them in research work has been frequently stressed and no doubt will continue to be stressed even more. The increasing importance has necessitated a much more serious consideration of periodical problems than was formerly thought essential. Many periodical divisions, like Topsy, just grew, and suddenly have waked up to find themselves unable to cope with the questions of the present day.[7]

Unfortunately Wulfekoetter did not pursue the organization of serial functions in general, but digressed to a detailed account of her own library's system. Five years later another librarian avoided the trap of my-library-does-it-good and recommended an overall solution for managing serials.

On June 24, 1935, J. Harris Gable, the Superintendent of the Serial and Exchange Department of the State University of Iowa Libraries, read a paper before the College and Reference Section at the American Library Association Conference in Denver, which was published five months later in the *Library Journal*. Gable's nine years of serials work, a thorough study of the literature devoted to serials during the past 60 years, on site inspections of systems used in large libraries, and the responses to a questionnaire sent to 125 representative libraries convinced him that a library with more than 1,000 subscriptions should have all serial functions within one department. From his observation and research Gable had concluded that the dispersal of serial activities resulted in "(1) considerable waste of money, (2) great lack of efficiency, (3) considerable duplication of functions, and (4) insufficient service to the public."[8] Libraries were not getting a good return on the money spent for purchasing and administering serials.

Gable did not regard the sorry state of serials as a diabolical plot devised by the staffs of the catalog, order, reference, and circulation departments. It was basically caused by the dramatic increase in the number and importance of serial titles. Library schools were not prepared to offer courses on the subject and no adequate guides were available to practicing librarians. Libraries were, therefore, left on their own to struggle with the flood of continuing publications. Almost every department within a library was assigned certain duties relating to serials. Assistants given these tasks had no special training and often resented the extra work. Serials were relegated to second class status and treated accordingly.

By bringing together all serial operations—selection, ordering, receiving, cataloging, binding, and public service—Gable was certain that the following benefits would accrue to the library:

> (1) the work may be more easily and efficiently done where the records are kept, (2) the work may be done by trained serials workers, (3) the evil of over departmentalization can not appear, (4) there is no unnecessary duplication of records, (5) the same persons handle all the necessary records, thus eliminating possibility of error or duplication of material, and (6) the service to the public is greatly improved.[9]

Although Gable believed his proposal was a vast improvement over current serial practices, he did not consider his plan the final solution to all the problems. He hoped that his efforts would arouse interest and encourage development of better methods and structures for handling serials.

Gable's commitment to improve the processing and servicing of serials did not stop with the presentation of his unified organizational concept. Two years later the American Library Association published his *Manual of Serials Work*. In her review of the manual, Carolyn F. Ulrich found some sections and the index not sufficiently complete. However, her overall reaction was one of approval and praise for Gable's endeavor.

> In spite of these limitations, the *Manual* is a direct service to libraries. Also, this volume is such a welcome contribution to the study and use of serials that it should go a long way toward developing the effective use of them and toward a wider study of them. Its merits far outweigh its faults and it will take an important place in the literature of its field.[10]

The publication of Gable's paper and manual did indeed awaken widespread interest in the appropriate administrative structure for serials. The variation and fluctuations found in the opinions, survey reports, and theories which appeared in library literature strongly resembled serials' own erratic behavior. While the contributors to this body of literature frequently reached similar conclusions, the reasons were often different.

Fred B. Rothman, Supervisor of the Serials Division of New York University's Washington Square Library, agreed with Gable that a unified serials organization was the ideal arrangement. However, Rothman felt Gable had approached the problem from the wrong direction. The New Yorker advocated an integrated department based on the needs of the user. If the organizational structure provided patrons with easy access to all types of serials, then it would follow that concentration of serial processing functions would resolve the technical problems associated with this material.

Patrons' requests would be funneled to one location in the library, the serials department. Here, staff experienced in the ways of corporate entries and changing titles could bring prompt relief to users struggling with serials perplexities. To further coordinate all serial activities, the check-in file would be declared the official serials catalog, thus, eliminating the need for updating the public catalog cards as individual issues were received. The card in the general catalog would be stamped "For complete record see Serials Catalog."

Once Rothman had presented the case for placing serials reference, serials circulation, and the primary serials information file together, it followed naturally, in his way of thinking, that the cataloging, acquisition, and binding of serials would become residents of the same enclave. While Gable envisioned a distinct department with staff members assigned specific responsibilities, e.g., cataloging or reference,[11] Rothman proposed a cadre of personnel trained in all aspects of serials.

> All the perplexities of serial routine are centralized at one point. Checking in and cataloging are combined in most instances, eliminating duplication of labor. The ideal of interdepartmental exchange of assistants among the acquisition, cataloging, and

circulation departments is achieved. The division can do the work with fewer assistants than would otherwise be required since the assignments can be adjusted as the need varies. As the pressure of work in serials moves from the point of acquisition to cataloging and then to circulation, the staff can be shifted accordingly. Furthermore, the supervisor of the division is in a position to put through the material in greatest demand at the particular time when it is most needed without the necessity of an exchange of memoranda from department to department.[12]

What could delight a library director more—better service with fewer staff! Lest the chief administrator be too joyful, Rothman added words of caution. A separate division whose functions cross those of all other units could only be successful with the firm, open support of the library administration.

As Chief of the New York Public Library's Periodicals Division, Ulrich expressed views similar to Rothman's in her July 1941 *Library Journal* article. Because of her position and experience Ulrich focused on the treatment of a particular type of serials, periodicals. She, like Rothman, began with the public servicing aspects and then moved to the technical activities. In proposing the centralization of materials, records, and specially trained staff, Ulrich appeared to hesitate and backtrack only when recommending that the total authority for purchasing and payments be transferred to the periodicals division. "It might be better to have the purchasing office of periodicals with the Periodicals Division, all bills and purchases to be approved by the Acquisition Department."[13] Perhaps Ulrich was willing for the Periodicals Division at New York Public Library to forego complete fiscal control in order to have full responsibility in servicing periodicals for readers.

Beatrice V. Simon, librarian and special lecturer at McGill University, showed no reluctance in enunciating the structure of serials departments and the role of serials librarians. The unit must encompass all serial operations and the librarians must be "a vital force in the thinking world . . . or become even more slavish to our techniques."[14] The idea, with its concomitant routines that Simon declared should be immediately discarded, was the concept that a library was a collection of individual books. Because serials were forced and manipulated to fit into this monographic mold, all facets of serials handling were inadequate and created obstacles for the patrons.

The three areas Simon enumerated as demanding prompt and continued attention were: (1) acquisition and preservation of the serial records of our civilization; (2) sensible and adequate methods of caring for these in our libraries; and (3) methods and means of making the best possible use of the information in them.[15] Since Simon in 1946 considered the principle of concentrating all serial functions in a single department to be an accepted fact, her solutions to the above problems were based on this operational pattern.

Librarians responsible for acquiring and preserving the serials collection must recognize the basic differences between book and serials selection and purchase. First, most libraries after buying a monograph would not attempt to obtain all earlier editions, although a commitment might be made to buy future editions. Second, it seldom mattered if six libraries in the same locale purchased the same book. With serials, the decisions to try for a complete run of a title and to duplicate holdings of nearby institutions were of major importance. Serials' ongoing consumption of the budget, space, and staff time warranted knowledgeable and judicious evaluation of serial orders. Simon urged serials librarians and library administrators to promote cooperative agreements. The tool, the *Union List of Serials,* was available to make local, regional, national, and international sharing of serials resources a reality.

Simon's approach to resolving the other two problem areas was again to divorce serials from the rituals prescribed for books. By stopping the unnecessary classifying of serials two goals would be achieved. Serials and books could no longer be shelved together, and serials would be inexpensively and naturally arranged by their titles, volumes, and dates. Simon, in agreement with Rothman, insisted that the check-in record should be the source for holdings, current receipts, payments, and binding information. Duplicate files meant increased costs and decreased efficiency and service. The catalogers of serials should concentrate on providing sufficient data to identify a particular title. Bibliographical details, such as the changing of editors and places of publication, cluttered the cards and confused the patrons. Simon would only accord in-depth bibliographic description to the "rare odd literary curiosities."[16]

The final step in utilizing the information within serials was the development of a reference staff that not only knew the serials collection and the tools to access it, but also understood the habits and contents of the serials themselves. According to Simon this could only be accomplished by:

> (1) adequate preliminary training in library schools; and (2) a definite, planned program for the in-service development of promising serials librarians. Here, the self-contained serials division is, again, the answer. It takes years to develop a good serials librarian, but a carefully integrated program which utilizes every step in serials work as a training experience will help speed the process immeasurably.[17]

While Simon believed that the integrated serials department had been established as the preferred organizational structure, Guy R. Lyle found the prevailing practice in most libraries was to distribute serial functions among various departments. Louis Round Wilson and Maurice F. Tauber concurred with Lyle's findings. The cost of a separate department and the need for the proper physical conditions, as well as a large staff, led them to the conclusion that only a few large university libraries would be able to maintain an independent serials division. When the staff, funding, and structural requirements were met, the three authorities on library administration concluded that centralized control of technical serial operations would be advantageous.

Wilson and Tauber were also willing under these favorable circumstances to have the serials department be the reference source for specific information on serials. However, they continued to emphasize that users be able to obtain knowledge from all the library's resources.

> In libraries having both a general reference department and a serials department, it is essential that there be close cooperation in the guidance of readers who need information on their projects, regardless of whether the information is in books, documents, or serials.[18]

Lyle did not propose the assignment of any reference activity to the separate serials unit. All reference services should be in the reference department. Since patrons' needs could not be predicted or limited to one type of material, Lyle believed that a staff trained in all formats could best serve the users.

Andrew Osborn in 1955 declared "it is difficult to lay down hard and fast rules for the location of serial functions."[19] The traditional divided structure with serial specialists in the acquisitions and catalog departments had apparent advantages. Essential cataloging tools, especially the card catalog and the shelflist, were not duplicated. Name and subject control were enhanced. All types of publications followed a more consistent classification pattern. By combining the acquisition, receipt, and payment of books and serials libraries were reflecting the approach of many vendors. Dealers' shipments and invoices frequently contained both types of materials and the single library facility expedited the unpacking and processing. Osborn balanced the arguments for distributing serial functions by quoting Rothman, Sidney Ditzion, and Simon's statements in support of an integrated division, then added his own comment that a centralized department "performs a useful service by highlighting the fact that serials have grown so enormously in number and consequentiality in the twentieth century."[20]

Osborn viewed the development of a separate serials organizational entity as only one segment of a broader issue, the departmentalization of libraries. Prior to the late 1930s and early 1940s there was little literature devoted to library organization.[21] Donald Coney, in a 1938 paper presented at the Library Institute of the University of Chicago, attributed this lack, not to administrative disinterest or indifference, but to the time consumed by daily routines.[22] In his September 1943 article Herman H. Henkle, the Director of the Library of Congress Processing Department, exhorted librarians to become aware "of the important body of professional knowledge which has been developed in the field of public administration and business management."[23] Henkle praised library administrators that were beginning to apply these principles and reminded them that the primary basis for departmentalization should be function. While the champions of separate serials divisions rallied to the support of departmentalization, they marched under the banner of format, not function.

Despite the enthusiastic endorsement of the advocates of centralized serials departments, surveys did not find this a movement that was sweeping the library world. One of the early published reports was prepared by Pearl Holland Clark in 1930. The preeminence of periodical literature among researchers had in Clark's opinion created a two-fold problem for librarians. First, extreme care and caution had to be exercised in the selection of this type of publication. "Second, the development of an efficient technique for handling the issues of such publications after they are acquired by the library, with a view to making them as fully accessible and widely serviceable as possible was necessary."[24] The questionnaire Clark sent to representative college and university libraries attempted to evaluate the quality of periodical service by measuring the completeness of the sets held by the libraries. The 85 responses revealed that a wide variety of methods existed for obtaining and controlling periodicals and other classes of serials. In reporting her results, Clark made no mention of discovering any library with a department devoted to serial activities. She stressed the need for the various departments that were involved with serials to coordinate and expedite their functions.

Ten years later Rothman and Ditzion presented in the March 1940 *College and Research Libraries* the findings of their survey of the serial operations in 126 college, university, and public libraries. At the conclusion of the study their overall feeling was that there was "a decided trend toward centralization. This trend has taken so many forms that it can hardly be called a prevailing practice."[25] The modi operandi of the institutions surveyed included at one extreme a library that had its serial functions scattered through the order, catalog, and circulation departments. At the other end of the spectrum was a university library that had all serial activities contained in a single department. Reference and circulation, cataloging and classification, binding, receipt, and acquisition were all responsibilities of its serials department.

Between these opposing positions the authors found a broad range of serial practices. Certain libraries had their serials divisions in charge of all tasks except cataloging and classification. In others, the reference and circulation of serials were not assigned to the serials unit. Often each type of serial was treated differently with periodicals distinguished from all other library materials. As more classes of serials gained in stature, some libraries added a continuations division, a serials division, and/or a documents division to their already established periodicals division. In a number of the responding libraries, when part of a serial was obtained as a gift or by exchange and the remainder was purchased, the issues from the different sources were not processed by the same department.

This diversity in serial operational structures did not weaken Rothman and Ditzion's conviction that the trend was towards concentrating serial functions in one department. They based their opinion on the statistics collected during their survey.

> Twelve of twenty-two large college and university libraries have a serials division which is staffed by from three to nineteen persons. Seven of these are independent departments which are coordinated in various ways with other departments of the library. Substantially the same situation, with some variations, is found among the medium-sized libraries where seven out of fifteen libraries reported that they had a serials division.[26]

Because of limited staffing, the small college libraries and the medium and small public libraries could not have a formal organizational structure, but they had centralized serial tasks.

From this data Rothman and Ditzion had discerned the trend to integrate serial functions, while Osborn from 1939 on saw only "a slight tendency to centralize serial activities to the extent that a full-fledged serials department is created, coordinate with acquisition, cataloging, and other departments."[27] Osborn made this statement in the second edition of his book, which was published 30 years after Rothman and Ditzion's article. Perhaps the variance in assessments could be attributed to time, perspective, semantics, or a combination of the three.

During the late 1940s and throughout the 1950s, reports of serial practices in specific institutions continued to appear in the library literature. George Hartje's 1949 unpublished master's paper at the University of Illinois Library School was the basis for the School's *Occasional Papers,* number 24. The eight libraries Hartje investigated were selected because "they were thought to have something to contribute to the effort to establish a serials division at the University of Illinois Library."[28] His study focused on the status of serial checking records in each of the institutions. While the LC and the Libraries of the Universities of California, Missouri, and Pennsylvania had centralized these records, the University Libraries at Columbia, Louisiana State, Michigan, and Minnesota continued to maintain a number of checking files. Only one library, the University of Missouri's, had begun a separate serials catalog which eventually would contain main entry and holding cards for all serial titles in the University Libraries. None of the libraries examined by Hartje had brought all their serial functions together in a single administrative unit.

Because of this fragmentation of serial operations, librarians involved with these publications had informally banded together to have serial work recognized as a distinct component of the library structure. By June 23, 1942, these unofficial groups had evolved into the Serials Round Table of the American Library Association. In its early years the Serials Round Table struggled to expand its membership and develop its own identity. At a Midwinter meeting in 1950 John H. Moriarty of Purdue University Libraries suggested "that there was need for closer exchange of information," and then proceeded to offer "the services of Purdue University Library to help get started a serial for serials."[29]

Moriarty's proposal came at an opportune time. The postwar years had seen a tremendous expansion in the number, problems, and costs of serials. Serials librarians eagerly awaited the arrival of a medium dedicated to them and their charges. *Serial Slants,* Volume I, Number 1, was issued in July 1950 and continued until October 1956 when it merged with the *Journal of Cataloging and Classification* to become *Library Resources and Technical Services.*

Throughout its six years of existence, its modest appearance remained unchanged—no slick paper and only an occasional small picture of a contributor graced its pages. "However, the new energy which *Serial Slants* had instilled in serial workers was a positive force."[30] All who had a concern or interest in serials had a medium for expressing and promulgating their ideas. Reports, such as Hartje's, that had been published in other publications were frequently summarized in *Serial Slants.* A perusal of the cumulative index in volume seven confirmed that no serial topic lacked adherents and opponents.

The divergency in serials organizational structures was evident in the articles appearing in *Serial Slants.* In the October 1951 issue Neal Harlow of the University of California at Los Angeles described the UCLA Serials Conference. This was an internal organization instituted by the library administration to increase the efficiency and effectiveness of their serial operations. Since serial functions were distributed among several of the library's departments, the heads of these units as well as the supervisors of the departmental subdivisions that performed the daily serial tasks joined with the associate librarian to create policies, resolve problems, and initiate new serial programs.

> Such is the structure and function of the UCLA Serials Conference. It meets only when serials problems are pressing enough to warrant bringing together nine persons of diverse departments, schedules, and interests. It is a Library-wide, nine-man Serials Authority. Its conclusions are final and binding, at least until the next meeting.[31]

In the next issue of the same volume, Edgar G. Simpkins explained the current serial practices at the Linda Hall Library of Science and Technology in Kansas City, Missouri. The library had only been in existence for six years when the report was published in January 1952. At this time the collection included 10,000 serial titles with 3,000 of these being currently received. A visible Kardex file had become the serials catalog, the sole repository for all bibliographic, ordering, checking, and binding information. The catalog was arranged alphabetically by title. This same title, together with the publication's enumeration and chronology, constituted the classification system for all the library's serial holdings. Since the library had been designed as a research facility limited to science and technology, it was not deemed necessary to establish multiple records and a complex classification scheme.

An article describing a larger and more diverse serials collection was contributed to *Serial Slants* in April 1955 by Sam Hitt, the head of the Serials Department at the University of Missouri. Hitt credited Ralph Parker, University Librarian, for the emergence in 1948 of a separate serials department. Centralization of serial records and responsibilities was proposed and then implemented to end the mismanagement and neglect of the constantly increasing serials collection. Initially, the department contained receipt; cataloging (except cataloging revision); binding of serials; and the government documents section. Four years later conditions changed and the disarray in the acquisition of serials became the dominant concern. The serials catalog remained in the department, but the serials cataloger was transferred to the catalog department. A staff member from the acquisition department became head of the serials department and brought with him the serial payment records to be interfiled in the Kardex. While the library administration seemingly endorsed the concept of a serials department, seven years after its inception certain serial functions were outside the department's jurisdiction.

This reluctance to integrate all serial operations after the establishment of a separate department was not unique to the University of Missouri. A survey conducted in October 1959 by Gloria Whetstone, the head of the Serials Department at North Carolina State College, found this to be the norm among the 16 libraries that returned usable questionnaires. Whetstone had queried libraries with holdings of between 4,000 and 6,000 periodicals on their serial procedures. The satisfactory responses came from the libraries at the universities of Alabama, Colorado, Duke, Iowa, Johns Hopkins, Maryland, New York, North Carolina, North Carolina State, Oklahoma, Oregon, Pennsylvania State, Rutgers, Texas, Virginia, and Wayne State.

Six of these libraries had separate serials departments, nine had separately administered serials units within a larger department, and one library reported that its acquisitions and cataloging departments shared responsibility for serials.[32]

Although Colorado, Johns Hopkins, North Carolina State, Oklahoma, Rutgers, and Texas had replied positively to the question of whether the library had a separate department, none had a structure that encompassed all the technical and public serial functions. The patterns Rothman and Ditzion reported in 1940 had not changed significantly 21 years later. Only one library with a serials department and two with serials subdivisions had the full responsibility for ordering serials. Colorado, North Carolina State, Oklahoma, and Rutgers had central serials records located in their serials departments. Johns Hopkins was contemplating developing this type of file, but Texas had no plans for forming one. A public serials catalog was maintained by both North Carolina institutions and the libraries at Alabama, Duke, and Virginia. In one library with a serials department this unit was responsible for the binding of all library materials. Other libraries split this activity among serials departments and subdivisions, subject divisions, and departmental libraries. Rutgers alone among the 16 responding libraries had assigned its serials department a public service role, and it was limited to the unbound periodicals.

The 16 respondents to Whetstone's survey characterized serials' status within the organizational structure of libraries. By 1960 libraries had not rushed to embrace and implement the concept of confining all serial functions in one department. However, library administrators were recognizing the importance and complexities of serials by giving serial responsibilities to specific administrative units and/or staff. Whether a particular serial operation was part of a separate serials department or a subdivision of a department based on function could depend upon the physical facilities; the personalities of staff members; funding; and, of course, happenstance.

What the advocates for total centralization could not achieve on the institutional level, they did attain within their national professional association. In 1957, 22 years after Gable's presentation, the new Resources and Technical Services Division of the American Library Association was organized with sections for acquisitions, for cataloging and classification, and for serials. The provision for a separate serials section acknowledged the cohesiveness of serials librarians and their insistence that serials were different. The rallying cry had remained the same for over 20 years—*vive la différence!*

NOTES AND REFERENCES

1. "Periodicals," *Illinois Monthly Magazine* 1 (1831): 302–03.
2. "Proceedings (of the Conference of Librarians), First Session," *Library Journal* 1 (1876): 94.

3. Ralph Munn, "The Library Mission of Magazines," *Wilson Bulletin* 7 (1929): 59.

4. Ibid., 60.

5. Paul Bixler, "Selection and Acquisition of Special Types of Materials," in *The Administration of the College Library,* by Guy R. Lyle (New York: H. W. Wilson Company, 1944), 373–74.

6. Michael Gorman, "Crunching the Serial," *American Libraries* 11 (July/August 1980): 416.

7. Gertrude Wulfekoetter, "The Organization of a Periodical Department," *Library Journal* 55 (1930): 448.

8. J. Harris Gable, "The New Serials Department," *Library Journal* 60 (1935): 869.

9. Ibid., 870.

10. Carolyn F. Ulrich, "Serials Work," *Library Journal* 62 (1937): 335.

11. J. Harris Gable, *Manual of Serials Work* (Chicago: American Library Association, 1937), 38.

12. Fred B. Rothman, "Pooh-Bah of the Serials Department," *Library Journal* 62 (1937): 458–59.

13. Carolyn F. Ulrich, "Some Problems Presented by Current Developments in the Periodicals Field," *Library Journal* 66 (1941): 597.

14. Beatrice V. Simon, "Let's Consider Serials Realistically," *Library Journal* 71 (1946): 1301.

15. Ibid., 1297.

16. Ibid., 1300.

17. Ibid., 1300–01.

18. Louis Round Wilson and Maurice F. Tauber, *The University Library,* 2nd ed. (New York: Columbia University Press, 1976), 235.

19. Andrew D. Osborn, *Serial Publications: Their Place and Treatment in Libraries* (Chicago: American Library Association, 1955), 21.

20. Ibid., 31.

21. Connie R. Dunlap, "Organizational Patterns in Academic Libraries, 1876–1976," *College & Research Libraries* 37 (1976): 395.

22. John Minton Dawson, "Department Interrelationship: The Many in One in Action as well as in Reorganization of the ALA," *Library Resources & Technical Services* 1 (1957): 155.

23. Herman H. Henkle, "Principles and Practice of Administrative Organization in the University Library," *College & Research Libraries* 4 (1943): 284.

24. Pearl Holland Clark, *The Problem Presented by Periodicals in College and University Libraries* (Chicago: University of Chicago, 1930), 2.

25. Fred B. Rothman and Sidney Ditzion, "Prevailing Practices in Handling Serials," *College & Research Libraries* 1 (1940): 166.

26. Ibid., 167.

27. Andrew D. Osborn, *Serial Publications: Their Place and Treatment in Libraries,* 2nd ed. rev. (Chicago: American Library Association, 1973), 51.

28. George N. Hartje, "Centralized Serial Records in University Libraries," *University of Illinois Library School Occasional Papers* 24 (1951): 4.

29. William H. Huff, "A Summary of Some Serial Activities, 1942–1966," *Library Resources & Technical Services* 11 (1967): 303.

30. Ibid., 305.

31. Neil Harlow, "Serials Conference at UCLA," *Serial Slants* 2 (1951): 16.

32. Gloria Whetstone, "Serial Practices in Selected College and University Libraries," *Library Resources & Technical Services* 5 (1961): 284–85.

THE INTEGRATED SERIALS DEPARTMENT

Joline R. Ezzell

The appropriate place within the library organization for the processing of serials has been debated for many years, both in print and in public forums. Recent programs within the Serials Section of the American Library Association have brought together both proponents and opponents of the integrated serials department. Many arguments have been advanced for the separate serials department but before summarizing them it may be helpful to describe this type of department and to see whether such an arrangement is based on organizational theory.

The components of a fully integrated serials department are preorder and precatalog searching, ordering, serials check-in, invoice approval, serials cataloging, shelflisting, maintenance of manual and machine records for serials, bindery preparation, withdrawal and transfer of serial materials, and the supervision and staffing of a current periodicals area, if such exists. Although serials departments in the past included selection responsibilities, they generally do not include this responsibility now unless it is delegated

Advances in Serials Management, Volume 1, pages 67–82.
Copyright © 1986 by JAI Press Inc.
All rights of reproduction in any form reserved.
ISBN: 0-89232-568-2

to serials specialists. However, serials department staff may do biblio-graphic searching to assist collection development staff in making selection decisions. Once such decisions have been made, any necessary additional preorder searching will be completed by serials department staff.

Vendor selection for supply of serial titles is made in the integrated serials department. Once the order is placed, all necessary records of the order and of fund encumbrances are made, and filed if necessary. Upon receipt of the material, serials staff check in the item(s) and approve in-voices for payment. Since many serial orders are for subscriptions or standing orders, the check-in process is repeated as additional issues or volumes are received. Invoice approval is also repeated with the receipt of volumes or as the subscription renewal comes due. The actual ac-counting function is rarely part of the integrated serials department, being more frequently located within the acquisitions department; in a separate unit; or, in academic libraries, elsewhere within the institution.

The types of items which are checked in by the serials department may vary among libraries. Serials and periodicals will certainly be included, and newspapers may be handled by the serials department. Although they are not serials, monographic set volumes may also be checked in by the serials department, because they are received in parts over time and lend themselves well to many serials procedures. The check-in process involves recording exactly what issue has arrived. Good check-in procedures also call for recording the date on which the item was received.

Claiming is an integral part of serial operations and frequently a part of the check-in procedures. Claims are issued when gaps are noted in serial holdings (preferably immediately after a skipped issue is detected). In addition to this type of claim, another type must frequently be made; the claim for titles which have ceased coming. Unless staff have excellent memories and can recognize when a title has stopped coming, the need for making these claims can be discovered only through a periodic review of the check-in file.

Precatalog searching may be done for new serial titles, depending on the level of detail of preorder searching which was done. Where preorder searching includes only identifying the item as a publication, precatalog searching may be the first instance of verification of the entry in biblio-graphic sources. The cataloging of new serial titles is also a responsibility of the integrated serials department.

Many records are maintained for serials. These may be manual or au-tomated, or a combination of both. If one of these records is a manual shelflist, serials department staff will update it as additional volumes of serials are received. If the library keeps a machine record of its serial titles, the serials department will have responsibility for updating and maintaining it. Similarly, the maintenance of any card catalogs of serial titles will be done by the serials department. The withdrawal of serial materials from the collection or their transfer from one location to another within the library are also tasks appropriate to the serials department staff.

The amalgamation of records of serial holdings from several libraries into a single joint list, called a union list, has become common in recent years. Preparation of the records for submission to the union list headquarters or of the union list itself is a proper function of the serials department.

In most libraries the majority of the materials bound, either in-house or by a commercial binder, are serials. Therefore, the bindery preparation operation is logically a part of the serials department.

Many serials departments also have a public service function. Their staffs provide reference service of the serials collection, or a portion of it, at a public service desk or assist patrons using the collection in a periodicals reading area. They may assist the patron in locating serial materials to which s/he already has a reference, or in using periodical or serial indexes and abstracts to find appropriate citations.

The integrated serials department, then, is a mixture of acquisitions, inventory, cataloging, and reference functions.

Is there a theoretical basis for gathering these several functions into one unit devoted to a particular format? Can management theory assist us in understanding this arrangement?

Grouping into departments is a fundamental means to coordinate work within the organization. Historically, there are several bases for grouping within an organization: grouping by knowledge and skill, by work process and function, by time (shift work), by output (products made or services rendered), by client, and by place.

Neil Kay calls organization by function "U-form" organization, and the existence of quasi-autonomous operating divisions organized by product "M-form" organization. The advantages he cites in adopting the M-form of organization are (1) the formation of natural decision units, and (2) the combination of richly interacting parts and the separation of weakly interacting parts.[1] Such a product or service structure allows staff to develop an *esprit de corps*.[2]

Modern organization studies describe two types of work structures, functional grouping and flow grouping. In the functional grouping mode, work is divided according to the type of operation performed. Workers and supervisors are specialists in the type of operation for which they are responsible. Materials move from area to area, department to department in the order of the operations performed.

In flow grouping, on the other hand, workers and equipment are arranged in a flow set up by product. Workers and supervisors are specialists in a particular product line. The organizational unit is responsible for the completion of this product line rather than being responsible only for specific parts of many products. Within the group everyone can see the whole process, and a team spirit is developed among the staff.

Henry Mintzberg, who recorded some of the above ideas in his recent book on the design of effective organizations, also suggests that the method chosen for grouping operating tasks should reflect natural workflow interdependencies and interdependencies related to specialty.[3] When like specialists are grouped together, he noted, they learn from each other and become more adept.

The alternatives of functional grouping and flow grouping are not unlike the alternatives in libraries of organization by function and organization by format. Under functional organization, departments are structured around types of activities, with one department responsible for all acquisitional activities, another for all cataloging activities, and so forth. Organization by format recognizes differences in some formats of library materials and is an acknowledgment that these formats require special handling. Generally with format organization all functions appropriate for the particular type of material are performed in the department created for that format.

Mitsuko Collver presents an interesting argument for the integrated serials department in her article "Organization of Serials Work for Manual and Automated Systems."[4] In regard to the importance of the interdependencies of tasks in choosing an organizational structure, her opinions are similar to those of Mintzberg. Collver bases her conclusions on James Thompson's theory of grouping activities according to levels of interdependence. The highest level of interdependence he identifies is reciprocal interdependence, in which each function has repeated inputs from, and interaction with the other functions. Collver argues, and rightly so, that serial materials meet the test of reciprocal interdependence since they involve title, publisher, or frequency changes; size or format changes; and cessations or suspensions of publication, which necessitate the repetition of cataloging and record creation. Thompson believes that it is essential for people whose actions are reciprocally interdependent to be grouped together as a team, leading Collver to conclude that all serials functions should be so grouped.

Whether one chooses to accept the traditional theories of grouping outlined by Mintzberg, in which serials may be considered a product, or the conclusions of Mitsuko Collver, it is clear that there is a theoretical basis for the establishment of serials departments in libraries.

The debate for and against separate serials departments has raged for many years. It has not been won; the debaters still present their arguments, as have Thomas Leonhardt in a 1984 issue of the *RTSD Newsletter*[5] and Sue Anne Harrington and Deborah Karpuk in the Winter 1984 issue of *The Serials Librarian.*[6]

The primary reason for formation of a separate serials department is the nature of the format itself. Serials are not monographs and they cannot successfully be treated so. They have an ongoing nature. Their acquisition is never complete, as it may be for a monograph; their acquisition is, in a sense, perpetual. Whereas monograph acquisition generally involves payment for a single order at time of receipt, the acquisition of serials frequently means payment in advance of receipt. Records for the receipt and payment of a title must be maintained over a longer time than that required for monographs, as questions about past receipts or payments frequently arise.

Two other characteristics of serials set them apart from monographs. First is their changeability. They often change title, change issuing body, split into parts, or merge with other serials; they may also suspend publication or cease publication altogether. Second, they are characterized by a numbering system which can be a date, a numerical or alphabetic designation, or a combination of the two. Both of these characteristics set serials apart and make their handling different of necessity from that of monographs, particularly the single volume monograph.

Bibliographic records must be created and maintained for the serial titles on standing order or subscription. These records must include both bibliographic and acquisitional information. Detailed records of the library's holdings of each title must be kept and must be available to library patrons in a comprehensible form. Title changes must be detected and recorded with links made between the various titles, for the benefit of both the staff and library patrons.

Work with serials requires good communication among all those involved. Staff ordering serials must give information to those receiving them. The staff checking in issues of new titles often have important instructions or bibliographic and publishing information to pass on to serials catalogers. Catalogers, in turn, may have information to communicate to the bindery preparation staff, such as the number of issues per volume, numbering peculiarities, or unpublished issues. Good communication is needed also between the check-in staff and the employees servicing the periodicals reading room or providing reference service for serials (if they are not one and the same staff). Particularly in the case of problem titles (and all libraries have their problem titles!), such communication is essential.

It is possible for communication to take place when the several serials functions are separated into various departments within the library, but it is not as natural and easy as when they are joined into an integrated serials department. Although the same mission is shared by these staff members and their long range goals may be identical or similar, it is likely that short range goals and objectives, as well as priorities, differ, and differ to such an extent that patron service is affected adversely. When all those handling serials are part of the same team sharing objectives and working together closely on a daily basis, such communication is nearly automatic. The lines of responsibility are clear and the functions performed by the individuals are widely known. Alerting appropriate staff within the department to problem titles is much easier when the individuals are fellow department members, when the focus of the work is the same for all (i.e., handling serial publications), and when the staff are all close at hand.

Another reason for the combination of serial functions into one department is the greater ease afforded in planning, policy-making, and the development of procedures. In an integrated serials department, the head of the department can coordinate the many functions which must be performed, taking into account ebbs and flows in workload among the areas. Planning for any changes in the handling of serial materials (such as introduction of a new check-in system) will require little coordination with staff members in other departments and the heads of those departments. It may require informing staff in other departments, but not the time-consuming type of coordination required when staff in several departments must be introduced to a change and retrained. The development of policies and the writing of procedures are likewise simplified in terms of logistics when all staff involved are in the same department.

With all of this debate about the merits of serials departments, what is the prevailing structure of libraries, and particularly those with good-sized serials collections? Has it changed over time?

Several surveys to investigate serials departments in libraries have been completed in the past. In 1940, Fred Rothman and Sidney Ditzion reported in *College and Research Libraries*[7] the results of their survey of practices for handling serial publications. The survey included 126 college, university, and public libraries. The authors reported great diversity among these libraries in handling various types of serial publications. During the time period of the survey, the organizational structure in libraries was frequently determined by the source of the material as well as its format. Of the large college and university libraries responding to the questionnaire 55 percent had serials "divisions"; 58 percent of these, or 32 percent of the total, were independent departments. Many of those libraries without serials divisions had a periodicals division or reading room which was responsible for periodicals check-in, circulation, and sometimes bindery preparation.

Results from another survey, of 76 medium and large academic libraries, were reported in 1962.[8] Of the libraries responding 49 percent had serials departments, and the remaining 51 percent had serials sections which were part of other departments. Of those libraries with separate serials departments, 34 percent performed "all of the functions of the selection, ordering, and handling of serials" (the specific functions are unspecified).[9] The variations among the departments which did not handle all of these functions were numerous. Two out of every three libraries with a serials department reported satisfaction with it; however, over half of those without a serials department were dissatisfied with their present arrangement.

A survey conducted in 1974 by Martin Ward to study 17 London libraries, mainly university and polytechnic, revealed that most of these libraries had a separate serials unit.[10] Ward found no meaningful correlation between the chosen organization for serials control and either type of library or size of the collection.

In 1976, Donald Dyal sent 66 questionnaires to community college, college, and university libraries, as well as to the state library and the public libraries of several large cities throughout Texas.[11] His survey included questions concerning organization, public service, automatic data processing, check-in, claiming, binding, selection, searching, and ordering. He did not include any questions about serials cataloging, since he believed it to be "so kaleidoscopic that it should be handled in a separate study." Of those responding 74 percent had separate serials departments, but there was no correlation between the number of serials processed and the presence/absence of a serials department. Of those libraries without a serials department, 77 percent of them placed serials functions within the acquisitions department and 22 percent placed them within a public service department. Half of the serials departments which existed administered a public service area. Seventy-two percent did preorder searching, 61 percent did ordering of serials, 46 percent were responsible for bindery preparation, and 94 percent included claiming among their duties.

Dyal found little in common concerning serials functions among the Texas libraries. There was little uniformity as to what materials were handled by the serials department and how check-in was done. These results of the survey led Dyal to conclude, "If there is a science of serials, it has been hidden from our view and subjugated by tradition and pragmatism."[12]

Victoria Johnson's dissertation, entitled "Organization of Serials Departments in University Libraries," is a report of the findings of a survey of serials departments in 48 university libraries (mostly members of the Association of Research Libraries) which she conducted in 1972.[13] She noted a continuing trend toward a centralization of serials functions into serials departments, and several distinct patterns of organization of these departments. The most frequently observed two patterns were departments containing either ordering, check-in, and claiming, or all of the above plus binding preparation.

She also learned that check-in and claiming functions were performed in all 48 serials departments which she studied. Serials cataloging was done in 41.7 percent of the departments, and maintenance of a periodicals reading room in 27.1 percent. There was no correlation in the study results between size of the serials collection and the organizational pattern of the department. In summary, she found, in addition to a movement toward a common organizational structure, some movement toward standardization of routines.

This, then, gives us an idea of the structure of the past. The majority of large academic libraries had either serials departments or serials sections within other departments. What is the arrangement today? Are serials departments still the prevalent form of organization for handling serial materials? To answer this question, a survey was conducted among the heads of technical services of the 117 members of ARL in the fall of 1984. A questionnaire (See Appendix) was sent, asking, first, whether the library presently had a serials department. Where there was not such a department, respondents were asked whether a serials department had ever existed in the past and if so the reasons for its being disbanded. They were also asked whether a serials department was planned for the future. Respondents with serials departments were asked to specify how long the department had been in existence, to identify which serials functions were performed therein, and to indicate in which other department(s) the remaining serials functions were performed.

One follow-up letter was sent in addition to the original questionnaire. One-hundred nine responses were received, for a 93 percent return rate. Two of the respondents indicated that it would be inappropriate for them to complete the questionnaire, leaving 107 usable responses. Forty-three respondents (40 percent) did not have a separate serials department; 64 (60 percent) had one. The percentages are reversed when one studies the nonacademic ARL members as a group. Of seven non-academic respondents, four (57 percent) do not have a serials department. The figures for the Canadian universities are much the same as for the nonacademic libraries; of the 12 respondents, seven (58 percent) do not have a serials department.

Of those libraries which do not presently have a serials department 24 (56 percent) had one at some time in the past. Four of the libraries without a serials department plan to create one in the future.

The heads of technical services were asked to indicate whether their serials department had been in existence for 0–5, 6–10, 11–15, 16–20, or more than 20 years. To compile the mean age of the departments, the figure of 22 years was used for all those departments which had been in existence for more than 20 years. The mean age of the 64 serials departments is 18 years. Nearly half of those libraries with serials departments have had them for over 20 years (30 libraries). The majority of the departments are either less than five years old or over 15; few departments among these ARL libraries came into existence during the 1970s.

Respondents were asked to indicate which of the following functions are part of their serials departments: ordering; preorder searching; precatalog searching; check–in of serials, periodicals, newspapers, or sets;

claiming; serials cataloging; maintenance of machine records for serials; catalog maintenance; shelflisting of serials; binding; union listing; transfer and withdrawal of serial materials; supervision and staffing of a current periodicals reading room; other (to be specified by the respondent). The maximum number of these functions which could have been included in the serials department described on the questionnaire (excluding "other") is 16.

The median number of functions handled by these serials departments is 11. Three libraries have responsibility for the maximum number of functions; in contrast, one library performs only three of the functions, and interestingly enough, it has been in existence for the shortest time period (0–5 years), and is perhaps still evolving. The responses indicate that those serials departments which are young have the least variation in the number of functions carried out. With the exception of the one with only three functions, the young departments are responsible for between 9 and 14 functions. In contrast, those departments in existence for over 20 years have a larger range in the number of functions which they handle, varying from 6 to 16.

Some type of check–in function is done by all libraries. (This is identical to the results in Johnson's survey.)[14] Most frequently carried out among the respondents is periodical check-in (98.4 percent), followed closely by check-in of serials (96.9 percent), maintenance of machine records for serials (85.9 percent), check-in of newspapers (82.8 percent), ordering of serials (81.3 percent), and the handling of the transfer and withdrawal of serial materials (79.7 percent). The function least likely to be included in the ARL serials department is the supervision and staffing of a current periodicals reading room (42.2 percent); this figure is an increase, however, over that in the 1972 survey. Fewer than half of the serials departments (48.4 percent) include check-in of sets or catalog maintenance among their responsibilities.

The percentage of serials departments responsible for ordering serials in this survey is considerably higher than that found by Johnson, but more of the serials departments in her study had responsibility for preorder searching (70.8 percent vs. 65.6 percent). This difference may be due to the creation in the intervening years of special units in technical services divisions devoted solely to bibliographic searching; five respondents in the present study noted that preorder searching is done in such a unit in their libraries. Of the serials departments in this study 64 percent include serials cataloging (only 41.7 percent of the departments in Johnson's study included it), and the identical percentage of departments include binding, whereas in the 1972 study only half of the departments performed this function.

Several libraries cited functions other than those listed above as part of their serials departments. Many different responsibilities were listed by respondents as "other" on the questionnaire: bookkeeping, handling the exchange program or receipt of gifts, book repair/mending, maintenance of the bound periodical stacks, staffing a service window for access to in-process material, reconversion of serial records, maintenance of a series authority file, collection management and development for serials, supervision and staffing of a microform reading room, serials reference, participation in the CONSER project, and circulation of unbound serials.

Respondents with a serials department were asked to identify, for the functions listed on the questionnaire which were handled in the library but not in the serials department, the department in which they were accomplished. When not performed in the serials department, both ordering and preorder searching are most often carried out in the acquisitions department. A few libraries have a special searching unit which does both preorder and precatalog searching. In three libraries collection development staff are responsible for preorder searching. The public services staff do preorder searching in one library. Precatalog searching of serials, when not done by the serials department, is most frequently done in the catalog department, although the acquisitions department has responsibility for it in three libraries. Newspapers may often be checked in by staff in a separate newspaper or newspaper/microforms department. In one library the documents department checks in newspapers, in another the responsibility belongs to branch libraries, and in two others it is handled by a current periodicals unit. Monographic set volumes are checked in by the acquisitions department in 27 libraries, nearly as many as those in which this type of material is handled by the serials department. Claiming of serials is almost always done in the serials department, though the acquisitions department staff claim serials in three libraries.

Two-thirds of the serials departments include the cataloging of serials among their activities. All but two of the remaining libraries assign serials cataloging to the catalog department. In nine libraries machine records for serials are maintained in the catalog department rather than the serials department. Catalog maintenance (card catalogs) is done more often outside of the serials department than in it, and most frequently by the catalog department. In many libraries the serials and catalog departments have shared responsibility for catalog maintenance. Some respondents noted that the catalog maintenance done in the serials department is limited to catalogs located in the serials department or catalogs of serial materials. Three libraries have a separate catalog maintenance/management department.

Shelflisting of serials in 18 libraries is done by the catalog department. Five libraries do not shelflist serials at all; most of them use their check-in records as a detailed holdings record.

Bindery preparation, when not handled by the serials department, is handled by a separate department in eight libraries, is included in a preservation department in five, and in other libraries is handled by circulation, bibliographic control, cataloging, central technical services, support services, processing, or preparations departments—a great variety of host locations among respondents.

Forty-four of the libraries participate in union lists. Serials departments are responsible for reporting holdings in over three-fourths of these, with the catalog department responsible in most of the other libraries.

In the few libraries where the serials department is not at least partially responsible for the transfer and withdrawal of serial materials, the catalog department most often does this work. It is interesting to note that the public services area has responsibility for this function in one library.

The responses to the question concerning location of responsibility for supervision and staffing of a current periodicals room reveal, among other things, the creativity with which public service areas are named. Less than half of the serials departments handle this function. Among the many other areas where it is located, the circulation department is the most common site. Other locations mentioned in the questionnaire responses are various subject reference areas in the library, the periodicals room (a unit unto itself), various public service areas throughout the library, the reference department, access services, the public service area, readers' services, central collections services, information services, and current journals/micro media. It is impossible to know what functions these variously named departments encompass without further investigation, but some, at least, may be reference departments. One respondent indicated that this function might be moved from the reference department at some point, although the new location was not stated. Three libraries do not have a current periodicals reading area. Another respondent noted that this function had been part of the serials department for about 10 years prior to 1983–1984, when current periodicals were distributed to individual libraries on campus and the responsibility for their service devolved to each library; no reason was given for this change.

Of the 43 libraries which do not have a serials department, 22 of them had one at some time in the past. Reasons for their elimination vary. In one instance, the reasons are unknown to the respondent, as the department was disbanded nearly 10 years ago by a different administration. In most cases the work done by the serials department was reassigned by function into acquisitions and catalog departments. One library indicated that this change was made to permit better use of professional staff, faster processing of materials, and integration of files. Other respondents replied that the elimination of the department was a result of a desire to redeploy staff and/or divert salary funds. Several respondents stated that the serials department was disbanded to effect a more efficient workflow or flexibility in staffing. A few respondents mentioned a change in ideology within the library from organization by format to organization by function. One purpose of the reorganization of the serials department, according to two respondents, was to promote greater consistency between monographic and serials cataloging practices by placing all cataloging activities in one department, and to standardize the philosophy of cataloging. In one library the implementation of an online catalog facilitated the integration of bibliographic control and cataloging in the library, resulting in the dispersal of serial functions.

Of the libraries without serials departments six have thoughts of, or plans for, creating one. Half of these had a serials department at one time in the past. Thus, formation of a serials department would be a return to an earlier practice. The technical services director of one of these libraries stated that there were plans to create a serials department because serials at that library are not receiving enough emphasis. The proposed department will include ordering; preorder and precatalog searching; check-in of serials, periodicals, newspapers, and sets; claiming; and maintenance of machine records for serials. All remaining functions will continue to be carried out in the catalog department except for binding, which will remain with the binding and conservation department, and supervision of the current periodicals reading room, which will remain with the current periodicals and microforms department.

Another library is considering creating a serials records unit when the library reaches the point of implementing the serials check-in module of an online integrated that will also include an online catalog, circulation, and acquisitions. The unit will include serials catalogers and serials ordering/receiving staff. This organizational change may extend to other parts of technical services as well. In this library, the disbanding of a previous serials department occurred only two years after its creation because of poor implementation of the change.

A third library which had a serials department in the past but which no longer has one is considering the creation of a periodicals department in the future, to bring together check-in, cataloging, and a current periodicals room, though it "would not include subscriptions or serials being classified." The technical services head noted that this change, though it was less than 50 percent certain to occur, might come with online check-in as part of an integrated automated system.

One of the libraries which has never had a serials department plans to create one when it obtains an integrated automated system in the near future. Its proposed department will include all functions noted in the questionnaire except for binding and union listing. The increasing influence of automation on practices and procedures has led another library to plan for a serials department. The head of technical services of the last library in this group noted that several section heads in technical services believe that accuracy and greater efficiency in handling serials will result if a smaller, closer-knit and more knowledgeable group works with these publications. Its proposed serials department will include all of the functions on the questionnaire except for the check-in of sets and the supervision and staffing of a current periodicals room.

Is there a relationship between the number of serials on standing order and the existence of a serials department? The only two conclusions which can be reached from this survey are that those ARL libraries with 5,000 or fewer standing orders are unlikely to have a serials department (75 percent do not) and that ARL libraries with 15,001–20,000 standing orders are the ones most likely to have a serials department. In libraries with collection sizes either larger than 20,000 or between 5,001 and 15,000 the likelihood is less predictable.

There is little correlation between the length of time the serials department has been in existence and the number of functions for which it is responsible. In fact, the two libraries with the smallest number of functions (three and six) are one of the youngest and one of the oldest departments. The majority of departments handle between nine and 14 functions. As noted earlier, greater variation in the number of functions occurs in older departments.

Conclusions about ARL libraries which can be reached from the survey are the following:

1. The majority of ARL libraries responding have a serials department.
2. Very few serials departments handle all functions related to serials.
3. Serials departments continue to be formed, reformed and disbanded.
4. Automation, and in particular online check-in, will have an effect on the handling of serial material, though the nature of that effect is uncertain. Many libraries are already beginning to think about and plan for the implementation of automated serials check–in. It is interesting to note that some of the survey respondents predict such automation will result in the formation of a serials department, while others predict it will lead to the demise of their serials department as an entity.

Many of the questionnaire responses indicated that where no serials department exists, there is still a serials unit within the acquisitions department. This structure of having specialists for check-in of serials, at the very least, is an acknowledgement that serial material is different from monographic material. Serials are not checked in by staff who also check in firm–order monographs; in other words, the staff members who check in serials are not generalists who check in any type of material—serial, monograph, or newspaper—which comes to them. There is a recognition in these libraries that the handling of serial material requires special training and is best done by staff dedicated to that activity. One technical services head stated, in fact, that the staff within the newly combined department formed from the acquisitions and serials departments have more or less the same responsibilities that they had before the merger.

In summary, there is a basis in organizational theory for arrangement of departments within the library by format. Such an arrangement is a grouping by specialty, or product, rather than by process. It also takes into account the reciprocal interdependencies in dealing with a particular format. The results from the survey of ARL libraries show that the separate serials department is common in the large academic library of today, being present in 60 percent of the libraries responding to the questionnaire. In addition, another 5.6 percent of the libraries responding intend to create such a department, several as a result of the introduction of automation. Finally, the separate serials department is an excellent organizational arrangement both in terms of efficiency of work processes and task coordination.

APPENDIX:

Questionnaire

Please limit your responses to the main library. Do not include responses for branch libraries.

1. How many serials/periodicals do you have on standing order?

_____

2. Does your library have a serials department?
   yes _____ SKIP TO QUESTION 5   64   (60%)
   no _____ If no,   43   (40%)
3. Has your library ever had a serials department?
   yes _____ If yes, why was it disbanded? Please explain briefly:
   24 (56%) _____

   _____

   _____

   no _____
4. Are there any plans to create a serials department in the near future?
   yes _____ Please state briefly the reasons for creating one:
   4 (9%) _____

   _____

   no _____ PLEASE RETURN THE QUESTIONNAIRE IN THE ENVELOPE PRO-
   VIDED.
   39 (91%)

5. Indicate by circling below the length of time your serials department has been in existence.

0–5 years   8   (13%)   16–20 years   10   (16%)
6–10 years   8   (13%)   20+ years   30   (48%)
11–15 years   6   (10%)

6. Please circle all of the following functions included in your present or proposed serials department.

ordering	52 (81%)
searching (preorder)	42 (66%)
searching (precataloging)	45 (70%)
check-in of: serials	63 (98%)
periodicals	62 (97%)
newspapers	53 (83%)
sets	31 (48%)
claiming	61 (95%)
serials cataloging	41 (64%)
maintenance of machine records for serials	55 (86%)
catalog maintenance	31 (59%)
shelflisting of serials	38 (59%)
binding	41 (64%)
union listing	36 (56%)
transfer and withdrawal of serial materials	51 (80%)
supervision and staffing of a current periodicals reading room	27 (42%)

other (please specify) ⎯⎯⎯⎯⎯⎯⎯⎯⎯⎯⎯

7. For all of these functions which are performed in the library but not in the serials department, please indicate below in which department they are accomplished.

ordering ⎯⎯⎯⎯⎯⎯⎯⎯⎯⎯⎯⎯⎯⎯⎯⎯⎯⎯⎯⎯⎯⎯⎯⎯⎯⎯⎯⎯⎯⎯⎯
searching (preorder) ⎯⎯⎯⎯⎯⎯⎯⎯⎯⎯⎯⎯⎯⎯⎯⎯⎯⎯⎯⎯⎯⎯⎯⎯⎯⎯
searching (precataloging) ⎯⎯⎯⎯⎯⎯⎯⎯⎯⎯⎯⎯⎯⎯⎯⎯⎯⎯⎯⎯⎯⎯⎯
check-in of: serials ⎯⎯⎯⎯⎯⎯⎯⎯⎯⎯⎯⎯⎯⎯⎯⎯⎯⎯⎯⎯⎯⎯⎯⎯⎯⎯⎯
         periodicals ⎯⎯⎯⎯⎯⎯⎯⎯⎯⎯⎯⎯⎯⎯⎯⎯⎯⎯⎯⎯⎯⎯⎯⎯⎯⎯
         newspapers ⎯⎯⎯⎯⎯⎯⎯⎯⎯⎯⎯⎯⎯⎯⎯⎯⎯⎯⎯⎯⎯⎯⎯⎯⎯⎯
         sets ⎯⎯⎯⎯⎯⎯⎯⎯⎯⎯⎯⎯⎯⎯⎯⎯⎯⎯⎯⎯⎯⎯⎯⎯⎯⎯⎯⎯⎯⎯⎯
claiming ⎯⎯⎯⎯⎯⎯⎯⎯⎯⎯⎯⎯⎯⎯⎯⎯⎯⎯⎯⎯⎯⎯⎯⎯⎯⎯⎯⎯⎯⎯⎯⎯
serials cataloging ⎯⎯⎯⎯⎯⎯⎯⎯⎯⎯⎯⎯⎯⎯⎯⎯⎯⎯⎯⎯⎯⎯⎯⎯⎯⎯⎯⎯
maintenance of machine records for serials ⎯⎯⎯⎯⎯⎯⎯⎯⎯⎯⎯⎯⎯⎯
⎯⎯⎯⎯⎯⎯⎯⎯⎯⎯⎯⎯⎯⎯⎯⎯⎯⎯⎯⎯⎯⎯⎯⎯⎯⎯⎯⎯⎯⎯⎯⎯⎯⎯⎯⎯⎯⎯⎯
catalog maintenance ⎯⎯⎯⎯⎯⎯⎯⎯⎯⎯⎯⎯⎯⎯⎯⎯⎯⎯⎯⎯⎯⎯⎯⎯⎯⎯⎯
shelflisting of serials ⎯⎯⎯⎯⎯⎯⎯⎯⎯⎯⎯⎯⎯⎯⎯⎯⎯⎯⎯⎯⎯⎯⎯⎯⎯⎯
binding ⎯⎯⎯⎯⎯⎯⎯⎯⎯⎯⎯⎯⎯⎯⎯⎯⎯⎯⎯⎯⎯⎯⎯⎯⎯⎯⎯⎯⎯⎯⎯⎯⎯
union listing ⎯⎯⎯⎯⎯⎯⎯⎯⎯⎯⎯⎯⎯⎯⎯⎯⎯⎯⎯⎯⎯⎯⎯⎯⎯⎯⎯⎯⎯⎯
transfer and withdrawal of serial materials ⎯⎯⎯⎯⎯⎯⎯⎯⎯⎯⎯⎯⎯⎯
⎯⎯⎯⎯⎯⎯⎯⎯⎯⎯⎯⎯⎯⎯⎯⎯⎯⎯⎯⎯⎯⎯⎯⎯⎯⎯⎯⎯⎯⎯⎯⎯⎯⎯⎯⎯⎯⎯⎯
supervision and staffing of a current periodicals reading room
⎯⎯⎯⎯⎯⎯⎯⎯⎯⎯⎯⎯⎯⎯⎯⎯⎯⎯⎯⎯⎯⎯⎯⎯⎯⎯⎯⎯⎯⎯⎯⎯⎯⎯⎯⎯⎯⎯⎯
other (those specified in answer to question 6.) ⎯⎯⎯⎯⎯⎯⎯⎯⎯⎯⎯⎯
⎯⎯⎯⎯⎯⎯⎯⎯⎯⎯⎯⎯⎯⎯⎯⎯⎯⎯⎯⎯⎯⎯⎯⎯⎯⎯⎯⎯⎯⎯⎯⎯⎯⎯⎯⎯⎯⎯⎯
⎯⎯⎯⎯⎯⎯⎯⎯⎯⎯⎯⎯⎯⎯⎯⎯⎯⎯⎯⎯⎯⎯⎯⎯⎯⎯⎯⎯⎯⎯⎯⎯⎯⎯⎯⎯⎯⎯⎯

THANK YOU FOR YOUR TIME IN COMPLETING THIS QUESTIONNAIRE. PLEASE
USE THE ENCLOSED STAMPED SELF-ADDRESSED ENVELOPE TO RETURN
YOUR RESPONSE.

Joline R. Ezzell
Head, Serials Department
Duke University Library
Durham, N.C. 27706

NOTES AND REFERENCES

1. Neil Kay, *The Evolving Firm: Strategy and Structure in Industrial Organization*
(New York: St. Martin's Press, 1982).

2. Ibid.

3. Henry Mintzberg, *Structure in Fives: Designing Effective Organizations* (Englewood
Cliffs, NJ: Prentice-Hall, 1983).

4. Mitsuko Collver, "Organization of Serials Work for Manual and Automated Systems," *Library Resources & Technical Services* 24 (1980): 307–16.

5. Thomas W. Leonhardt, "The Place of Serials in Technical Services." *RTSD Newsletter* 9 (1984:7): 84–85.

6. Sue Anne Harrington and Deborah J. Karpuk, "The Integrated Serials Department:
Its Value Today and in the Future." *Serials Librarian* 9 (Winter 1984): 55–64.

7. Fred B. Rothman and Sidney Ditzion, "Prevailing Practices in Handling Serials,"
College and Research Libraries 1 (1940): 165–69.

8. Robert W. Orr, "The Selection, Ordering, and Handling of Serials," In *Selection
and Acquisition Procedures in Medium-Sized and Large Libraries*, ed. Herbert Goldhor,
Allerton Park Institute, no. 9 (Champaign, IL: Illini Union Bookstore, 1963).

9. Ibid., 72.

10. Martin Ward, "Observations of Serials Management in Seventeen London Libraries,"
Library Association Record 77 (1975): 247.

11. Donald Dyal, "Survey of Serials Management in Texas," *Texas Libraries* 38 (1976):
164–72.

12. Ibid., 172.

13. Victoria Arend Johnson, "Organization of Serials Departments in University Libraries" (Master's Thesis, University of Chicago, 1973).

14. Ibid.

DECENTRALIZATION OF SERIALS FUNCTIONS

Ruth C. Carter

It seems fair to say, on the topic of centralization versus decentralization of serials activities within either a single library or libraries in general, that there is not one best approach. Nor is there any single approach that will stand the test of time without debate. Anything that by definition involves both format and function cannot be given any single best treatment. Individuals who are primarily oriented to format will say that all serials processing and services must be brought together (centralized), and individuals with function as their uppermost concern will look to an organization which features function over form.

In addition to the previously mentioned, which suggest one approach within any given institution, there are many large institutions which have multiple branch or departmental libraries, adding another dimension to organizational complexities. For example, Library A may have a centralized serials department in the main library and may do all ordering, check-in, and claiming from a central location; Library B may have de-

Advances in Serials Management, Volume 1, pages 83–99.
Copyright © 1986 by JAI Press Inc.
All rights of reproduction in any form reserved.
ISBN: 0-89232-568-2

centralized check-in and claiming for its branches but have centralized ordering; and Library C may have total decentralization of serials activities. The advent of large scale integrated automated systems which include serials activities has the potential to increase the prevalence of the organizational model represented in Library C's activities.

Coupled with the obvious fact that there are a number of viable configurations for serials activities within a given institution is the also obvious fact that in any institution the organizational structure will vary over a period of time. It seems a simple truism that: any particular library organization, including those components for functions involving serial publications, is valid only at a certain point in time, at a particular institution. In fact, a corollary would be that the execution of any activity, including those related to serial publications—whether principally approached by function or format—evolves in any single institution over time. At the same time that there is a tendency toward evolution in organizational structures in a single institution over time, there appears to be a cyclical pattern in the library world at large.[1]

The purpose of this paper is to examine the state of serials librarianship from the perspective of decentralization of serials activities. The first step will be to survey briefly the decentralized serials activities as reported in the literature. Second, the current trends in this area, including advantages and disadvantages of various organizational structures, will be assessed.

For the purpose of this article, decentralization of serials means the separation of any aspect of activities related to serials processing, control, and access. It may be that most aspects are brought together or it may mean that most are separated by function or service orientation, i.e., technical services as compared to public services. It should be noted, however, that most references to centralization versus decentralization of serials activities are directed in large measure to technical services considerations—primarily whether acquisitions or cataloging are together or separate.

It is probable that a library is considered to have decentralized serials whenever it has no department or major unit with serials as the only descriptive word in its title. Although the emphasis in this paper is on the technical services aspects of serials, it is not limited to technical services in scope. A full range of possible configurations will be discussed.

According to Potter,[2] there were no centralized serials departments in modern academic libraries prior to the 1930s. The first attempts to create separate serials departments took place in the 1930s at the Minneapolis Public Library and New York University. There are a number of reasons why recognizable serials departments were slow to develop. Libraries were smaller, most technical services personnel performed a variety of functions including public services activities, there were fewer serials, the existing serials were less complex, and cataloging rules tended to bring all title changes for a given publication together. In fact, the *A.L.A. Cataloging Rules for Author and Title Entries* issued in 1949[3] called for what can be described as earliest title cataloging. It prescribed entry of periodicals that had ceased publication under an earlier title if the earlier title was used longer than the latest title.

The first step toward creating separate serials departments was establishing staff within acquisitions and cataloging units who specialized in serials. Gradually this led to bringing all staff with a specialization by format in serials together in one department. This article will not attempt an in depth review of the history of serials departments, as that topic is covered in detail by Cook[4] in another paper in this volume. However, to help set the stage for the discussion of various configurations of decentralized serials activities that exist in the 1980s, a brief look at the literature on organizational structures to support serials activities in the 1970s and first half of the 1980s will be considered.

The second edition of Andrew Osborn's classic *Serial Publications: Their Place and Treatment in Libraries,*[5] published in 1973, included a chapter devoted to the organization of serials work. Osborn stated that three main areas of serials activities are commonly large enough to require one or more staff members dedicated to serials. These are: serials acquisitions, serials cataloging, and the current periodicals room which may be supplemented by a document or a newspaper room. He suggested that any of the three areas could assume the major responsibility for serials and be named the serials section or serial division, etc.[6]

Osborn noted that from 1939 forward there has been a slight tendency to centralize serials activities and create a serials department. "Realignments which culminate in the formation of a [serials] processing department commonly have as an objective the correlation of what could otherwise be overlapping serial functions in the traditional acquisition and catalog departments."[7]

In general, Osborn tried to outline the pros and cons of the various possible approaches to organization of serials activities. He concluded that although outright centralization may not be the answer, there should be coordination of serial functions "to eliminate areas of overlap, to provide adequate staff and quarters for all phases of serials work, and to conserve for the future all the files of serials."[8]

The third edition of *Serial Publications* was published in 1980. Osborn[9] did not update the chapter on organization for serials activities, rather, he succeeded in leaving the whole topic somewhat murky.

In 1976 Dyal[10] reported on a survey undertaken that year of academic libraries in Texas. The survey was on the general topic of serials management. At that time, 74 percent of the libraries reported having a separate serials department. However, there was no uniformity on such topics as:

how materials are checked in, what materials are handled by the serials department, or whether binding belongs with serials. Dyal noted that "there appears to be no consensus of management which has an empirical basis."[11] He suggested that despite some commonality of practice there are many differences. They are so great that there is no single approach to management of serials; or, if there is one, it is a well kept secret.

A similar survey was conducted in 1974 of 17 London libraries of varying types. At that time most of the libraries had a separate serials unit.[12] The London survey results also demonstrated that there was a wide variety of practices even among very similar libraries. In a number of cases the divergent practices resulted simply from "historical" factors at the particular institutions.

Writing in 1979, Weber[13] began by noting that service is the primary role for any serials unit regardless of the status of the unit in the organization. He commented that many of the difficulties in processing serials stem from the fact that they are continually changing. As Weber pointed out, personnel who work mostly with monographs tend to put serials aside because they often present many problems. That is one reason why administrators who understand serials bring various aspects of the serials activities together. The mere fact of having staff who know the whole range of serials and their problems contributes to a more efficient workflow and pride in work. In general, Weber argued for centralization of serials functions.

McKinley's 1980 article had the provocative title, "Serials Departments: Doomed to Extinction?"[14] The answer to the question is never really provided by McKinley. She notes, however, that "function has to all appearances triumphed over form," and then describes some of the activities that might be incorporated into a serials department if there is a serials department. A key point is that no matter how broad a serials department might be, it could never include all services and activities for all types of serial publications in a given institution.

After summarizing the thoughts of a few writers on the topic of centralization versus decentralization, McKinley discusses some aspects of serials activities that are constants regardless of the organizational structure. She concludes that serials specialists and an informal communication system are essential components of an efficient and effective serials processing system.[15] In McKinley's opinion, even when there is decentralization of serials functions, a communication system of serials specialists will develop to facilitate efficient serials processing.[16]

"Form or Function? An Analysis of the Serials Department in the Modern Academic Library," by William Gray Potter, appeared in 1981.[17] Potter outlined what he considered to be problems associated with centralized serials departments. He then, almost facetiously, discussed incorporation of monographs processing into serials processing. As he noted, regarding the circulation of serials, "If a system can provide for the circulation of serials, it can handle the circulation of monographs with ease."[18] This was followed by a summary of arguments in favor of organizing processing by function.

Among the major reasons that Potter cited for organizing by function were first, ordering, cataloging and binding are much the same regardless of the format of the material being acquired, cataloged or bound; second, form should be subservient to function, including providing assistance to library clientele. He stated, "The point is not that serials should be subservient to any other format, but that serials processing should not have been divorced from the other processing functions to begin with."[19]

In Potter's view, well designed serials control systems only add to the argument for a functional organization because automation integrates separate functions into one system; a central database can be accessed from a variety of points on a campus, and can perform a variety of functions. He said, "Decentralized access to a centralized file obviates any lingering need for segregated processing."[20] Potter prophesied that while maintenance of serials records is still mostly centralized, it may be decentralized soon.

A number of articles in the early 1980s, including that by Collver in the Fall 1980 issue of *Library Resources & Technical Services*[21] provided arguments in favor of centralization of serials processing. A less definitive point of view was presented in Jo Ann Hanson's 1984 article, "Trends in Serials Management."[22] Hanson noted that the history of organizing for serials activity has shown a cyclical pattern. In fact, it is only the relatively recent growth of serials and academic research libraries in the twentieth century that have worked to suggest a need for organizational units dedicated to handling serials.

For the purposes of discussion, Hanson separated the issue of serials functions in branch libraries from the division of serials processing within the main library. She properly noted that the makeup of what constitutes a "serials department" varies, as does its location. The one core element seems to be serials check-in. In citing three research libraries which recently decentralized serials functions, Hanson noted that the technical processes for serials at the City University of New York, University of Oregon, and University of Illinois have been divided among cataloging, acquisitions, and a processing/binding unit.[23] In two of the three, check-in is now associated with acquisitions; in one of them it has gone with cataloging. In all three cases public service aspects are handled by public service units.

One point currently receiving attention is that serials control benefits from increased participation by catalogers. As Hanson stated, "Coordinating check-in, binding, and payment records with permanent holdings records, coping with title, series, and numbering variations, and creating needed cross-references are within the province of cataloging.''[24]

Nowhere is the importance of the catalog record seen more clearly than in OCLCs union listing capability. All union list holdings must be attached to the appropriate bibliographic records. Catalogers are essential to interpret the online bibliographic records. The regional Serials Institutes to be held around the country in 1986 and 1987 and jointly sponsored by the Library of Congress and the Resources and Technical Services Division of the American Library Association focus on the serials catalog record and its uses. The Institutes should bring out the fact that serials cataloging is not an end in itself and virtually all services and functions within the library have a stake in how a serial title is cataloged.

Not all the literature of the 1980s argued for or saw a trend toward centralization of serials functions. Jennifer Cargill, in an article published in 1982, declared ''there is now a clear trend in many libraries to eliminate separate serials departments and to merge personnel and duties into other departments.''[25] Cargill described a number of advantages in decentralization of serials activities and their merger with functional departments. These included: streamlining of work, assignment of new duties to staff freed from various tedious routines, more positive images for technical services personnel, improved performance of the organization, and increased opportunities for cross training staff.[26]

Marcia Tuttle's *Introduction to Serials Management* (1983) has a brief section on the organization of serials functions. Tuttle suggested that it may be selection of serials that is most often the aspect of serials activities that is missing from an integrated or centralized serials department. As Tuttle noted, ''Serials are involved in so much of the library's activity that it may be unrealistic to attempt to restrict every contact with them to one department.''[27]

In late 1984 Thomas Leonhardt, then column editor for *Technical Services Management* in the *RTSD Newsletter* wrote a column with the title, ''The Place of Serials in Technical Services.'' His opening words were: ''I don't have any proof that function is generally a better way to organize library work than by form or format, but it seems a logical conclusion when staffing, workflow, and work tools are taken into consideration. This opinion goes against all but a few of the published articles on the place of serials in the library.''[28]

Leonhardt conceded that serials may present problems not applicable to monographs but stated that they were not a justification for removing serials from the mainstream of acquisitions, collection development, circulation, or reference. In discussing the coordination and communication problems that must ensue if there is a separate serials department, Leonhardt alluded to the fact that in essence this creates "two heads of cat-aloging and two heads of acquisitions."[29] Leonhardt suggested that the appropriate person to coordinate the various serials and monographic activities is the technical services administrator in conjunction with the administrators of other areas. And, as he so rightly pointed out, there must be coordination and communication even within a central serials unit.

The 1985 article by McKenna and Carter[30] was written and in press more than a year before Leonhardt's column article appeared. It documented the change at the University of Pittsburgh from a centralized serials department to a functional organization. In general, the authors did not state that one approach is necessarily better than the other. Rather conditions and circumstances at a particular point in time were critical factors in decisionmaking relating to organizational structure. They agreed that any success the decentralized structure has had results, in substantial part, from maintaining staff positions that are dedicated to serials. From the viewpoint of McKenna and Carter, both organizational approaches can work effectively.

ORGANIZING FOR SERIALS ACTIVITIES

The literature discusses changes, and, to some extent, trends in the organization of libraries to process and provide access to serials publications. Before discussing the advantages and disadvantages of greater or lesser decentralization of serials activities in any one library, it is worth considering the range of possible organizations. At least, that is, considering the range of the most probable configurations, because there are many different ones.

Functions in libraries that relate to serial publications include:

- cataloging and classification of serials
- creating and maintaining union list(s) of serials
- placement of serial subscriptions
- renewal of serial subscriptions
- acquisition of serial publications via gift or exchange or on deposit
- check-in of serials
- back-order of serials
- binding of serials
- end processing of serials
- catalog maintenance for serial publications
- selection of serial titles
- reference service

In many libraries, especially smaller ones, a processing distinction is made between periodicals and/or newspapers and other serials. Often, periodicals and newspapers are not cataloged and classified but are simply shelved and recorded under main entry or title. Another common distinction may be a division by whether the serial is held in hard copy or microformat or is received and treated as a government document. In short, there are many possible combinations when considering the place of serial publications in any library or library system. In fact, when the complexity of multiple branches is added to the organizational structure of a library, the possible permutations are almost endless.

Most commonly, discussions on decentralization of serials activities center on a functional approach versus a format approach. In this basic scenario the cataloging of serials takes place with other cataloging; the acquisition of serials takes place with other acquisition activities; processing of serials, including binding, takes place with other processing; and public service activities are part of a traditional public services unit.

An entity called the Serials Department is probably not constituted the same way in any two libraries. It is almost impossible to say that any specific activity constitutes a core activity and is nearly always present in a recognizable Serials Department. Perhaps it is reasonable to start by grouping the major activities into four categories: acquisition, cataloging, processing (including binding), and public services. A named serials department may include all four functions; or, it may be minus one or two. Even a generalization is risky, but when a serials department is not comprehensive, the aspect most likely to be separate is the public service function. A second likely candidate for division is cataloging. It is not uncommon for most or all serials activities to be together with the exception of cataloging.

Thus, even when a unit is called a Serials Department there may be many activities related to serials that take place outside of that department's purview. However, generally, this would not be decentralization of serials in terms of the overall organization. That situation exists when there is no identifiable serials department or section that brings together at least two of the four functions.

When serials activities are separated by function there may or may not be specialists by format within a functional organization. When staff dedicated to serials do exist there are very often identifiable serials units within a department or division; for example, units called Serials Acquisitions or Serials Cataloging are common. Another frequently used term has been Serial Record(s). When Serial Record is used, it often includes the check-in function and the inventory function. The Serial Record Division at the Library of Congress also includes descriptive cataloging for serials.

Creating and maintaining a union list of serials for a library can fall into a number of different places organizationally if there is no serials department. The responsibility for union listing can rest with reference staff or bibliographers. Most frequently, however, it will be associated with serials acquisitions, serial records, or serials cataloging.

Binding functions in a library usually encompass both monographic and serial publications. When there is a serials department, binding is often included. When a serials department does not exist, binding can be in various places. Often it will be either with some sort of processing unit or with acquisitions. Another location for binding is with preservation departments, when they exist.

There is not even a uniform approach to the location of public service aspects of serials. This is particularly true for the periodical and newspaper subset of serials. It is not uncommon for libraries to have a separate area for unbound periodicals. Such a unit can be almost any place in a library without a serials department. In many cases it will be associated with periodicals check-in; often it will be part of a public services department.

As there is no one organizational structure that can best provide for serials processing and access in large libraries, it is obvious that each of the basic approaches has advantages and disadvantages. This article will try to assess both the advantages and the disadvantages inherent in the decentralization of serials in the organizational structure of a library.

ADVANTAGES OF DECENTRALIZED SERIALS FUNCTIONS

1. Functional organizations bring together individuals performing the same or similar functions and improve communication and exchange of information about technical details such as cataloging rules, procedures for processing invoices, staffing public service units and similar rules, procedures, files, or problems. This is true whether the function is acquisitions, cataloging or serving patrons.

2. There is often one less department head in a functional organization since there is no separate serials department. Depending on viewpoint and the effectiveness of an organization, this situation can result in a cost savings without a loss in efficiency.

3. Training for automation may be reduced because most individuals will need to receive detailed training in only one function.

4. There will be less duplication of files or procedural manuals for the same information.

5. Each function can be carried out independently without manpower being diverted to the crisis of the moment, as can happen with centralization by format.

6.   The library does not have several individuals, each claiming to have an equal stake in setting policy for a particular function.

7.   If decentralization of serials includes direct receipt and check–in of materials at multiple locations, there may be less duplication of effort and faster patron access to materials.

8.   There should be less duplication of work tools than in organizations where the same functions are performed in more than one department.

DISADVANTAGES OF DECENTRALIZED SERIALS FUNCTIONS

1.   There is often one less department head. This may result in the loss of the natural check and balance in determining policy and procedures for the major functions such as acquisitions and cataloging.

2.   Some processing efficiency may be lost as some individuals may need to handle more different types of material.

3.   Loss of specialization may result in an inability to solve problems rapidly or, even to identify problems accurately and in a timely manner.

4.   A network of serials specialists may evolve and staff may find that many of their questions can best be answered outside of their own work unit.

5.   When decentralization of serials does not result in some units or positions with expertise in serials, serials work may tend to be neglected as it is often more time consuming per item handled.

6.   Decentralization of serials can result in duplicate record keeping, especially in a manual environment.

EFFECT OF AUTOMATION

With few exceptions, the introduction of automation throughout a library, in the current world of integrated systems (or even separate systems that can interface), will result in some organizational change. It is true that automation limited to creating a machine readable subscription file or a locally maintained union list of serials or the like probably would not cause major organizational waves. However, automation limited to a single file with a single purpose was characteristic of automation of the 1960s and 1970s, and is not usually the case today, except for microcomputer applications.

In libraries large enough to be candidates for separate serials departments, automation in the 1980s is increasingly directed to comprehensive automation that directly links many library files and records. Any library introducing large scale automation, must of necessity, review its organization. McKinley states unequivocally that "Automation will have a profound effect on the *general organization structure* of a library."[31]

The type of change in terms of organization for serials activities is not fixed. As with most other aspects of matters related to serials in an organization, there are as many answers as there are libraries. Nor is it by any means predetermined that all organizational changes will be toward either greater or lesser decentralization of activities. Libraries that are centralized will probably look at less centralization, and those that already have decentralized serials may consider bringing certain activities back together on a format basis.

Introduction of automation forces a review of existing practices. If it doesn't, it should. Or, as Montague stated, "It has been utterly possible to use the automated system as inefficiently and ineffectively and with as little knowledge of what is going on as with the manual system."[32]

In addition to the built in impetus to review and revise workflow and organization upon the introduction of new technology, the actual design of the system may heavily influence a library's organization. For example, if a separate subscription system is selected, such as one available from a commercial subscription vendor, it will tend to influence organizational decisions in the direction of having a clearly defined major section or department dedicated to serials. On the other hand, the selection of an integrated system with serial subscriptions and renewals as one subset of an acquisitions module, along with a bibliographic database for all types of material, may tend to encourage a functional organization.

An integrated system provides for a shared bibliographic record among the various functional modules. By effectively eliminating duplicate bibliographic records between acquisitions and cataloging and stand alone circulation files, library automation is reducing the need to keep serials in a single department. Serial records can be accessed from terminals in many locations, both in technical services and public services, including branch libraries. As Hanson indicated, automation leads to a reconsideration of all technical services functions.[33] It also blurs the lines between technical and public services, including the work distinction between public and technical services.

Furthermore, as was expressed by McKinley, if a particular aspect of serials activity is not being automated, there is *no* impact on the library operations and organization.[34] At least as basic is the definition of "Serial" by an individual library. In some libraries this is not a simple "either it is or it is not a serial" decision. A number of libraries have different processing steps based upon whether a title is a periodical or newspaper, or a serial that is classified, or a monographic series. Documents present another dimension for consideration.

One influence of automation on serials has been to strengthen the recognition of the central importance of the bibliographic record. Most automated systems, including those of the bibliographic utilities such as RLIN and OCLC, require a bibliographic record before a check-in record, acquisitions record, or union list record can be built. Early circulation systems often carried little bibliographic information while newer systems link circulation records to full bibliographic records.

The relationship of various serials activities to the catalog record was illustrated by Carter in discussing union lists of serials in the OCLC online environment. She noted "In general, bibliographic activities and record selection are becoming central to online union lists."[35] When the University of Pittsburgh Libraries reorganized on a functional basis in 1981, the union list of serials activities were grouped together with serials cataloging. That decision has been upheld many times in the subsequent four years.

Introduction at the University of Pittsburgh of an integrated automated system, scheduled to begin in mid-1986, is forcing a new examination of procedures and workflow. Issues such as the provision of training on a continuing basis, who needs to consult various serial records, who can answer questions about the serials collection, and which activities are interdependent in terms of specialized knowledge and skills, are all factors in the re-examination of the existing organizational structure.

It is too soon to predict the specific changes that will occur at the University of Pittsburgh in its efforts to provide all necessary services in regard to its serial collection. However, it is safe to say there will be some change and that some activities related to serials that are currently separate will be brought together. Whatever new group or work unit focusing on serials is created may not be a department. And, it will have different components than have ever been together in a definable serials section at that university at any time in the past. This topic will be considered below.

CURRENT TRENDS

As of the mid-1980s there appear to be several trends in considering the decentralization of serial functions.

1.   There is some movement toward functional organizations, i.e., there is increasing decentralization of serials within a number of institutions.
2.   Introduction of large scale automated systems may be going hand in hand with a long term requirement to reduce ongoing personnel costs. One way this can be achieved is by eliminating the position of a separate serials department head.

3.   There is an increased acknowledgment of the centrality of the cataloging or bibliographic records. This is seen by such things as the association of union listing activities with cataloging and the association of serials check-in with cataloging.

4.   Automation reduces the need for duplicate files, because data input at one place can be accessed at multiple points.

5.   Automation can facilitate distribution of activities such as serials check-in and claiming. For example, receipt of periodical issues and their check-in has been on a distributed basis for years at the University of Pittsburgh. Only the initial order and renewal of periodical subscriptions is centralized. An automated system will only enhance the existing organizational structure because information will be available throughout the system. And, whether a change might be suggested toward more centralization or toward more decentralization, there are always pragmatic considerations such as changing the address to which mail is sent. Considering that a few mailing label changes for Pittsburgh orders have not been achieved since initial notification in 1968, this is not an insignificant consideration.

6.   Change will continue in spite of anything else. Change is inherent in organizations. It may come fast, it may proceed slowly, or it may occur only occasionally, but change is a fact of life. Nothing in life or in the organizational structure of a library or any other institution is forever static. Automation can only accelerate organizational change, although even change stimulated by automation is usually evolutionary in nature.

7.   Organizational patterns that develop may be new to any particular institution. For example, the University of Pittsburgh has had a centralized Serials Department which did not include any aspect of public service. As of this writing it has a decentralized structure with cataloging and union listing part of a Cataloging/Technical Services Department. The Current Periodicals Room is also associated with Technical Services. However, serials/periodicals check-in is part of Order Services which reports separately. Again, while it is premature to predict the future, there is some reason to think that the serials/periodicals check-in function will be joined with serials cataloging/union listing and the Current Periodical Room to form a Serials Control Section. The ordering of serials and periodicals might continue to have a functional orientation but a large portion of activities dealing with serials and/or periodicals may be brought together.

8.   Some libraries that are currently centralized for serials are considering changing to a functional structure; likewise, some libraries with a functional organization are considering implementing a separate serials department. This topic will be discussed further in the section below which deals with the survey conducted by Joline Ezzell in 1984.[36]

9.   In the organizational structure for serials activities as in serials themselves, the only thing predictable is change!

SURVEY ON ORGANIZATION FOR SERIALS ACTIVITIES

Joline Ezzell, in research for her article "The Integrated Serials Department," (in this volume), surveyed 117 members of the Association of Research Libraries (ARL) of which 109 responded.[37] Ezzell has generously shared the results of her survey with this author, and the following remarks are interpreted from those survey returns.

Question three of Ezzel's survey was: "Has your library ever had a serials department: If yes, why was it disbanded: Please explain briefly." Nineteen respondents replied that they did not now have, but previously had a serials department.

A variety of reasons were given for disbanding serials departments. However, they fall into several broad categories. These are:

1. A functional organization, i.e., cataloging, acquisitions, and access services were seen as more efficient in terms of workflow and resulted in less duplication of files, etc.

2. A functional organization resulted in the elimination of the head position for a serials department, fewer staff overall, and, in effect, reduced administrative overhead. In some cases this was a direct result of the need to save money, or, alternatively, to provide needed leadership in a particular area.

3. Staff were better used, especially professionals. There was more flexibility in using staff and more opportunities for staff development. There was also a need to bring staff together philosophically.

4. There was no specific reason; rather, a functional split between acquisitions and cataloging just seemed to work best in a particular environment.

Question 5 of the survey was: "Are there any plans to create a serials department in the near future?" Those who answered yes were asked to state briefly the reasons for the decision. There were four "yes" answers to this question. The reasons given for planning for the creation of a serials department were:

1. "Hope of an integrated automated system in the mid term future."

2. "We are in the beginning stages of implementing an integrated system that would include an online catalog, circulation system, acquisitions and serials check-in. When we reach the stage of implementing serials check-in, we may decide to create a serials records unit that would include catalogers and serials ordering/receiving staff."

3. "Several section heads think that there would be better accuracy and

efficiency in the area of serials if a smaller, closer–knit, more knowledgeable group worked with them."
4. "Serials are not receiving enough emphasis."

Thus, of the 18 survey respondents who do not have a serials department
at the present time, only four are actively thinking of creating one. A fifth
institution does not think it will create a full fledged serials department,
but may bring certain functions together within the purview of a unit of
the catalog department. This may be serials cataloging and receipt, union
listing, and the current periodicals service area.

CONCLUSIONS

As long as serials exist, which, despite Michael Gorman's assertion that
serials are "the biggest problem in librarianship,"[38] there will be a division
of opinion on whether to approach the processing of serials organizationally
by format or by function.

The physical representation will undoubtedly change for some serials,
for example, they may be issued on diskette, or videodisc or only available
online. However, the fact that a serial is expected to be issued indefinitely
will always present the need for some routines that take into account the
ongoing and repetitive nature of serial publications.

From this author's personal experience, either a distinct serials department or a functional organization can be effective. *There is no single
best approach.* What is best for any particular institution will vary over
time, and what is best at any given time will certainly vary from institution
to institution.

Many factors go into the decision on how to organize at any given time.
These include, but are not limited to, skills of available personnel, history
of serials in the organization, availability of funds, system or systems used
in automation of records (if any), current trends in organization, and the
perceived need for either organizational change or stability. As McKenna
and Carter point out, organizational change in and of itself can be beneficial.[39] When the shift was made to a functional organization at the University of Pittsburgh Libraries, everybody involved had to rethink basic
assumptions and learn new skills. This would be just as true if the change
were going from a functional organization to a centralized serials department.

In a time when there is considerable attention paid to staff development
and job satisfaction, changing the organization may be one way of keeping
staff at all levels stimulated. This can be especially significant for those
in department head or supervisory positions.

In conclusion, it seems clear that there is no strong trend either toward or away from decentralizing serials activities in large or medium size libraries. It also seems obvious that to provide effective public and technical services for serials collections a number of factors are required. The two most important may be: staff who specialize in serials (regardless of their organizational location) and dynamic and positive leadership at the department level (whether that is one leader in a centralized serials department, or two or more leaders in a functional organization).

NOTES AND REFERENCES

1. Jo Ann Hanson, "Trends in Serials Management," *Serials Librarian* 8 (Summer 1984): 7.

2. William Gray Potter, "Form or Function? An Analysis of the Serials Department in the Modern Academic Library," *Serials Librarian* 6 (Fall 1981): 85.

3. *A.L.A. Cataloging Rules for Author and Title Entries*, 2nd edition (Chicago: American Library Association, 1949), 10.

4. Jean G. Cook, "Serials' Place on the Organizational Chart: A Historical Perspective," *Advances in Serials Management* 1 (1986): 53–66.

5. Andrew Delbridge Osborn, *Serial Publications: Their Place and Treatment in Libraries*, 2nd edition (Chicago: American Library Association, 1973).

6. Ibid., 51.

7. Ibid.

8. Ibid., 64.

9. Andrew Delbridge Osborn, *Serial Publications: Their Place and Treatment in Libraries*, 3rd edition (Chicago: American Library Association, 1980), 57–73.

10. Donald H. Dyal, "A Survey of Serials Management in Texas," *Texas Libraries* 38 (1976): 164–72.

11. Ibid.

12. Martin Ward, "Observations of Serials Management in Seventeen London Libraries," *Library Association Record* 77 (1975): 247.

13. Hans H. Weber, "Serials Administration," *Serials Librarian* 4 (1980): 15–24.

14. Margaret M. McKinley, "Serials Departments: Doomed to Extinction?" *Serials Librarian* 5 (Winter 1980).

15. Ibid., 17.

16. Ibid., 24.

17. Potter, "Form or Function," 85–94.

18. Ibid., 91.

19. Ibid.

20. Ibid.

21. Mitsuko Collver, "Organization of Serials Work for Manual and Automated Systems," *Library Resources and Technical Services* 24 (1980): 307–16.

22. Hanson, "Trends," 7–13.

23. Ibid., 9.

24. Ibid., 10.

25. Jennifer Cargill, "Serials: Separate or Merged?" in *The Serials Collection: Organization and Administration* (Ann Arbor, MI: Pierian Press, 1982), 15.

26. Ibid., 15–22.

27. Marcia Tuttle, *Introduction to Serials Management* (Greenwich, CT: JAI Press, 1983), 12–14.

28. Thomas Leonhardt, "The Place of Serials in Technical Services," *RTSD Newsletter* 9 (1984): 84–85.

29. Ibid., 85.

30. Florence M. McKenna and Ruth C. Carter, "Serials Workflow in a Library without a Centralized Serials Department," in *Projects and Procedures for Serials Administration* (Ann Arbor, MI: Pierian Press, 1985), 39–50.

31. Margaret M. McKinley, "Victims, Villains or Victors: The Impact of Serials Automation on a Library Organization," *Serials Review* 10 (Summer 1984): 47.

32. Eleanor Montague, "Automation and the Library Administrator," *Journal of Library Automation* 11 (1978): 320–21.

33. Hanson, "Trends," 10.

34. McKinley, "Victims," 47.

35. Ruth C. Carter, "Cataloging Decisions on Pre-AACR2 Serial Records from a Union List Viewpoint," in *Union Lists: Issues and Answers* (Ann Arbor, MI: Pierian Press, 1982), 77–80.

36. Joline Ezzell, "The Integrated Serials Department," in *Advances in Serials Management* 1 (1986): 67–82.

37. Ibid.

38. Michael Gorman, "The Current State of Standardization in the Cataloging of Serials," *Library Resources and Technical Services* 19 (1976): 301–13.

39. McKenna and Carter, "Serials Workflow," 49.

PERIODICAL PRICES:
A HISTORY AND DISCUSSION

Ann Okerson

There is nothing new under the sun. Witness the following excerpt from a library survey:

> Librarians are suffering because of the increasing volume of publications and rapidly rising prices. Of special concern is the much larger number of periodicals that are available and that members of the faculty consider essential to the successful conduct of their work. Many instances were found in which science departments were obliged to use all of their allotment for library purposes to purchase their periodical literature which was regarded as necessary for the work of the department.[1]

This complaint is taken from a report prepared in 1927 for the Association of American Universities. One of the concerned institutions was Cornell University, where a list of 633 periodical subscriptions increased in price by 182 percent between 1910 and 1925.[2]

Although the price of serial publications is one of the "hot" issues of librarianship, the present generation is not aware that it has been a significant problem for decades. Many of today's working librarians remem-

Advances in Serials Management, Volume 1, pages 101–134.
Copyright © 1986 by JAI Press Inc.
All rights of reproduction in any form reserved.
ISBN: 0-89232-568-2

ber only the bountiful budgets of the 1960s and the subsequent budget agonies during years of more-than-inflationary subscription price rises.

Paradoxically, now that the Western nations are recovering from the recent recessionary periods, the interest and controversy which surrounds the subject of serial prices is not abating. On the contrary, more segments of the library community are being drawn into the act and the cost of library materials (particularly serials), has emerged, next to automation, as one of the great library concerns of the past 15 years; it promises to continue so to the end of the century.

In this paper, I will survey the literature on chief issues of serial pricing. The discussion is influenced by a background of 15 years in serials librarianship. Research prior to 1970 is generally outside the scope of this article. The discussion stems also from the perspective of a "medium-sized" academic library, that is, one of approximately 1.5 million volumes and 13,000 active serials, of which about half are periodical subscriptions. It comes from a largely Canadian perspective. The drying up of library funds which affected the United States in the early 1970s was delayed by perhaps 5 years in Canada; the recent U.S. recovery has been slow to cross the border, if it has yet begun. The gap between the Canadian and U.S. dollar, which on June 30, 1970, was 3.5 percent has, as of December 1985, widened to almost 40 percent. In these ways, the Canadian experience is more like that of non-U.S. Western nations; the impact of spiralling prices has been debilitating to countries with an economy less robust than that of the United States. But the high cost of materials is a serious problem common to all countries and all types of libraries, and all librarians will feel an immediate recognition of the matters described below.

I have chosen to limit the discussion of serial prices to periodicals (used interchangeably with the word "journals"), defined here as items appearing (regularly or irregularly) more than once a year and characterized by prepayment for the year, followed by receipt of the numbers or issues. This definition omits the entire arena of "standing order" serials: the annuals, editions, monographic series, and sets published over a long period. Although many librarians are of the persuasion that if a title is intended to be published indefinitely—or for an extended time—it is a serial, libraries differ greatly in their working practices regarding the so-called "continuations," and budgeting and payment procedures are very diverse. Non-subscription serials are far more difficult to define and describe financially than their periodical cousins.

It is fair to say that no author or index has attempted to come to grips with standing orders, either as a subset of serials or monographs, or as a category by themselves.

The rather exciting related issues of usage of periodicals, weeding, and the future of serials as a medium, all tempting, must be left to other discussions, although all have a close relationship to cost.

First, we will consider the question of what periodicals have cost over the past 15 years, and the methods of determining this. We will then look at librarians' responses to costs, followed by the contribution of subscription agents and publishers to periodical prices. Prior to conclusion, we will discuss the timely, major issue of dual pricing.

WHAT HAVE JOURNALS COST?

This question precedes any discussion of periodical pricing. When a library manager examines the cost of journals, usually as part of the exercise of predicting the following year's budget, he or she investigates past performance, which is then used to project future cost. Of course, the historical information is tempered by other relevant factors: new orders placed within the existing year which will become part of the new base, cancellations, foreign exchange behavior, predicted inflation, the best advice of one's vendors, and so on. The exercise of compiling a renewals budget considers many pieces of information and modifies them with experience and intuition. Even with the best data, the manager can be surprised at mid-year by world economics outside expectation or local events which were not predictable.

Most libraries keep accounts for serials expenditures within their institution, by individual title, by subject break-down, or as a grand total. It is fair to say that although many library accounting systems are now automated, very little manipulation has been done to give the manager data on which to base budget prediction. Most prediction is still done manually, intuitively, and politically.

Excellent assistance is now being provided by the major subscription agencies. The Faxon Company, for instance, is able to add library fund numbers to individual subscription orders and provide historical information regarding local increases. Later in this paper, a library describes the use of Swets & Zeitlinger services in a similar way. Unfortunately, in order to obtain comprehensive information by this method, one would have to place all one's library subscriptions with one or two vendors, which libraries are generally unwilling or unable to do. Nonetheless, vendor information is valuable; vendors deal with many more publishers and pay many more invoices than individual libraries. They should always be approached for assistance. Publishers of journals have not been helpful in the same way. So far, no publisher has offered to generate statistical or historical price information for even its large library customers.

The longest–running, most widely available, and most broadly-based subscription information has come from a handful of indexes published in library journals. There are at least three major English-language sources of information about what periodicals cost year by year. Publication of these indexes generally does not appear at precisely the best time for new fiscal predictions, but some preliminary information is available. The price indexes available to librarians are described below.

ALA/RTSD Library Materials Price Index Committee Index (ALA Index)

It is published annually in the *Library Journal (LJ)* in articles entitled "Price Indexes for (year): U.S. Periodicals and Serial Services."[3-18] The first year of compilation was 1950, using 1947–49 periodical prices as a base. The *LJ* began regular annual publication of the indexes in the October 1, 1962, issue. By that time, a new base (1957–59) was in use. Further substantial rises in the price of periodicals led to still another base, that of 1967–69, and finally 1977–79, in use at present. The ALA Index has been consistently maintained over the years by a relatively small number of devoted librarians and largely coordinated in recent years by Norman B. Brown of the University of Illinois, Urbana-Champaign, in conjunction with Jane Phillips and William Huff of the same library. (See *LJ* August 1985 for a fuller history of publication.)[19] The ALA indexes have appeared in July, August, or September issues of *Library Journal.*

In 1981, the Price Index Committee also began sponsoring a preliminary survey of these same subscription costs and publishing them in *RTSD Newsletter*[20] early in the calendar year in order to provide a more timely aid to the budgeting process. The preliminary figures have tended to be higher than the final figures, and the difference between early and final indexes can be great. The final ALA price indexes are also repeated in the following spring in the *Bowker Annual,* along with price indexes for monographic materials.[21-26]

The ALA Index appears in two sections: Periodicals and Serial Services. Each periodical included meets certain criteria. That is, it must meet an American National Standards Institute (ANSI) definition for a periodical as one published continuously under the same title, more than twice a year, appearing indefinitely, and consecutively numbered or dated (newspapers and services are excluded). The periodical must be of U.S. origin, although it may be simultaneously published in another country, in which case the U.S. imprint should be the first one. The indexes include titles of interest to libraries, particularly most of the titles indexed by the H. W. Wilson Company in its publications.

In the Periodicals portion of the index, the prices are presented by general subject categories, giving average price and percentage increase over the previous year. An overall percentage is also calculated.

Serial Services also meet certain criteria for inclusion in the second part of the ALA Index. The ANSI definition of a serial service is "a periodical which revises, cumulates, abstracts, or indexes information in a specific field on a regular basis."[27] For inclusion, the service must be in printed form and a U.S. publication or primarily a U.S. publication. In both the Periodical and the Service indexes, titles are added or replaced as necessary, and prices are normally as charged by the publisher during the index year. In the Serials Service section, average price increases are given for eight general subject categories, along with "combined" increases and a single average price.

The findings of the ALA Indexes for periodicals and services are shown in Chart I.

The ALA Indexes do not attempt to establish the reasons for price increases. Their purpose is to report figures with as much objectivity as possible. Clearly, the rise in periodical prices over the charted 16 year period is extraordinary. For example, a periodical subscription costing $10.00 in 1970 would cost, on the average, $56.65 by 1985, an increase of more than 5.5 times. Similarly, a serial service costing $100.00 in 1970 would cost $350.80 by 1984, an increase of 3.5 times. Year after year, almost without fail, the highest price increases in periodicals have been in the sciences, commonly chemistry, physics, mathematics, engineering, medicine, and zoology; that is, the sciences, with competition in the non-

Chart I. ALA Price Indexes, Periodicals and Services, Increases 1970–1985, as reported in Library Journal

Year/ Issue	Periodicals			Services		
	No. of Titles	Avg. Price	Percent Increase	No. of Titles	Avg. Price	Percent Increase
July 1970	2372	10.41	—	1124	85.44	—
July 1971	2415	11.66	12. up	1139	90.05	5 up
July 1972	2537	13.23	13. up	1182	95.38	6 up
July 1973	2861	16.20	22. up	1238	103.45	8 up
July 1974	2955	17.71	9 up	1307	118.03	8 up
July 1975	3075	19.93	12.5 up	1347	118.03	8 up
Aug. 1976	3151	22.52	12.9 up	1382	129.47	9.7 up
July 1977	3218	24.59	9.2 up	1432	142.27	9.9 up
July 1978	3255	27.58	12.2 up	1426	153.95	8.2 up
Sept. 1, 1979	3314	30.37	10.1 up	1450	171.06	11.1 up
July 1980	3358	34.54	13.7 up	1470	194.21	13.5 up
July 1981	3425	39.13	13.3 up	1477	219.75	13.2 up
Aug. 1982	3544	44.80	14.5 up	1494	244.52	11.3 up
Sept. 1, 1983	3674	50.23	12.1 up	1524	274.72	12.4 up
Aug. 1984	3731	54.97	9.4 up	1537	295.13	7.4 up
Aug. 1985	3731	59.70	8.6 up	N/A	—	—

sciences from labor/industrial relations and law. The lowest have been children's periodicals, along with literature, philosophy and religion, and physical education.

The sciences have not only shown the highest increases; they have also been many times more expensive than other disciplines. In our general academic library collection, one third of the journals are in the sciences and use two thirds of the renewals budget, and note–comparing with colleagues suggests this is not atypical. Clearly, scientific publishing has become big business in a way that other areas have not. We will return to this topic later.

In the early to mid–1970s, librarians began to note that the rate of periodical increase was becoming as high as, or often higher than, the rate of increase in book prices. This awareness both surprised and dismayed librarians, although it is now so much the norm that one hardly remembers why. According to a news note in *LJ,* February 1, 1973,

> "The result in many cases has been a long, hard look at duplicate subscriptions and titles which are no longer in steady demand. And new acquisitions of periodicals are under particularly sharp scrutiny . . . A recent article in the *Washington Library Newsletter* . . . expresses the dismay . . . In 1971–72, after a cutback in funds, the library found itself spending three times as much for serials as for books and sees little chance of ever reducing the proportion of a better than 50–50 split."[28]

Comparison of book and periodical prices is shown in Chart II. Some further library reactions to high price increases are discussed later.

With the 25th ALA Periodical Price Index in 1985, responsibility for compilation transferred to the Faxon Company with the blessing of the Library Materials Price Index Committee. Faxon calls upon its large periodicals data base which includes the latest prices charged by publishers, as well as upon software which is able to manipulate the information into data useful for libraries, thus removing much of the painstaking manual preparation which was involved earlier. For the present, the base of titles and general methodology remains the same. Prices used by Faxon exclude discounts and service charges. Faxon also makes available additional breakdowns and information on rates of change.

A questionnaire was included with the latest Index, asking how the information can be made more timely and relevant in the future. In coming years, some changes to the ALA Indexes will evolve. For a fuller discussion of the switch, see the 1985 survey article.[29]

B. H. Blackwell Periodical Price Index[30]

This index is produced by the bookseller and subscription agency of the same name in Oxford, England. It was first published in the August 1966, issue of the *Library Association Record* and since 1977 has been published in the May issue. The survey is based on a market basket of titles which are purchased by "learned" libraries. Important journals are chosen without discrimination as to language, price, or country of publication. The sample size is smaller than the ALA survey, i.e., about 2,000 titles as compared to 3,700. The survey is particularly useful for several reasons: it does not limit itself geographically or by currency, it presents periodicals from a worldwide rather than a U.S. perspective and thus more closely approximates an academic subscription list, and it is published early enough in the year that it can be an aid to the budgeting process.

Prices in the index are given in sterling currency. The United Kingdom, like most Western nations, has recently had a weaker currency than the United States and is also more greatly affected by publication prices outside its own country. Thus, the Blackwell Index gives an even more dramatic presentation of the behavior of periodical prices over the years. A B.H.B. summary is given in Chart III, along with U.S. rate of exchange on or around January 1 of that year, as taken from the currency conversion tables in the *New York Times.*

The B.H.B. Index also attempts no judgments about the reasons for price rises, although extra volumes and supplements in sciences periodicals (1970) and currency fluctuation (1972, 1973, 1975, 1982) are mentioned. If U.S. increases during this period were large, increases to the British

Chart II. **Bowker Annual** Published Price Indexes, Comparison of Book Increases to Periodical Increases

Year	Edition of Bowker	Periodicals		Books	
		Avg. Price	Percent Increase	Avg. Price	Percent Increase
1970	1971	10.41		11.66	
1971	1972	11.66	12. up	13.25	13.7 up
1972	1973	13.23	13. up	12.99	- 2. down
1973	1974	16.20	22. up	12.20	- 6.5 down
1974	1975	17.71	9. up	14.09	15.5 up
1975	1976	19.93	12.5 up	16.19	14.9 up
1976	1977	22.52	12.9 up	17.39	7.4 up
1977	1978	24.59	9.2 up	19.22	10.5 up
1978	1979	27.58	12.2 up	19.30	00.4 up
1979	1980	30.37	10.1 up	23.96	24.1 up
1980	1981	34.54	13.7 up	24.64	2.8 up
1981	1982	39.13	13.3 up	26.63	8.1 up
1982	1983	44.80	14.5 up	30.34	13.9 up
1983	1984	50.23	12.1 up	31.19	2.8 up
1984	1985	54.79	9.4 up	27.84	-10.7 down
					(preliminary figures)
1985	N/A	59.70	8.6 up	N/A	N/A
		(Library Journal)			

Chart III.   B. H. Blackwell Price Index, Periodicals, Increases
1970–1985, as reported in Library Association Record

Year	No. of Titles	Average Price	Percent Increase	U. S. Exchange	Equivalent U. S. Price
1970	1728	11/10/9	14.2 up	2.40	27.72
1971	1689	13.14	15.6 up	2.39	31.40
1972	1691	14.34	8.9 up	2.55	36.57
1973	1671	16.78	16.2 up	2.35	39.43
1974	1661	19.78	17.6 up	2.31	45.69
1975	1753	23.64	21.1 up	2.35	55.55
1976	1752	30.11	27.1 up	2.03	61.12
1977	1752	38.28	26.9 up	1.70	65.08
1978	1762	41.98	9.7 up	1.90	79.76
1979	2007	44.18	9.2 up	2.03	89.69
1980	2007	46.81	5.8 up	2.24	104.85
1981	2007	52.41	12.2 up	2.38	124.74
1982	2007	64.00	22.3 up	1.94	124.16
1983	2007	72.82	14.2 up	1.62	117.97
1984	2007	84.73	16.3 up	1.42	120.32
1985	2007	100.81	19.3 up	1.16	116.94

were phenomenal. A subscription costing £10.00 in 1970 would cost, on average, £92.59, an increase of over nine times. Based on U.S./Sterling exchange rates over the years 1970–1985, the average periodical price on the B.H.B. Index in U.S. currency was $27.72 in 1970 and $116.94 in 1985. Thus, the same mix of titles increased to U.S. libraries by 4.22 times over the same period that they increased to the U.K. market by 9.26 times.

As in the United States, science/technology and medicine generally accounted for higher price increases but not to the same extent as in the United Kingdom. Some reasons for this may be apparent later (see discussion on dual pricing of periodicals).

Obviously, English libraries, generally not as large or as well-funded as their U.S. counterparts, have had a far more difficult 15 years. On the other hand, the pound sterling dropped to its lowest value ever against the U.S. dollar in 1985, close to par. During the second half of the year, that situation changed and at the end of December 1985, the rate is approximately 1.44 dollars to the pound (compare to 1.16 in January). U.S. and Canadian libraries have been badly damaged during the 1985 autumn renewal period by the wild change in exchange rate, which has caused an immediate increase of 24 percent over Autumn 1984 renewals, even assuming no subscription price increases. With routine increases, the rise in British prices will be in the region of 30 percent.

Faxon Price Index

The Faxon price index is published by the subscription agency of the same name, located in Westwood, Massachusetts. It has been published in a less regular fashion than either the ALA or B.H.B. indexes, beginning with the October 1974 study, which covered 1972–1974.[31-38] The titles in Faxon's index are based on "easily definable authority groups." That is, some 30 major indexing and abstracting services are consulted and the titles indexed by them are the ones used in compilation of Faxon statistics. The index uses "weighted" prices, in which the popularity (i.e., number of Faxon subscribers) of each journal is factored.

The Faxon Index presents figures in a variety of permutations. The first table gives average prices by subject; that is, by indexing or abstracting service. Table II breaks customer subscriptions into price ranges of $3.00 increments. Table III provides data on savings effected where subscription periods of greater than one year are offered by the publisher. Table IV gives average prices paid by different types of libraries. Table V tells the reader how many titles retained the same price as the previous year, and how many increased, decreased, or changed category. In Table VI, the average price by subscriber category is shown, based on number of titles invoiced. Table VII compares domestic and foreign prices. Finally, Table VIII provides price by a number of LC subject classifications. Tables I, II, and III are the most useful in a library's budget preparation; the rest are useful to specific libraries in particular situations. A summary of Faxon price increases is given in Chart IV. Chart V then summarizes a comparison of ALA, B.H.B. and Faxon indexes.

Local Indexes

Obviously, the differences between the above indexes in any given year can be great, and choosing a particular one can have a tremendous impact on a library's renewals budget estimates. Therefore, libraries have found it desirable to attempt in-house calculations. Some libraries have done this in very simple ways; some have compiled sophisticated statistical data.

Relatively little has been written about indexes kept within individual libraries; various methods are possible, depending on local requirements and staff resources available for the job.

In 1981, Frederick Lynden wrote a plea for detailed cost studies in libraries, particularly the costs of materials.[39] He listed sources available for price information and suggested areas where research has been inadequate. Taking up Lynden's challenge, the D. H. Hill Library at North Carolina State University, Raleigh, performed its own calculations of av-

Chart IV.   Faxon Periodical Price Indexes, Summary, 1972–1985

Year	Average Price (University)	Percent of Change
1972 1973 1974	No overall, only by separate category	
1975	34.55	
1976	38.94	12.7 up
1977	41.85	7.5 up
1978	45.14	7.9 up
1979	50.11	11.0 up
1980	57.23	14.2 up
1981	67.81	18.5 up
1982	73.89	9.0 up
1983	78.04	5.6 up
1984	83.47	5.7 up
1985	86.10	4.4 up

erage periodical costs by using the invoices from two major suppliers, Faxon and Swets & Zeitlinger.[40] These suppliers added Hill's local call numbers to the customer subscription file and the library used the call number breakdown to estimate average costs in subject areas by LC classification number. The Library then compared NCSU averages with Faxon

Chart V.   Comparison of ALA, B. H. Blackwell, and Faxon Index Increases

Year	ALA	B. H. Blackwell	Faxon
1970	11.8 percent up	14.2 percent up	
1971	12.0	15.6	
1972	13.0	8.9	
1973	22.0	16.2	
1974	9	17.6	
1975	12.5	21.1	
1976	12.9	27.1	12.7
1977	9.2	26.9	7.5
1978	12.2	9.7	7.9
1979	10.1	9.2	11.0
1980	13.7	5.8	14.2
1981	13.3	12.2	18.5
1982	14.5	22.3	9.0
1983	12.1	14.2	5.6
1984	9.4	16.3	5.7
1985	8.6	19.3	4.4

published averages. Some very close similarities were evidenced, along with pronounced differences. The authors concluded that local studies are a useful exercise, although we are not told if these were continued.

An important piece of local library research was published in 1983 by Mary Elizabeth Clack and Sally Williams of Harvard College Library.[41] In 1978, Sally Williams had published the results of a first study in which Widener Library prepared a periodical index based on internal payment records and compared it with the ALA and B.H.B. indexes.[42] The correlations were used to predict Harvard's 1977 average prices. The Clack/ Williams study updates the former study from 1978–1982, continues its comparisons with the two major indexes, and draws certain conclusions.

Widener's principal objective was to obtain accurate budget forecasting, without using large amounts of staff time to maintain the in-house data. The authors clearly demonstrate that local price indexes are, indeed, different from composite published indexes. Nonetheless, Widener found that by using regression analysis, it was possible to calculate correlation coefficients between local prices and the two published indexes. In addition, the published indexes lend credibility to library arguments for better funding, particularly in years where overall increases may be higher than local increases.

The study concluded that national indexes can (because of acceptable margin of error) and should be used to predict local increases, provided that local compilations are done every few years as a cross-check on the validity of the published indexes. Widener determined that for Harvard's purposes, the major indexes can be used in combination with developed formulae for five years. In the sixth year, the library will do its own price-gathering and, if necessary, re-calculate the slope of the regression line.

Clack and Williams emphasized that this decision was taken after 12 years of internal price index maintenance. The authors recommend that the number of years of internal index-keeping to establish accurate predictors using linear regression is around nine.

Two other valuable articles assist in serials budget forecasting. While these are not specifically price indexes, they are noted here. In 1980 Guilbert Hentschke and Ellen Kehoe proposed a model for determining the costs of subscribing to periodicals for a one-year versus a three-year period.[43] The problem is described as a capital budgeting one whose objectives are lowest library subscription costs over a six-year period. The formulae are well–described and applicable to other libraries. The conclusion reached seems obvious, i.e., that three-year subscriptions can produce significant savings. However, the authors carefully discuss the limitations of multi-year subscriptions. While they may provide a hedge against rising prices, they are only valuable in a static subscription situation. Otherwise, the library is locked into journals which it may need or wish to cancel. The initial subscription charges are also very high and must be funded somehow. It appears that the availability of the three-year subscription for the academic or scholarly journal is declining, even in the short period since this study was published.

Finally, Dennis Smith describes the University of California system's attempt to establish a sufficient base budget for its campuses and to predict future cost increases.[44] Convincing, objective data were needed for the political authorities who assign funds to the library system. A library committee developed an acquisition model and used the indexes published in the *Bowker Annual* to seek appropriation increases. A second committee, The Task Group on the Cost of Library Materials, was then created "to design and recommend methods for documenting increases (or decreases) in the actual costs of library materials."[45] Much of the committee's work focused on nationally published price indexes. While noting the limitations of the indexes, the Committee decided to accept these, with modifications that were necessary within the California system. The University has had great success in its negotiations with the State for several years, by understanding published indexes and adapting them to University of California library collections.

For libraries that wish to develop their own periodical price indexes, the latest version of ANSI Z39.20-1983, the *American National Standard for Library and Information Sciences and Related Publishing Practices— Library Materials—Criteria for Price Indexes*[46] is the first guide. It describes the purpose of creating price indexes and sets specific rules and definitions for various types of library materials. The foreword suggests that improved data collection is required. It also notes that published indexes are not intended to substitute for local indexes.

The consensus of publications connected with periodical price indexes is that librarians have found any and all published data useful. In spite of the problems associated with the ALA, B.H.B., and Faxon indexes (having to do with size of samples, mix of titles, countries and currencies), they have been the best there is. No doubt, many librarians use them in convincing their administrations of the need for budget increases.

The most intelligent use of the major indexes combines them with local studies. There is, to echo Lynden, still a great demand for more and better information and further research. It appears that in the future the capabilities of serial and fiscal automation may begin to give libraries internally what they have been unable to achieve by manual calculation. It is hoped that the evolution of such skills within specific libraries will lead to studies on how best to use these powerful new tools.

LIBRARIANS RESPOND TO HIGH PRICES

The prevalence of double-digit figures in published periodical price indexes and the effects on library budgets elicited comment from many librarians. Michael Kronenfeld and James Thompson used the ALA indexes to examine the relationship of periodical price increases to the U.S. Consumer Price Index (CPI) from 1967/69–1979.[47] First they summarized the ALA overall indexes, along with 10 subject categories. Then they listed the CPI for each year examined. For each year they calculated the value of U.S. journals as a percentage of CPI dollar value in each category and graphed the results.

The first two graphs chart the increase in CPI along with the increase in periodical prices by subject area. These clearly show that even the subjects with the lowest rate of increase rose more quickly than the CPI, while those with the greatest rate of increase (chemistry and physics, labor and industrial relations) rose almost three times as quickly. The second pair of graphs shows the lower value of the dollar over the studied time period. The 1979 consumer dollar is worth less than half of the 1967 dollar. The library/periodicals dollar of 1979 buys about 30 percent of what the 1967 dollar bought. That is, not only has the buying power of the dollar been severely eroded, but for libraries it has eroded at a rate far more severe than inflation indexes suggest.

It would be useful to compare journal price increases with the CPI to see if consistent correlations exist between the two. A quick comparison suggests that there is no correspondence. However, the available data are "too noisy" for accurate calculations. How the rate of general inflation affects periodical price increases is a useful subject for further examination.

The *Library Resources & Technical Services* annual review articles on trends in serials librarianship noted such statements as "The University of California, Riverside, estimated that, assuming a steady-state allocation in 1973/74 dollars with 12 percent inflation on the average and a continuing proportion of renewals and new titles, by 1978/79 95.8 percent of the total book budget would go to serials."[48] The 1976 review article noted a comparison of increase in periodical prices from 1970 to 1975 (92 percent) to the U.S. CPI for the same period (38.6 percent) to the increase in appropriations of 79 Association of Research Libraries members (36.5 percent) and noted that significant funds had to be transferred from monographic to serials budgets.[49] "Taking into account the increased inflation rates presented . . . in order to maintain the status quo in serials collections by the late 1980s, libraries will have ceased purchasing monographs entirely."[50]

The Association of College and Research Libraries reported that the cost of U.S. hardcover books purchased by academic institutions rose by 81 percent between 1971 and 1978, and the cost of U.S. periodicals increased by 122 percent during that time.[51] An updated survey of medical journals shows that a list of 111 titles which cost an average of $11.81 per title in 1963 and $14.00 in 1968, increased to $59.67 in 1983.[52] This was compared to the CPI and a dollar that had only 20 percent of the buying power of the 1963 dollar. Even so, a library whose budget had increased at the CPI rate in those 20 years would be able to purchase only 65 percent of its 1963 periodicals.

Several authors touch on what is the ideal balance in a library materials budget between book and serial acquisitions, and numbers such as 50 percent[53] and two thirds[54] have been suggested as desirable. Such a proportion is not universally definable, for it depends on type of library collections, type of library, and what the local definition is of a serial publication. Varma suggests that a sensible guideline is the percentage a particular library employed in days without severe financial restraint.[55]

Librarians around the world contributed to cries of anguish over high periodical prices. A Canadian business librarian discusses the problems of rapid increase in cost of serials and finds the average price increased from 1975 to 1981 by 76.2 percent.[56] Blake and Meadows discuss cancellation strategies in British universities as a result of high prices and large price increases.[57]

An article from India poignantly stated "the hard fact of life is that everything except the purchasing power of money is increasing manifold."[58] The two authors then describe a difficult situation in Punjab University. Both this article and one by Saxena and Khan, University of Roorkee, emphasize the currency problem in developing nations, whose money drops in value every year against major currencies.[59] For instance, the rupee was worth more than three times less against the Dutch Guilder in 1978–79 as opposed to 1966–67 and almost 80 percent less than the U.S. dollar. If things have been tough all over, they have been much worse for the countries that most need educational resources.

Edelman says that "librarians are suckers for numbers."[60] He believes that librarians' basic philosophy and guilt about inadequate collections after World War II contribute to their inclination to purchase far too many periodicals. Librarians carry out a custodial function and have allowed faculty to make too many subject-related decisions. De Gennaro, in a rousing and now very-well-known article, blames much of the problem of exaggerated prices, far above national inflation, on librarians.[61] Librarians tend to be orderly to a fault: they love perfect runs of serials and do not like to break or interrupt a set. They are gullible: they allow publishers to take advantage of their need for tidiness. They are insecure:

they allow faculty to bully them into keeping titles for which there is no demand. They are trusting: they do not quarrel with publishers who charge absurdly high prices. De Gennaro states that "journals are the sacred cows of librarianship." He suggests various remedies, and generally rallies librarians to assertiveness. Although he overstates the case, many of his recommendations have since been followed. The cynic would say that librarians were forced into action by circumstances, not by initiative.

Librarians have begun to fight back, and they began doing so for a number of reasons, listed here.

1. Budgetary cuts have taxed the ability of even the most willing administrators to preserve materials budgets. Political and economic problems outside institutional control caused these problems.
2. The decrease of available funding over the last 10–15 years has forced librarians to be selective about what is bought. The need to choose has called for community-wide input and resulted in the politicization of budget issues, which has in turn put librarians on the spot and forced them to be articulate and accountable.
3. In the tough financial environment, librarians have become more businesslike. The "new" library manager is expected to have financial skills. The competition for good jobs has led to advanced degrees and MBA's.
4. Automation and the increased availability of computing resources in the library and in the home have provided powerful tools for librarians to begin understanding, if not controlling, finances.
5. The literature, although not exhaustive, has been more vocal about price increases.
6. Increased automation of the major vendors has brought them into the arena, where they have become significant contributors to price information.
7. The decrease in available funds has come at the same time as not only increased numbers of periodicals being published, but also an increase in varieties and types of information available to libraries; library budgets are pulled in more directions simultaneously.
8. Bibliographic networking and union lists have made resource sharing possible.
9. Lack of funds makes new buildings or stack additions unlikely or impossible.

The various ways in which librarians have responded to the large price increases have been:

1. Usage studies, which have shown that a far larger-than-expected proportion of library materials (including periodicals) are little used,

have confirmed the suspicion that a number of subscriptions are supporting only one faculty member's research.
2. Cancellation of subscriptions, beginning with duplicates and then becoming bolder, cancelling unique copies.
3. Weeding of collections.
4. Limiting new subscriptions by more critical selection, or forcing cancellation of a low–use periodical to buy a more desirable one.
5. Regular review of existing subscriptions.
6. Monitoring invoices for extraordinary price rises.
7. Relying on delivery from external sources instead of internal holdings (Interlibrary Loan, online access, document delivery services). For example, hundreds of online searches through *Chemical Abstracts* are possible before the cost of the subscription is reached.
8. Co-operative collection development, in its early stages.
9. High priority for serial retrospective conversion, to enhance resource-sharing across campuses and between institutions.
10. Challenging publishers over specific issues and publicizing outrageous behavior.

FACTORS IN PRICE INCREASES

Is the Subscription Agent a Culprit in High Prices?

It has been suggested that he is. In 1971, Frank Clasquin, Vice-president of the Faxon Company, wrote an article replying to a librarian concerned about a possible 5–10 percent agency service fee to be charged for periodicals.[62] Clasquin defends the subscription agency service charge, first stating that three to four years earlier it had been the general practice for the agent to offer library discounts.

Obviously, the agency needs to stay solvent, and the cost of operating a subscription business utilizes about 10–12 percent (at that time, and according to agents the margin holds in 1985) of publisher's price. It is widely known that publishers' discounts to subscription agencies have been diminishing over the years; formerly they were high enough for libraries to receive a net discount, but for the past 10 or more years customers have been paying subscription agents a surcharge over publishers' list price. This charge is generally an amount that compensates the agency for operating costs and provides it the profit necessary to stay in business comfortably. In some instances, the agency quotes its subscriber a straight percentage fee; in others, the service charge varies with mix of titles. A library with a high percentage of popular discounted journals may pay a zero charge; a library with a high ratio of scholarly titles may incur a service charge of 5–10 percent (or more).

Other factors affect the percentage charged. A large customer library may receive special consideration from a vendor. A library which arranges to prepay its renewal invoice particularly early in the year, i.e., June or July instead of October or November, may receive a discount or a "bonus." A library which sets up a "deposit" account with a vendor may pay a reduced fee. In these instances, the bookseller is compensating the library for the use of its money, a feature very attractive when interest rates became unusually high in the early 1980s. The library never receives interest from its administration for budget funds remaining unspent in its accounts, so there is incentive for forwarding funds to a supplier in advance. Some libraries receive additional vendor services such as checking–in and re–shipping and pay an extra charge for these.

We have never seen routine service charges in excess of six percent, although some librarians have complained of double-digit charges. Our experience also was that earlier service charges, that is, in the 1970s, were higher than those today, and that efficiencies in supplier routines and competition have made them more reasonable. Librarians must know what the library is being charged. Librarians must inquire what the fee policy is and whether the service charge is built into each individual title or added as a separate line. If the former, the percentage should be discovered; if the library prefers one or the other method, it must ask its vendor.

There does not appear to be much substance to complaints that the agent's fee is usurious. Many agencies have gone out of business or been subsumed by other companies simply because their profitability was inadequate, as in the case of Macmillan parting with Stechert Macmillan (to Faxon). Huff gives an interesting history of subscription agencies and a state-of-the-situation review as of the mid–1970s.[63] Most of the eight agencies he names as medium-sized independents are either no longer in business or no longer independent.

Two authors present interesting considerations of the usefulness and cost–effectiveness of subscription agents. Coplen attempts to compare the agent's service charge to the cost of doing the same work internally.[64] He suggests that the cost of paying a single subscription invoice may be $7.00–$10.00 (basic estimated charge of $3.55 for "legitimate" invoices, and taking into account junk mail and problems). Huibert Paul recommends a critical look at subscription agents and their service fees.[65] He suggests that the reason publishers have stopped giving agency discounts is that they no longer value such services. Another way to look at this, of course, is that publishers either feel the library is a captive subscriber whatever the periodical costs, and/or publishers' automated systems can cope with a variety of direct orders as effectively as with a handful of agents' orders, so they would like to make all the profits themselves. In fairness, the discount situation is of more concern in the United States, where the middleman has never been as entrenched as in Europe. In the United States, some publishers are even offering discounts to librarians who purchase directly from them. At the same time, U.S. agents have asked for equal treatment with European agents, which has had the effect of lowering European discounts, rather than raising North American discounts.

Paul lists various problems and headaches of dealing through a subscription agency, few of which can be gainsayed: additional charges and transactions during the course of a year, failure to offer multi-year options, checking of renewal lists, peculiar non-library entries, no relationship of invoices to what is actually being published, and elaborate claiming requirements. What he does not say is that the same or comparable problems happen in dealing directly with publishers.

If a library has a periodical renewal list totalling $500,000 and it is placed with a subscription agency charging a five percent fee, this fee will be $25,000 or (assuming a price of $59.70 per title as in the ALA Price Index for 1985), $2.99 per title. The fundamental question is, is $25,000 saved internally by ordering via a subscription agent?

Like Mr. Paul, we have not done detailed statistical analyses of the precise internal costs of placing orders directly, but like him we have solidly-based observations. They are that in five areas agencies save staff time:

1. By removing the need to keep publisher address files continually up-to-date. The agency has multiple dealings with publishers to the library's one and can normally supply an order or process a claim from its data base. The library does not have time to check addresses and update them on a continual basis.

2. By acting as a funnel for orders, claims, mail, and other correspondence, which can be bundled into pre-addressed envelopes on a regular basis. Some agencies can now be accessed on-line without the tremendous costs of forms, letters, or postage and without the time delay.

3. By reducing the number of checks written and accounts maintained.

4. By providing management/price information as specified by individual libraries.

5. By dealing with foreign publishers, in foreign languages and foreign currencies, and providing associated services. This is the area in which overseas agents can be most helpful. Even where language not a barrier, time often is, and the agent can solve such problems.

One of the characteristics of the low-budget years was that not only were materials budgets reduced, but so were staff budgets. In fact, it was normal to attempt to reduce staff size in order to preserve materials budgets. Libraries have emerged from this era with leaner staffing, and the only way to compensate has been to pay vendors (out of the materials budget) to absorb some of the work previously done within the library. (Approval plans are another example of work being done by suppliers.) Even if the subscription agent's work could be done as effectively in-house, it is doubtful that funding for such provision could be provided in most institutions in the 1980s.

A serious defense of agency size and service charge is presented by Wayne Thyden, Vice-president of EBSCO Subscription Agency.[66] He asserts that by dropping agency discounts, publishers have passed costs to the library community. He presents a convincing case for modest fees. It is incorrect to blame subscription agents for the large price increases of periodicals, although it is necessary to know what the effect has been. In fact, as we will see later, some subscription agents have made serious efforts to help libraries pay lower prices.

What is the Publisher's Role in Pricing of Journals?

It is not easy to determine how publishers set journal prices. Various cost studies exist, but to draw conclusions is difficult because of contradictory philosophies and methodologies. Several methods are employed: publishers calculate costs and desired profit based on projected number of sales, determining the subscription price necessary to achieve this goal; or, publishers charge what the market will bear (for example, this appears to be the case with many business and medical publications, as the user community is perceived to be prosperous and willing to pay a great deal); or, some publishers operate without profit motive. Publications of the latter type usually fill creative or cultural needs. Many of them are undercapitalized and more likely to be erratic in appearance or to go out of business. They are generally not culprits in high prices.

Several articles have dealt with publisher price-setting. John Jarvis (of John Wiley and Sons, Ltd.), discusses planning for a brand new journal and states that worthwhile profits are achieved no earlier than four to five years into publication, in spite of the attractive cash flow situation of regularly collecting income in advance every fiscal year.[67]

An IEEE conference in 1973, representing the academic librarian, the special librarian, the nonprofit scholarly publisher, and the commercial scholarly publisher, captured the issues which continue to be critical today.[68] The academic viewpoint, from Walter Fraser of Rutgers, was that there exists an atmosphere of "soak the librarian," or if publication costs soar, "let's raise the institutional price." He suggested that rising rates would kill certain journals and that to let the marketplace totally determine what remains in publication is not necessarily desirable.

Joe Kuney (of John Wiley, U.S.) suggested that libraries had been paying too low a differential for a long time. The representative from the American Institute of Physics suggested that if libraries did not support marginal journals, these would not continue publication. Discussion then focused on sources of publishing revenue for the learned society publisher and the proportion available from member subscribers (usually individuals), nonmembers (usually institutions, i.e., libraries), advertising, and page charges (see Scal[69] for history and definition of page charges, which are a way of charging the author or his sponsoring institution for a portion of cost of publication). The practice described during the conference was that of charging members the cost of producing their copies, whereas nonmembers bore basic production cost (editorial, composition, and production). The differential between nonmember and member subscription costs within the AIP was at least four to one; that is, a nonmember would pay at least $40 for a subscription that cost a member $10.

Price-setting also takes into account those "break points," the psychological barriers which deter one or another category of subscribers. The institutional deterrent is much higher than the individual deterrent; thus, the institution is levied a much higher price. The situation is exacerbated in commercial publishing by lack of membership fees and by need for profit. Therefore, commercial publishers usually charge a substantially higher price than nonprofit or society publishers for the same type of publication. To librarians it appears that in subscribing to the publications of professional societies they are subsidizing a number of member activities from which they do not benefit, while in subscribing to expensive commercially-published journals they are supporting what may be excessive profits.

One librarian actually defended publishers' mega-inflationary price increases by demonstrating that between 1959 and 1969 these could be explained by increased numbers of pages.[70] He showed that 20 physics journals increased in size as well as in cost. Taking physical growth into account, these journal prices actually increased by 55 percent over 10 years, not 202 percent as indicated by gross subscription cost. It is interesting to note that this is not an argument commonly used by publishers.

C & EN published a special report in May 1983, "Troubled Times for Scientific Journals," which described the state of scientific periodical publishing in the early 1980s.[71] According to the author, there has been a severe decline in journal subscriptions. Overall circulation of American Chemical Society journals fell from 119,827 in 1969 to 86,082 in 1982. The American Institute of Physics reports that its subscriptions have been falling two to three percent per year recently. Personal members have dropped their ACS subscriptions twice as often as non-member (i.e., library) subscribers. At the same time, because non-members often pay 3 to 7.5 times more for a subscription than individuals, emptier library pocketbooks have had an enormous impact.

Publishers have been hammered by rising costs of producing journals in labor, paper, and postage, and they have attempted to economize by using cheaper or lighter paper stock, changing to in-house typesetting or asking for camera-ready copy, purchasing improved presses, cutting internal costs, and subcontracting distribution functions. It is not clear to what extent production costs have increased or how much they have contributed to price increases, but higher prices have been laid at their door. These higher prices have led to cancellations, which lead to greater price increases. (It is interesting to speculate on the world's remaining subscription to a given journal, which then costs an infinite amount of money.)

In the battle with lost subscriptions and revenue, publishers have attempted to compensate and achieve higher market share by creating new, often more and more specialized, journals, each with smaller numbers of subscribers. The waters of pricing are muddied by copyright and photocopying, as well as the dubious merits of some new publications. Page charges are still highly controversial; advertising is barely a factor in funding highly specialized publications; electronic publishing poses threats to conventional publishing. All in all, if publishers are to be believed, the current situation for journals is pessimistic, or at best, uncertain.

Note that most of the foregoing discussions of high prices and super-inflationary increases concern scientific journals far more than those in the social sciences and humanities, which increase at a slower rate. Average prices by discipline are generally several times higher in sciences than non-sciences, with only a few exceptions. No study specifically deals with the reasons for this difference; however, several factors come to mind:

1. Science journals are generally more voluminous per title than those of other disciplines.
2. The science professions (also law) offer more jobs at higher salaries than the social sciences and humanities. They are associated with greater prosperity.
3. There are more emerging and advancing research areas in the sciences; many of these have commercial and industrial (profitable) applications.
4. Higher grants are awarded for scientific research.
5. Higher costs (such as refereeing, composition) are frequently associated with science publications.
6. Scientists are more number-conscious; the emphasis on citations has accelerated pressure for publication.

In general, librarians have been willing to accept publishers' explanations for high prices and might have continued to pay without argument, had the fiscal situation allowed. The traditions of public service and generous availability of materials within the library building have long been entrenched in library philosophy. There is an area, however, where librarians have become vocal about pricing, involving two-tier pricing structures. One type charges libraries a different, generally much higher, rate than individuals. The second discriminates between libraries on the basis of geographical location.

Prior to discussion, service-based pricing (as in the H. W. Wilson indexes) should be mentioned. In service-based pricing, libraries are charged according to the number of indexed periodicals to which they subscribe; this usually relates directly to size of library. There appears to be no complaint about this pricing method, and a higher cost for more indexing appears fair to librarians.

Dual Pricing, Libraries vs. Individuals

The first exploration of higher institutional versus lower individual subscriptions was undertaken by Wittig in 1977.[72] He surveyed 180 journal prices between 1966 and 1975 and determined that while only four percent had a two-price structure in 1966, the number had risen to 15 percent by 1975. A check on the four percent revealed that the first instances of dual pricing go back to at least the mid-1950s. In addition, the institutional rate was increasing at a higher average than the individual rate. Although publishers occasionally give a lower rate to libraries, this is extremely rare.

In many instances, the dual pricing is for publications of learned societies. The reasons for implementation of the higher library rate appear to be economic; that is, publishers attribute a loss of individual subscriptions to easy availability of library copies, combined with access to cheap, convenient photocopying facilities. Additionally, libraries have higher budgets than personal subscribers.

A brief exchange of letters in *Library Journal* took up the discussion of individual/institutional pricing differentials.[73,74] A member of the staff of the American Association for the Advancement of Science (AAAS) pointed out that any individual who pays dues may receive a subscription to *Science* at the lower rate. AAAS's rationale is that individual names are more valuable in advertising sales, and advertisers want to know specific readers' names and addresses. Also, institutions have more than one reader per copy.

While it is possible for libraries to obtain *Science* at a personal rate by posing as individuals, this method is impossible with many societies which have certain educational, professional, and affiliation requirements for membership. Some organizations allow academic departments, but not libraries, to take memberships. (The publications may then be housed in a departmental library or reading room, but seldom find their way to the general institutional readership. If they do, it is after a time lag.) Some publishers do not allow individual subscriptions unless the institution also subscribes at the institutional rate. One major study suggests that "a differential of perhaps 50 percent between institutional and individual subscriptions does not seem out of line."[75]

The reality is rather higher. Miller and Jensen surveyed dual pricing within the field of medicine.[76] They discovered that about 15 percent (281) of titles checked have dual pricing structures; the price differential was as high as 890 percent, with an average of 102.4 percent. Clearly, there is no consistent practice for determining what libraries ought to pay for periodicals and assigning rates appears almost arbitrary. Dyl suggests that dual pricing constitutes price discrimination and may be illegal.[77]

Koenig plays devil's advocate and argues that dual pricing allows individual subscriptions at an affordable rate, thus generating additional revenue for the publisher and keeping down the cost of the library's subscription.[78] He does not discuss inconsistencies of the practice nor the fact that many of the publishers are societies with goals beyond publication of journals. Although librarians are apparently prepared to pay a higher price than individuals, they expect some rationale for the pricing structure. In fact, the budgeting practices of publishers seem no more "scientific" than those of libraries. Like academic budgets, publishing budgets may be based on history, politics, intuition, and other objectives (as well as what the subscriber can be coerced into paying).

In any case, librarians collectively appear to have accepted the fairness of higher institutional rates based on serving a large public.

Dual Pricing, Geographically Based

Another practice which has existed for some time has relatively recently come under the critical scrutiny of librarians and has not been accepted with complacency. This is the behavior of European, most specifically (at present) British, publishers of charging substantially higher prices to their overseas customers, particularly U.S. and Canadian libraries. Libraries were aware of the practice for some years, but the first real publicity came in 1981 in a letter to its customers by the German academic bookseller and subscription agent, Otto Harrassowitz. In 1980, Springer New York had offered librarians a subscription price of approximately 10 percent below Springer Germany rates, presumably as an inducement for libraries to move subscriptions directly to Springer. In 1981, Springer New York raised the U.S. subscription rates to 15–45 percent above Springer Germany rates, for an average increase of 40 percent over 1980 fall renewals, or 30 percent higher than the European rate. Harrassowitz outlined events to its customers and pointed out to librarians the price protection afforded to customers who had continued to use the country-of-origin agent. Harrassowitz was disturbed at what appeared to be unethical behavior in

charging U.S. libraries an unnecessarily high differential price and in trying
to remove business from booksellers. Apparently, the U.S. office's behavior was not supported by the head office, as the New York operation
later reduced its price differential to a reasonable rate, around 10 percent.
(There is no suggestion by librarians that a differential which allows for
higher cost of doing foreign business is unfair.)

The next publicity given to geographically-based dual pricing used British publishing as an example. Larry X. Besant, Director of Linda Hall
Library in Kansas City, Missouri, and Siegfried Ruschin, Collection Development Librarian at Linda Hall, wrote a letter to the editor of *Nature*
in April 1984, questioning the practice of charging American libraries far
more than the basic subscription rate.[79] The exchange rates were also
publicized in *LJ*.[80]

This concern was shared at a meeting of directors of Missouri University
libraries, and Dr. Tom Shaughnessy, Director of the University of Missouri–Columbia Library, asked his Head of Serials, Deana Astle, to "do
something about it." Astle collaborated with Charles Hamaker, Collections
Development Librarian at the University of Missouri–St. Louis, to document the British dual-pricing practice. At the ALA Conference in Dallas,
June 1984, Astle and Hamaker were on the agenda of the Bookdealer/
Library Relations Committee of the Resources & Technical Services Division of the American Library Association. The voice of a few Missouri
librarians played a major role in creating a resolution subsequently passed
by the RTSD Board:

> Whereas, Libraries subscribing to some British periodicals are required to pay a
> U.S. subscription price which is significantly higher than the subscription rate charged
> to libraries in the United Kingdom as well as other overseas libraries, and
>
> Whereas it is expected that there may be some price differential due to fluctuations
> in exchange rates and postage costs, some British journal publishers have established
> prices in excess of what can be considered a normal differential, and
>
> Whereas the higher U.S. price is seriously affecting library budgets and their ability
> to continue to subscribe to needed British journals, and
>
> Whereas such practices are operating against the free flow of exchanging and dis-
> seminating information,
>
> Be it resolved, therefore, that the Board of Directors of RTSD request that the
> Executive Director of the American Library Association take action, in conjunction
> with other appropriate library organizations, including ARL, SLA, MLA, and IFLA,
> to convey to British periodical publishers the concern of U.S. libraries and to ask
> that British periodical publishers establish more equitable subscription rates for U.S.
> libraries.[81]

At that same conference, Jane Maddox of Otto Harrassowitz gave a
timely presentation to RTSD/Serials Section Discussion Group on the major types of distribution employed by European publishers and how these

patterns influence prices.[82] The agent's relationship to distribution types was also addressed.

Briefly, the publisher in the home country establishes a journal list price and may vary prices to different countries. The higher outside price may be connected with additional distribution expense in other countries. Basic practices are:

1. The European publisher is sole source for journal distribution and sets a price charged everywhere in the world.
2. The European publisher is sole source for distribution, but sets more than one price. Where the publisher has a higher price in certain countries, there may be an office in those countries which provides some services (apart from actual distribution, done from country of origin).
3. The European publisher may have his own distribution offices in other countries, which determine prices.
4. The European publisher may contract with a distributor in particular countries. That distributor sets the prices. Whether the publisher forces the library to purchase from the distributor or allows purchase from country of origin depends on policy.

In some cases, publishers may elect to bill a subscription according to address of invoice (in this way, the library can use a local agent and pay internal country price). In other cases, publishers are concerned with ultimate destination address and insist on charging the library the overseas rate, even where no additional expense to the publisher exists. The greatest outrage on the part of librarians is in cases where the publisher does not allow purchase in country of origin with local pricing. It appears that more publishers insist on charging according to the address of the end-user.

In the next dual–pricing series of events, the Faxon Company noted, in Fall 1984, that the price differential charged by Taylor & Francis, a U.K. scientific publisher, was extraordinarily high and called this to the attention of customers, suggesting a review of T & F journals. Meanwhile, ALA Executive Director Robert Wedgeworth began discussions with British publishers in attendance at the October 1984 Frankfurt Book Fair. British publishers also had the opportunity to present their position to a closed meeting of the January 1985 ALA Midwinter Bookdealer/Library Relations Committee.

Around this time, Astle & Hamaker published an article documenting recent British journal pricing patterns.[83] They examined the price lists of 17 publishers and demonstrated that U.S. libraries paid a two-thirds premium on the 548 titles compared to U.K. subscribers and one-third more than other overseas libraries. The authors contended that completely unrealistic exchange rates (as high as $3.20 during a period with bank exchange of $1.30) were being charged. Many publishers quoted an overseas rate and often a still higher special U.S. rate. A few publishers also set higher prices for West Germany and Japan. During the recent period when the pound was slipping badly, a number of British publishers were benefitting from dollars, yen, and Deutsch marks paid them by countries with strong currencies.

In the spring of 1985, Siegfried Ruschin's article appeared in *Serials Librarian*.[84] He pointed out that libraries with large numbers of science and technology publications have suffered most from the British dual pricing behavior, as a high proportion of the guilty periodicals are scientific. Ruschin notes that the practice appears to be spreading to other countries as well, partly because of changing distribution practices. He does not ask "for a price reduction, but merely to be allowed to pay the price established for the rest of the world."

On Friday, March 22, 1985, a seminar was held in London, England, sponsored by the Association of Learned and Professional Society Publishers and the Publishers Association, to discuss differential pricing of journals.[85] This was an opportunity for all interested parties, U.K. publishers, U.S. and U.K. librarians, and subscription agencies, to have their say. It appears, from reading the proceedings, that fundamental misunderstandings exist between American libraries and U.K. publishers. The latter believe that American librarians require a U.S. dollar price on their British journals. The fact that U.S. libraries state they find no problem with sterling payment seemed to be a surprise. It appears also that the basis for at least some of the discrepancy between sterling and U.S. rates came several years ago during the period of a falling dollar. At that time, there was reasonable correspondence between prices given in dollars and pounds. As the dollar gained in strength, the differential remained unchanged; both prices were increased by the same percentages even as the equivalency changed dramatically.

Part of the seminar considered the issue of "buying round," the English term for the practice of a subscription agent in the U.K. buying journals at local prices and reshipping/reselling them to overseas customers at lower than the publisher's price to the library in the subscribing country. The term appears to be used when the library's or agent's objective is to avoid paying the higher overseas rate. At least two British and one Dutch agent provide this service, with increasing protests and impedence from publishers. Other agencies will reship but comply with the specific publisher's pricing wishes. For this, the complying agencies have been criticized by some libraries and have lost some business. Some agents have attempted to keep the final destination address from the publisher, often without success. These discussions continue now and various parties are attempting to determine not only the ethics but also the legality of publishers' demand to know the end-user. It may be that the recent high rise in value of the pound sterling will render some re-shipping to now be more expensive than paying the overseas rate.

One of the publishers' arguments is that prices have to be set far in advance of the year of publication. Even so, it is difficult to understand how financial "futures" can have such an impact as many British-set U.S. prices suggest. It is easy to understand why North American librarians feel cheated.

After the U.K. seminar, it appeared that some progress had been made. Taylor & Francis agreed to hold U.S. prices at 1985 levels for two years. The British Medical Association said it would move from a three-tier to a two-tier price, charging U.K. libraries 15 percent less than the rest of the world. Both the Royal Chemical Society and Butterworth's were making adjustments in pricing. On the other hand, publishers in other countries are just beginning to show signs of charging a much higher price to American customers.

The issue is divisive and has caused considerable bad blood between certain agencies and publishers, librarians and publishers, and among subscription agents. To be charitable to publishers, it may be that they have not "cleaned up" as a result of high prices to the U.S. but have made up for leaner years. The additional income may have allowed them to keep rest-of-the-world prices lower than they might have otherwise been. One suspects that the above investigations and the increased communication between librarians and publishers will make publishers more accountable but that the result will finally be higher prices to the world at large rather than a lower price in the United States. Astle and Hamaker have been charged by ALA with a watching brief on dual pricing worldwide. Their followup article on British pricing is due to appear early in 1986 and will show that some progress has been made in fairer treatment for American libraries. Both their earlier study and the new one take place during periods of similar dollar/sterling exchange rates.

OTHER USEFUL STUDIES

Two excellent studies about scholarly communication deal in large part with journal publication and should be read by every concerned librarian. Although neither study has been updated into the 1980s, the journal publishing and library situations remain similar to what was described.

The first study was conducted by Bernard Fry and Herbert White under the auspices of the National Science Foundation at the Indiana University Graduate Library School.[86] It examined the relationship between libraries

and academic journal publishers during 1969–1973. It surveyed and analyzed library budgets, library responses to budget cuts, costs and revenues,
and library cooperation. Fry and White identified the beginnings of decreases in overall subscriptions resulting from lower library budget increases. In spite of cancellations, insufficient funding led to shifts from
monographic to serials budgets. The study measured net annual growth
of new journals to be only two percent, rather than the wild proliferation
that had been suggested by critics. It calculated that commercial publishers' gross profit during 1969–1973 rose to about 14 percent, or six percent
net, which is far from exhorbitant; it stated that the situation for non-
commercial scholarly publishing had entered a state of instability because
of reduced subscriptions. The authors believed that some subsidy, probably governmental, was required to keep the system alive and well. A
detailed bibliography is included with the study. Follow-up work in 1978
and 1979 reported a general continuation of earlier trends.[87,88]

The second study, the *Report of the National Enquiry on Scholarly
Communication,* was created to investigate dissemination of scholarly
knowledge, especially in the humanities and humanistic social sciences
during a time of financial crisis.[89] The crisis was the same one examined
by Fry and White, namely, fewer funds available to support scholarly
book and journal publishing, and the impact of this on spread of knowledge
in printed form. Various recommendations were made regarding cooperation, economics, marketing, and technology. A major section on scholarly journals discusses issues of pricing, as well as grave concern for quality.

CONCLUSION

In the course of this discussion, the following have been established:

1.   Periodical prices have grown rapidly, in the United States by over
     5½ times in the last 15 years.
2.   These prices are far in excess of the inflation rates (C.P.I.).
3.   No one has determined the relationship between subscription price
     increases and inflation rates, if there is a correlation.
4.   Major subscription price indexes exist but agree only approxi-
     mately with one another; the differences between them are great.
5.   Published price indexes assist, but only roughly, in local price
     forecasting.
6.   The tools and studies for serials budget forecasting are primitive.
7.   Subscription prices and price increases are heavily determined by
     type of library collection, i.e., general, scientific, etc.

8. Prices are heavily affected by foreign exchange rates, which have been erratic and unpredictable.
9. The country of publication and country in which a library is located thus are significant in determining size of price increases. The United States has been in a favored position, whereas emerging countries have not been readily able to afford resources.
10. Librarians can, to some extent, take action and affect the prices libraries pay for serials.
11. Choice of subscription agent may affect price paid by the library, but it is not the most significant factor.
12. Librarians' best results come from communicating with publishers and requiring them to be more open and accountable.
13. Libraries have learned to adapt to cancellation of periodicals.

Further areas for research are:

1. How to use increasingly available automated accounting systems in predicting and fine–tuning serials budgets.
2. How to adapt available indexes to local situations, or how to create local indexes which are useful.
3. How to correlate C.P.I. and journal inflation figures.
4. How to control non–periodical serial budgets.
5. How to determine when a subscription can be cancelled.

How much a library collects in a given fiscal year usually reflects the local budget situation, which in turn is a microcosm of the regional, and perhaps national and world, economic situation. As we move through the mid–1980s, Western economies appear to have reached a period of greater strength and stability. In 1985, the U.S. inflation rate decreased markedly and libraries saw the first signs of reduction in rate of subscription price increases. Librarians will be waiting to see if this is a continuing behavior and if increases will more closely approximate level of inflation. If, as is likely, subscriptions increase at a higher-than-standard inflation rate, librarians will continue to be faced with justifying increases larger than budget appropriators are prepared to fund; an improved economy may not solve the basic concern of how to afford the libraries our patrons historically have had.

If serials prices accelerate at a faster rate than both inflation and monographic price increases, can libraries contemplate a future in which most of the acquisitions budget is spent on serials? Probably not, and, therefore, will they accept further major reductions in serial holdings? Although we have been living with reduced library budgets for over a decade, many librarians are reacting to budgets rather than planning purchase strategies in advance. Fifteen years after the plentiful days of the 1960s, the time has come to accept financial restraint as the new operating environment.

NOTES AND REFERENCES

1. Hendrik Edelman, "Periodical Literature in a Changing Library Environment," *IEEE Transactions on Professional Communication* PC-20 (September 1977): 71.

2. Ibid.

3. "U.S. Periodicals and Serial Services: Cost Indexes for 1964," *Library Journal* 89 (1964): 2746–49.

4. Helen W. Tuttle, Norman B. Brown, and William Huff, "Price Indexes for 1970: U.S. Periodicals and Serial Services," *Library Journal* 95 (1970): 2427–29.

5. Helen W. Tuttle, William Huff, and Norman B. Brown, "Price Indexes for 1971: U.S. Periodicals and Serial Services," *Library Journal* 96 (1971): 2271–75.

6. Norman B. Brown and William H. Huff, "Price Indexes for 1972: U.S. Periodicals and Serial Services," *Library Journal* 97 (1972): 2355–57.

7. Norman B. Brown and William H. Huff, "Price Indexes for 1973: U.S. Periodicals and Serial Services," *Library Journal* 98 (1973): 2052–55.

8. Norman B. Brown, "Price Indexes for 1974: U.S. Periodicals and Serial Services," *Library Journal* 99 (1974): 1775–78.

9. Norman B. Brown, "Price Indexes for 1975: U.S. Periodicals and Serial Services," *Library Journal* 100 (1975): 1291–95.

10. Norman B. Brown, "Price Indexes for '76: U.S. Periodicals and Serial Services," *Library Journal* 101 (1976): 1600–05.

11. Norman B. Brown, "Price Indexes for 1977: U.S. Periodicals and Serial Services," *Library Journal* 102 (1977): 1462–67.

12. Norman B. Brown, "Price Indexes for 1978: U.S. Periodicals and Serial Services," *Library Journal* 103 (1978): 1356–61.

13. Norman Brown and Jane Phillips, "Price Indexes for 1979: U.S. Periodicals and Serial Services," *Library Journal* 104 (1979): 1628–33.

14. Norman B. Brown and Jane Phillips, "Price Indexes for 1980: U.S. Periodicals and Serial Services," *Library Journal* 105 (1980): 1486–91.

15. Norman B. Brown and Jane Phillips, "Price Indexes for 1981: U.S. Periodicals and Serial Services," *Library Journal* 106 (1981): 1387–93.

16. Norman B. Brown and Jane Phillips, "Price Indexes for 1982: U.S. Periodicals and Serial Services," *Library Journal* 107 (1982): 1379–82.

17. Norman B. Brown and Jane Phillips, "Price Indexes for 1983: U.S. Periodicals and Serial Services," *Library Journal* 108 (1983): 1659–62.

18. Norman B. Brown and Jane Phillips, "Price Indexes for 1984: U.S. Periodicals and Serial Services," *Library Journal* 109 (1984): 1422–25.

19. Rebecca T. Lenzini and Judith G. Horn, "Price Indexes for 1985: U.S. Periodicals," *Library Journal* 110 (August 1985): 53–59.

20. Judith G. Horn, "Library Materials Price Indexes: U.S. Periodicals Price Index Preliminary Report for 1985," *RTSD Newsletter* 10 (1985): 19–20 (As an example of preliminary ALA Index)

21. *Bowker Annual of Library and Book Trade Information* (New York: R.R. Bowker, 1971): 180.

22. *Bowker Annual of Library and Book Trade Information* (New York: R.R. Bowker, 1976): 206.

23. *Bowker Annual of Library and Book Trade Information* (New York: R.R. Bowker, 1977): 335.

24. *Bowker Annual of Library and Book Trade Information* (New York: R.R. Bowker, 1982): 400–01.

25. *Bowker Annual of Library and Book Trade Information* (New York: R.R. Bowker, 1983): 388–89.

26. *Bowker Annual of Library and Book Trade Information* (New York: R.R. Bowker, 1985): 474.

27. Norman B. Brown, "Price Indexes for '76," 1600–05.

28. "Rising Periodical Bills Worry Research Libraries," *Library Journal* 98 (1973): 374.

29. Rebecca T. Lenzini and Judith G. Horn, "Price Indexes for 1985," 53–59.

30. John B. Merriman, and others, "Comparative Index to Periodical Prices," published annually in *Library Association Record*. Data in this article kindly provided by B.H. Blackwell.

31. F.F. Clasquin, "Periodical Prices: A Three-Year Comparative Study," *Library Journal* 99 (1974): 2447–49.

32. F.F. Clasquin, "Periodical Prices: A 1975 Update," *Library Journal* 100 (1975): 1775–77.

33. F.F. Clasquin, "Periodical Prices: '74–'76 Update," *Library Journal* 101 (1976): 2015–19.

34. F.F. Clasquin, "Periodical Prices: 1975–77 Update," *Library Journal* 102 (1977): 2011–15.

35. F.F. Clasquin, "Periodical Prices: 1976–78 Update," *Library Journal* 103 (1978): 1924–27.

36. F.F. Clasquin, "The 1978–80 Faxon Periodical Prices Update," *Serials Librarian* 5 (1981): 81–90.

37. Gerald Lowell, "Periodical Prices 1980–1982 Update," *Serials Librarian* 7 (1982): 75–83.

38. Rebecca T. Lenzini, "Periodical Prices 1983–1985 Update," *Serials Librarian* 9 (Summer 1985): 119–30.

39. Frederick C. Lynden, "Library Materials Cost Studies," *Library Resources & Technical Services* 27 (1983): 156–62.

40. Nellie L. Waltner, et al., "Periodical Prices: A Comparison of Local and National Averages," *Library Acquisitions: Practice and Theory* 1 (1978): 237–41.

41. Mary E. Clack and Sally Williams, "Using Locally and Nationally Produced Periodical Price Indexes in Budget Preparation," *Library Resources & Technical Services* 27 (1983): 345–56.

42. Sally F. Williams, "Construction and Application of a Periodicals Price Index," *Collection Management* 2 (1978): 329–44.

43. Guilbert C. Hentschke and Ellen Kehoe, "Serial Acquisitions as a Capital Budgeting Problem," *Journal of the American Society for Information Science* 31 (1980): 357–62.

44. Dennis Smith, "Forecasting Price Increase Needs for Library Materials: The University of California Experience," *Library Resources & Technical Services* 28 (1984): 136–48.

45. Ibid., 140.

46. *American National Standard for Library and Information Sciences and Related Publishing Practices—Library Materials—Criteria for Price Indexes*, ANSI Z39.20-1983 (New York: American National Standards Institute, 1983).

47. Michael R. Kronenfeld and James A. Thompson, "The Impact of Inflation on Journal Costs," *Library Journal* 106 (1981): 714–17.

48. Hans H. Weber, "Serials '73—Review and Trends," *Library Resources & Technical Services* 18 (1974): 141.

49. Richard De Gennaro, "Escalating Journal Prices: Time to Fight Back," *American Libraries* 8 (February 1977): 69–74.

50. John R. James, "Serials in 1976," *Library Resources & Technical Services* 21 (1977): 217.

51. "Costs of Books and Periodicals Soar," *College & Research Libraries News* 4 (1979/80): 113, quoting D. Kenneth Halstead, *Higher Education Prices and Price Indexes, 1978 Supplement* (Washington, D.C.: U.S. Department of Health, Education, and Welfare, Office of Education, 1978).

52. Michael R. Kronenfeld and Sarah H. Gable, "Real Inflation of Journal Prices: Medical Journals, U.S. Journals, and Brandon List Journals," *Medical Library Association Bulletin* 71 (1983): 375–79.

53. Peter Gellatly, "Debits and a Few Credits: Can Serials Prices Be Controlled?" *Illinois Libraries* 60 (1978): 100–05.

54. Richard Morrill, "Serials Problems in Education Libraries," *Education Libraries* 6 (Summer 1981): 34–36.

55. D.K. Varma, "Increasing Subscription Costs and Problems of Resource Allocation," *Special Libraries* 74 (1983): 61–66.

56. Ibid.

57. Monica Blake and A.J. Meadows, "Journals at Risk," *Journal of Librarianship* 16 (1984): 118–27.

58. A.K. Anand and H.R. Chopra, "Subscription to Current Periodicals in University Libraries in India: A Discussion of Some Problems," *ILA Bulletin* 17 (1981): 205.

59. R.S. Saxena and S.K. Khare, "Impact of Exponential Rate of Growth of Periodicals and Their Cost in Scientific and Technical Libraries," *ILA Bulletin* 16 (January/June 1980): 63–75.

60. Edelman, "Periodical Literature," 71.

61. De Gennaro, "Escalating."

62. Frank F. Clasquin, "The Jobber's Side: Cost of Acquiring Periodicals," *RQ* 10 (1971): 328–30.

63. William H. Huff, "Serial Subscription Agents," *Library Trends* 24 (1976): 683–709.

64. Ron Coplen, "Subscription Agents: To Use or Not to Use," *Special Libraries* 70 (1979): 519–26.

65. Huibert Paul, "Are Subscription Agents Worth Their Keep?" *Serials Librarian* 7 (Fall 1982): 31–41.

66. Wayne Thyden, "Subscription Agency Size: Threat or Benefit?" *Serials Librarian* 7 (Spring 1983): 29–34.

67. John Jarvis, "Costs and Full Cost Recovery: Budgeting for Journals and Justifying New Journals," in *Learned Journals Pricing and Buying Round,* proceedings of a seminar conducted by the Association of Learned and Professional Society Publishers, and the Publishers Association, March 22, 1985, London (Letchworth, England: Epsilon Press, 1985), 1–9.

68. "Session V. Roundup and Critique," *IEEE Transactions on Professional Communication,* PC-16 (1973): 156–71.

69. Marjorie Scal, "The Page Charge," *Scholarly Publishing* 3 (1971): 62–69.

70. James M. Matarazzo, "Scientific Journals: Page or Price Explosion?" *Special Libraries* 63 (1972): 53–58.

71. Howard J. Sanders, "Troubled Times for Scientific Journals," *C & EN* 6 (May 30, 1983): 31–40.

72. Glen Wittig, "Dual Pricing of Periodicals," *College & Research Libraries* 38 (1977): 412–18.

73. "Double, Double, Publishers in Trouble," *Library Journal* 107 (1982): 158.

74. "Double, Double, Publishers in Trouble—Round II," *Library Journal* 107 (1982): 1202.

75. *Scholarly Communication: The Report of the National Enquiry* (Baltimore: Johns Hopkins University Press, 1979), 66.

76. Dick R. Miller and Joseph E. Jensen, "Dual Pricing of Health Sciences Periodicals: A Survey," *Medical Library Association Bulletin* 68 (1980): 336–47.

77. Edward A. Dyl, "A Note on Price Discrimination by Academic Journals," *Library Quarterly* 53 (1983): 161–68.

78. Michael E.D. Koenig, "Serials Dual Pricing: The Librarians' Hobgoblin," *Serials Librarian* 8 (Spring 1984): 25–28.

79. Larry X. Besant and Siegfried Ruschin, "Price of European Journals," *Nature* 310 (1984): 358.

80. "Foreign Journal Vendors and Price Gouging," *Library Journal* 109 (1984): 411.

81. Marcia Tuttle, "Seminar on Pricing of British Journals: Report," American Library Association, Resources and Technical Services Division, Document 85.24.

82. Jane Maddox, in an address to American Library Association, Resources and Technical Services Division, Serials Section Discussion Group, Dallas, June 1984, on types of distribution employed by European publishers and effect on journal prices.

83. Charles Hamaker and Deana Astle, "Recent Pricing Patterns in British Journal Publishing," *Library Acquisitions: Practice and Theory* 8 (1984): 225–32.

84. Siegfried Ruschin, "Why Are Foreign Subscription Rates Higher for American Libraries Than They Are for Subscribers Elsewhere?" *Serials Librarian* 9 (Spring 1985): 7–17.

85. *Learned Journals Pricing and Buying Round,* proceedings of a seminar conducted by the Association of Learned and Professional Society Publishers, and the Publishers Association, March 22, 1985, London (Letchworth, England: Epsilon Press, 1985).

86. Bernard M. Fry and Herbert S. White, *Publishers and Libraries: A Study of Scholarly and Research Journals* (Lexington, MA: D.C. Heath, 1976).

87. Bernard M. Fry and Herbert S. White, "Impact of Economic Pressures on American Libraries and Their Decisions Concerning Scholarly and Research Journal Acquisition and Retention." Final Report, National Technical Information Service PB283874. Bloomington: Indiana University Graduate Library School, June 1978.

88. Herbert S. White and Bernard M. Fry, "The Impact of Periodical Availability in Libraries on Individual and Library Subscription Placement and Cancellation." Final Report, National Technical Information Service PB90111883. Bloomington: Indiana University Graduate Library School, December 1979.

89. *Scholarly Communication: The Report of the National Enquiry.*

ADDITIONAL READING MATERIAL

Asser, Paul Nijhoff. "Some Trends in Journal Subscriptions." *Scholarly Publishing* 10 (1979): 279–86.

Clasquin, F.F., and Cohen, Jackson B. "Physics and Chemistry Journal Prices in 1977–78." *Serials Librarian* 3 (1979): 381–86.

Culliton, Barbara J. "AMA: Specialty Journals Must Lure Paying Subscribers." *Science* 178 (1972): 1070–72.

Dessauer, John P. "Library Acquisitions: A Look Into the Future." *Publishers Weekly* 207 (June 16, 1975): 55–68.

Katz, Bill, and Gellatly, Peter. *Guide to Magazine and Serial Agents.* New York: R.R. Bowker, 1975.

Lerner, Rita G. "The Professional Society in a Changing World." *Library Quarterly* 54 (1984): 36–47.

Walsh, John. "Journals: Photocopying is Not the Only Problem." *Science* 183 (1984): 1274–77.

White, Herbert S., and Fry, Bernard M. "Economic Interaction Between Special Libraries and Publishers of Scholarly and Research Journals." *Special Libraries* 68 (1977): 109–14.

White, Herbert S. "The Economic Interaction of Scholarly Journal Publishing and Libraries During the Present Period of Cost Increases and Budget Reductions: Implications for Serials Librarians." *Serials Librarian* 1 (1977): 221–30.

White, Herbert S. "Factors in the Decision by Individuals and Libraries to Place or Cancel Subscriptions to Scholarly and Research Journals." *Library Quarterly* 50 (1980): 287–309.

White, Herbert S. "Library Management in the Tight Budget Seventies: Problems, Challenges, and Opportunities." *Medical Library Association Bulletin* 65 (1977): 6–12.

White, Herbert S. "Publishers, Libraries, and Costs of Journal Subscriptions in Times of Funding Retrenchment." *Library Quarterly* 46 (1976): 359–77.

ANNOTATED BIBLIOGRAPHY OF 1982–85 BOOKS AND ARTICLES ON SERIALS

Marcia Tuttle

This annotated bibliography continues the 649-item Annotated Bibliography that appeared in the author's *Introduction to Serials Management,* published in 1983 by JAI Press. The cut-off date for the original work was early 1982; this supplement begins at that time and covers publications dated through 1985 that had appeared by mid-April 1986. However, many entries in the bibliography have publication dates earlier than 1982, because it was possible in this update to annotate each article in some works that had been listed only as collections (for example, the *Proceedings* of the United Kingdom Serials Group). Again, an author index follows the actual bibliography.

Some differences exist between this listing and the parent work. No "Working Tools" are included this time, but they are not necessarily excluded from future updates. The original bibliography had a large catchall

Advances in Serials Management, Volume 1, pages 135–230.
Copyright © 1986 by JAI Press Inc.
All rights of reproduction in any form reserved.
ISBN: 0-89232-568-2

section named "Networking and Library Cooperation." That has been broken into three more specific categories, "Resource Sharing and Union Lists," "Automation," and "National Programs." Further refinement of specific subjects needs to be done. For instance, serials publishing is placed in the first section, "General;" that topic has enough entries to be made a separate category in the future.

Finally, the author wishes to thank Libby Grey of the University of North Carolina at Chapel Hill Library Science Library, for her help in locating materials and her generosity in permitting extended use of the library and its resources.

I. GENERAL

1. Almagro, Bertha R. "Overpublication: Who is to be Blamed?" *Technicalities* 3 (February 1983): 7–8.

A plea for librarians, scholars, and publishers to take a stand against the proliferation of expensive, specialized journals.

2. Baumol, William J., and Braunstein, Yale M. "Empirical Study of Scale Economics and Production Complementarity: The Case of Journal Publication." *Journal of Political Economy* 85 (1977): 1037–48.

The journal publishing industry is used to test the concepts of economies of scale and scope and of subadditivity. In this instance, bigger may well be cheaper.

3. Beckhoefer, Arthur S. "Electronic Publishing: The New Newsletter." *Byte* 8 (May 1983): 124, 126, 128, 130.

Computer conferencing is the best "newsletter" format for stock market advice because of its immediate availability and opportunity for interaction between publisher and subscriber.

4. Boyer, Robert E. "Serials in the Small Public Library: Not Out of Control." *Library Resources and Technical Services* 29 (1985): 32–38.

"Practical suggestions for the small public library which is not preparing for automation, does not belong to a bibliographic utility, has a small staff, and has modest resources."

5. Broad, William J. "Journals: Fearing the Electronic Future." *Science* 216 (1982): 964–68.

The electronic journal may be the solution to the economic and delayed-publication problems of the traditional journal. Scientists and librarians welcome the possibility, but many editors are fearful.

6. Broad, William J. "The Publishing Game: Getting More for Less." *Science* 211 (1981): 1137–39.

The "paper inflation" is not a result of more research, but of the different ways people publish: shorter papers, more joint authorship, multiple publication of the same data.

7. Brown, David J. "Electronic Document Delivery by Publishers." In *Resource Sharing—Its Impact on Serials,* edited by Margaret E. Graham and Brian Cox, 15–25. Stratford-upon-Avon: UK Serials Group, 1982.

Publishers' revenue is threatened by talk of and library experiments in electronic document delivery. The publisher and the librarian must ensure that this issue does not equal the controversy created by the copyright question.

8. Campbell, Robert. "Survival of the Fittest: Adaptive Strategies in Journal Publishing." In *Financing Serials from the Producer to the User,* edited by David P. Woodworth, 27–39. Oxford, Eng.: Blackwell's for the UK Serials Group, n.d.

Rising costs of producing a scientific journal have forced curtailment of author benefits and implementation of lower production standards, while the publisher attempts to retain subscribers.

9. Carter, Carolyn J. "Serials Education and Training: The Student's Viewpoint." In *Serials '83: Proceedings of the UK Serials Group Conference,* edited by Rodney M. Burton, 96–103. Stratford-upon-Avon: UK Serials Group, 1984.

A student evaluates the year-long serials option available at Loughborough University of Technology in terms of its value in preparing future serials librarians for their jobs.

10. Charbonneau, Gary. "Taylor's Constant." *Serials Librarian* 7 (Fall 1982): 19–22.

The rate at which a random sample of current serials at Indiana University changed title is dubbed "Taylor's Constant," in honor of David C. Taylor, editor of *Title Varies.*

11. Compaine, Benjamin M. *The Business of Consumer Magazines.* White Plains, N.Y.: Knowledge Industry Publications, Inc., 1982.

A study of the U.S. popular magazine industry in 1981.

12. Conochie, Jean A. "A Decade of Serials Librarianship in Australia: An Overview." *Serials Librarian* 10 (Fall 1985/Winter 1985–86): 253–61.

The last decade has been characterized by change in Australian serials librarianship: automation, AACR2 and other international standards, the economy, and the establishment of the Australian Bibliographic Network.

13. Ding Choo Ming. "Access to Serials in Southeast Asia." *Libri* 35 (1985): 298–319.

Lacking a comprehensive union list of serials and an index for Southeast Asian journals, researchers must depend upon a variety of sources for access. There is a need for cooperative collection of "indigenous" serials to improve coverage within the area.

14. Dutta, S. "Synopsis Journals—Communication Media for a Transition Period." *Annals of Library Science and Documentation* 29 (1982): 45–50.

Supports the use of the synopsis journal on an economic basis.

15. Edgar, Neal L. "Andrew Osborn: The Father of Serials Librarianship." *Technical Services Quarterly* 1 (Spring 1984): 55–61.

Edgar's tribute to Osborn.

16. Feinman, Valerie Jackson. "Factors and Flexibility: The Form vs. Function Dilemma." In *Serials and Microforms: Patron-Oriented Management,* edited by Nancy Jean Melin, 149–58. Westport, Conn.: Meckler Publishing, 1983.

Practical advice on the arrangement and organization of serials functions in an era of change and technological development.

17. *Financing Serials from the Producer to the User: Proceedings of the UK Serials Group Conference held at University of Technology, Loughborough 3–6 April 1979.* Edited by David P. Woodworth. Oxford: Blackwell's Periodicals Division for the UK Serials Group, n.d.. (Serials Monograph No. 2)

Each paper presented at the conference is listed separately in the Annotated Bibliography.

18. Forbes, Dennis. "The Role of the Publisher." In *Information Chain,* edited by John A. Urquhart, 11–18. Stratford-upon-Avon: UK Serials Group, 1983.

In the future new means of dissemination of information will supplement the printed page. Forbes discusses several European experimental projects.

19. Freilich, Mary K., and Watkins, Steven G. "Ulrich's and OCLC's Online Databases: Acquisitions and Reference Sources." *Serials Review* 9 (Summer 1983): 65–66.

The two databases are compared for bibliographic information on new periodical titles. While neither is comprehensive, each has advantages.

20. *The Future of Serials: Publication, Automation and Management. Proceedings of the 10th Meeting of IATUL, Essen, Federal Republic of Germany, June 6–10, 1983.* Edited by Nancy Fjallbrant. Gotheborg: International Association of Technological University Libraries, 1984.

Each paper in this volume is listed separately in the Annotated Bibliography.

21. Garg, K.C., and Dua, R.K. "A Plea for the Rationalizing of the Publication Schedules of Periodicals." *Serials Librarian* 9 (Summer 1985): 89–97.

States the problems irregular publication schedules cause libraries and suggests standards that would resolve the problems.

22. Gellatly, Peter, ed. "Serials Librarianship as an Art: Essays in Honor of Andrew D. Osborn." *Serials Librarian* 6 (Winter 1981/ Spring 1982): 83–158.

Friends and admirers of Osborn discuss various aspects of his career and personality. Includes bio-bibliography. Articles are listed separately in the Annotated Bibliography.

23. Goldsmith, Maurice. "Reflections on the Role of Government in the Dissemination of Knowledge with Particular Reference to Journal Provision in Libraries." In *Financing Serials from the Producer to the User,* edited by David P. Woodworth, 1–9. Oxford, Eng.: Blackwell's for the UK Serials Group, n.d.

In the future scientists will require access to classified, condensed, and evaluated data. The librarian is in a position to provide this information.

24. Goodman, Susan L. "Serials Management at the British Museum (Natural History)." *Serials Librarian* 6 (Summer 1982): 15–24.

The Serials Section and the serials librarian's work in the context of a large special library.

25. Gordon, Martin. " 'Til the End of *Time." Technical Services Quarterly* 1 (Fall/Winter 1983): 149–53.

Projects a changed college library periodicals unit by the end of the century with fewer staff, more automation, and alternative means of article receipt.

26. Gorman, G.E. "Serials After 1984: Report on a Seminar Organized by the Acquisitions Section of the Library Association of Australia, Brisbane, 26 August 1984." *Library Acquisitions: Practice and Theory* 9 (1985): 271–78.
Summarizes in detail presentations on the Monash Price Index, serials automation, journal publishing, and resource sharing in Australia.

27. Gorman, Michael. "Dealing With Serials: A Sketch of Contextual/ Organizational Response." *Serials Librarian* 10 (Fall 1985/Winter 1985–86): 13–18.
Thoughts on the modern-day serial and its optimum treatment within the library. Advocates leaving the processing to technicians so the librarian can concentrate on the more meaningful issues.

28. Gorman, Michael. "Mutating the Genome." *Cataloging and Classification Quarterly* 3 (Winter 1982/Spring 1983): 19–25.
The problem with serials departments is the serial. Gorman proposes a radical change in publication of journal articles, the creation of a central clearinghouse that would match "articles" to personal or institutional profiles.

29. Graham, W. Gordon. "Managing Change in Professional Publishing." In *Information Chain,* edited by John A. Urquhart, 68–74. Stratford-upon-Avon: UK Serials Group, 1983.
In the context of the development of electronic publishing, Graham urges the publisher to anticipate and plan for change in order to maintain the quality of information being transmitted.

30. Gray, Edward. "A Few Cautionary Words About Electronic Publishing." *Journal of Micrographics* 15 (October 1982): 37–43.
An advocate of micrographics urges caution in adopting electronic technology. There will be a place for microforms and for paper, proven forms of communication.

31. Green, Paul Robert, Merriman, John B., and Woodworth, David P. "The United Kingdom Serials Group: Its History, Development, and Future." *Serials Librarian* 9 (Summer 1985): 107–11.
Covers the UKSG's beginning as an informal group to its current position as "the foremost authority on serials work in the United Kingdom."

32. Hanson, Elizabeth, and Linkins, Germaine C. "Serials Education in Library Schools." *Journal of Education for Librarianship* 23 (1982): 83–95.
Report of a 1980 survey of ALA-accredited library schools, including the coverage of serials in their curricula. Despite a dearth of serials courses, response from the schools was high and indicated interest in increasing attention to serials.

33. Hanson, Jo Ann. "Trends in Serials Management." *Serials Librarian* 8 (Summer 1984): 7–12.
An examination of past and present means of organizing library serials functions shows that the proper organization varies with the library's needs.

34. Harrington, Sue Anne, and Karpuk, Deborah J. "The Integrated Serials Department: Its Value Today and in the Future." *Serials Librarian* 9 (Winter 1984): 55–64.
Featuring the Serials Department of the University of Oklahoma Libraries, the article supports the centralization of serials functions, particularly in an automated situation.

35. Harrington, Sue Anne. "Serials Organization: A Time for Reappraisal." *Serials Librarian* 10 (Fall 1985/Winter 1985–86): 19–28.
Reviews the controversy as reflected in the literature and urges serials librarians to be prepared to adapt to changes caused by automation and the economy.

36. Holbrook, Carol, and others. "The Merging of Serials Units: A Case Study." *Journal of Academic Librarianship* 10 (March 1984): 29–32.
A project team approach was used in the merger of two serials units at the University of Michigan Library.

37. Hoppe, Eberhard. "Serials Management at a Traditional University in the Federal Republic of Germany." *Serials Review* 8 (Summer 1982): 79, 81, 83 (German text on facing pages).
The Library of the Technical University of Munich faces the same serials problems of inflation and access as American academic libraries.

38. Johnson, Karl E. "IEEE Conference Publications in Libraries." *Library Resources and Technical Services* 28 (1984): 308–14.
Survey results show that most libraries catalog these materials fully, through OCLC, and find that patrons benefit from series access.

39.   Johnson, Victoria A. "Organization of Serials Departments in University Libraries." Master's Thesis, University of Chicago, 1973.

Surveys in great detail 48 university libraries with separate serials departments. Results show common patterns, but wide variation in staffing and routines.

40.   Kapur, Shabad, Malhan, I.V., and Thakur, G.S. "Survey of Periodicals of Indian University Libraries." *Herald of Library Science* 20 (1981): 201–06.

Discusses results of a survey concerning problems of serials selection, acquisition, staffing, and management.

41.   Katz, William A. "The Fallacy of the Plugged-In Periodical." *Technical Services Quarterly* 1 (Fall/Winter 1983): 155–57.

A plea for planning and the use of common sense in adopting new technology.

42.   Katz, William A. "Osborn and that Elusive Definition." *Serials Librarian* 6 (Winter 1981/Spring 1982): 143–44.

Osborn resolved the eternal problem in a masterly and humorous way.

43.   Katz, William A. "Ten Years of Living With Magazines." *Serials Librarian* 10 (Fall 1985/Winter 1985–86): 281–87.

The editor of *Magazines for Libraries* reflects on change and lack of change in popular magazines during the last decade.

44.   Katzen, May. "How Rising Postal Rates May Curtail British Journals." *Scholarly Publishing* 14 (1983): 253–58.

British journal publishers, especially learned societies, face the need to decrease journal size to compensate for increased postal rates.

45.   Lanier, Don, and Vogt, Norman. "The Serials Department, 1975–1985." *Serials Librarian* 10 (Fall 1985/Winter 1985–86): 5–11.

Reviews literature of organization for serials work and predicts that the debate over centralization and decentralization will continue.

46.   Lea, Peter W. "Change or Decay? New Patterns in Serials Publishing." In *Management of Serials Automation,* edited by Peter Gellatly, 273–84. New York: Haworth Press, 1982.

Covers pressures upon publishers to devise alternatives to the printed journal, examples of new methods of publishing, and possible future patterns of serials publishing.

47.   Lenzini, Rebecca T. "Viewing the MLS from the Vendor's Perspective." *Illinois Libraries* 67 (1985): 494–96.
The person holding an MLS, especially with an emphasis in technical services or automation, is a valuable employee for a vendor, providing a communication link between the vendor and the library customer.

48.   Leonhardt, Thomas W. "Introducing Serials Education." *Serials Librarian* 10 (Fall 1985/Winter 1985–86): 211–14.
Advice for new serials librarians wanting to become professionally active, featuring the Serials Section of ALA's Resources and Technical Services Division.

49.   Line, Maurice B. "On-Demand and Online Publishing and the Bookseller: Life-Line, Death Knell, or Irrelevant?" *Bookseller* 4149 (June 29, 1985): 2629–31.
The impact on booksellers and subscription agents of the coming availability of scholarly materials on CD-ROM and other electronic means of dissemination of information.

50.   Liu, Ellen F. "Serial Collections in Taiwan, R.O.C.: Brief Sketches." *United Kingdom Serials Group Newsletter* 7 (December 1985): 35–36.
Covers current holdings, subscription services, and union lists of libraries in Taiwan.

51.   MacDougall, Alan. "Recent Research in Serials: Modelling of Journal v. Article Acquisition by Libraries." In *Serials '84: Proceedings of the UK Serials Group Conference,* edited by Brian Cox, 135–40. Stratford-upon-Avon: UK Serials Group, 1985.
Loughborough University of Technology Library is testing the hypothesis that a collection of articles would serve its patrons better and at lower cost than serial subscriptions.

52.   McGlasson, Sheila. "The Characteristics of Conference Proceedings." *UK Serials Group Newsletter* 5 (June 1983): 5–10.
Covers identification, acquisition, and cataloging, and presents problems (and some solutions) typical of this type of publication. Describes BLLD's efforts at bibliographic control of conference proceedings.

53.   McKenna, Florence M., and Carter, Ruth C. "Serials Workflow in a Library Without A Centralized Serials Department." In *Projects and Procedures for Serials Administration,* edited by Diane Stine, 39–50. Ann Arbor: Pierian Press, 1985.

Technical services aspects of serials functions at the University of Pittsburgh Libraries form a case study of functional organization.

54. Matson, Susan. "Informal Continuing Education for Serials:
     Keeping up with the Journal Literature." *Illinois Libraries* 63
     (1985): 458–62.
Practical and helpful guidelines for persons wanting to keep up with meetings and articles on serials. Lists journals most likely to have articles of
interest.

55. Melin, Nancy Jean. "Andrew Osborn: The Serials Specialist."
     Serials Librarian 6 (Winter 1981/Spring 1982): 139–42.
An appreciation of Osborn on behalf of those entering serials librarianship
in the early 1970s.

56. Melin, Nancy Jean. "Serials Research from the Writer's and Ed-
     itor's Point of View: A Paper Presented to the RTSD Conference
     Within a Conference at the Annual ALA Meeting, Philadelphia,
     July 11, 1982." *Serials Librarian* 8 (Winter 1983): 49–56.
Guidelines for practicing serials librarians, who are encouraged to do
needed research, then publish it.

57. Melin, Nancy Jean. "The State of the Art Survey and Trends in
     Serials Librarianship." In *Information Chain*, edited by John A.
     Urquhart, 101–09. Stratford-upon-Avon: UK Serials Group, 1983.
Melin concentrates on serials activity, economics of serials, automation
of serials, and needed research related to serials.

58. Merriman, John B. "The Serials Information Chain: Working
     Together Toward a Common Goal." In *Library Serials Stan-
     dards: Development, Implementation, Impact*, edited by Nancy
     Jean Melin, 125–30. Westport, Conn.: Meckler Publishing, 1984.
Merriman describes the evolution of the UK Serials Group from a 1975
Blackwell's conference on serials. He covers future plans of the Group
and encourages other countries to develop a similar means of providing
continuing education opportunities for persons working with serials.

59. Migneault, Robert L. "Serials: An Introductory Perspective."
     In *Projects and Procedures for Serials Administration*, edited by
     Diane Stine, 1–22. Ann Arbor: Pierian Press, 1985.
Reviews and analyzes the literature on library serials operations in the
traditional library. Emphasizes the variety of opinions.

60. Millson, R.J. "Learned Society Journal Publishing." In *Serials '84: Proceedings of the UK Serials Group Conference,* edited by Brian Cox, 92–99. Stratford-upon-Avon: UK Serials Group, 1985.

The United Kingdom has a multitude of small learned societies, all of which publish. Millson discusses the problems involved in disseminating specialized scholarly information.

61. Myers, James N. "Publishers' Services—A Librarian's View." *Bridging the Gaps: Proceedings of the Third Annual Meeting of the Society for Scholarly Publishing,* edited by Dave Dobson, 134–36. Washington, D.C.: Society for Scholarly Publishing, 1981.

A plea for an end to the adversary relationship between publishers and librarians, to enable the most benefit to both parties from a finite library materials budget.

62. Nelson, Milo. "Knowledge in Pieces: Future Trends in Serials Librarianship." In *Information Chain,* edited by John A. Urquhart, 112–21. Stratford-upon-Avon: UK Serials Group, 1983.

Serials librarianship in the 1980s faces a number of potential threats: the demand for immediate availability of information, economic reasons for restricting information, electronic response to space restraints, and preservation problems.

63. Nzotta, Briggs C. "Serials Librarianship in Nigeria, 1975–1985." *Serials Librarian* 10 (Fall 1985/Winter 1985–86): 269–79.

The efforts of librarians to acquire and make available serials in Nigerian libraries are frustrated by lack of funds—and of recognition by those controlling the funds—of the importance of serials.

64. Osburn, Charles B. "The Place of the Journal in the Scholarly Communications System." *Library Resources and Technical Services* 28 (1984): 315–24.

Throughout the centuries the journal has been the primary means of transmitting the knowledge that results from research and scholarship.

65. Ostwich, P.A. "What Has to be Costed in Record Keeping: Activities and Efforts." In *Financing Serials from the Producer to the User,* edited by David P. Woodworth, 56–63. Oxford, Eng.: Blackwell's for the UK Serials Group, n.d.

Thoughts on systems analysis, directed toward serials procedures.

66. Page, Gillian. "Economics of Journal Publishing: The Publisher's Viewpoint." In *Economics of Serials Management,* edited by

David P. Woodworth, 52–61. Loughborough, Eng.: Serials Group, n.d.

Concentrates on the variables of number of subscribers and number of pages, but touches on many other factors influencing the cost of producing and distributing a scholarly journal.

67. Pilling, Stella, and Wood, David. "Serials at the British Library Lending Division." *Serials Librarian* 10 (Fall 1985/Winter 1985–86): 239–52.

Covers history, policy, and procedures of serials activity at BLLD. Speculates about the future services of the facility in the light of technological developments.

68. Postlethwaite, Bonnie. "The Impact of AACR2 on Serials Processing: Beyond Cataloging." In *AACR2 Goes Public*, 54–63. Tucson: Art Libraries Society of North America, 1982. (Occasional Papers No. 1).

Emphasizes the effect the new code will have on users and on the multitudes of serials files; points out the decisions that must be made.

69. Preibish, Andre. "Serial Resources in Canadian Libraries, 1982 (Second Survey)." *Serials Librarian* 9 (Summer 1985): 23–32.

Following his own recommendation of further research, Preibish finds negligible growth of serials collections in Canadian university libraries. Public libraries are coping, and federal libraries are becoming national serials resource collections.

70. Preibish, Andre. "Serials Resources in Canadian Research Libraries in 1981." *Serials Librarian* 8 (Spring 1984): 29–41.

The survey provides initial data in an investigation of the adequacy of serials resources in Canada and raises the question of a national serial lending facility.

71. *Projects and Procedures for Serials Administration*, compiled and edited by Diane Stine. Ann Arbor: Pierian Press, 1985. (Current Issues in Serials Management. 5)

Each essay in this collection is listed separately in the Annotated Bibliography.

72. Rast, Elaine K. "Formal Continuing Education for Serials." *Illinois Libraries* 67 (1985): 453–58.

Describes the variety of conferences, institutes, etc., available in the 1980s to serials librarians in the U.S., Canada, and the United Kingdom.

73. Roen, Sheldon R. "Publishing the Society-Sponsored Periodical."
     *Bridging the Gaps: Proceedings of the Third Annual Meeting of
     the Society for Scholarly Publishing,* edited by Dave Dobson,
     178–80. Washington, D.C.: Society for Scholarly Publishing, 1981.
Emphasizes the relationship between the publisher and the society, and
the benefits to the society and the publisher of commercial production
and distribution of society-sponsored periodicals.

74. *Role of Serials in Sci-Tech Libraries,* edited by Ellis Mount. New
     York: Haworth Press, 1983. (Science and Technology Libraries,
     vol. 4, no. 1 (Fall 1983)).
Articles in this work are listed separately in the Annotated Bibliography.

75. Royal Society of London. Scientific Information Committee. *A
     Study of the Scientific Information System in the United King-
     dom.* London: The Society, 1981.
The variety of pressures on the scholarly scientific publication system
lead the Committee to recommend the urgent consideration of increased
public support for research and publication.

76. Sabosik, Patricia E. "Trends in the Marketing of Serials to Li-
     braries." In *Library Serials Standards: Development, Imple-
     mentation, Impact,* edited by Nancy Jean Melin, 77–84. Westport,
     Conn.: Meckler Publishing, 1984.
The H.W. Wilson Company's development and introduction of Wilsonline
illustrates publishers' marketing trends.

77. Sanders, Howard J. "Troubled Times for Scientific Journals."
     Chemical and Engineering News 61 (May 30, 1983): 31–40.
Reviews the reasons for increasing journal subscription costs, discusses
sources of income for scholarly journal publishers, touches on the pros
and cons of electronic publication.

78. Schmidmaier, Dieter. "Serials and 'Grey Literature' " In *The
     Future of Serials,* edited by Nancy Fjallbrant, 185–94. Goeteborg,
     Sweden: International Association of Technological University
     Libraries, 1984.
Defines and describes this complicated, elusive material and emphasizes
its significant role in the dissemination of scientific information.

79. *Serials '84: Proceedings of the UK Serials Group Conference
     Held at the University of Surrey, Guildford, England, 26–29*

March 1984. Edited by Brian Cox. Stratford-upon-Avon: UK Serials Group, 1985. (Serials Monograph No. 7)
Each paper presented at the conference is listed separately in the Annotated Bibliography.

80. *Serials Librarianship in Transition: Issues and Developments,* Edited by Peter Gellatly. New York: Haworth Press, 1986 (*Serials Librarian* 10:1/2).
Each article in this special issue is listed separately in the Annotated Bibliography. The work recognizes ten years of *Serials Librarian.*

81. Shackel, Brian. "Are Serials on the Way Out? An Electronic Communication Experiment." In *Information Chain,* edited by John A. Urquhart, 34–39. Stratford-upon-Avon: UK Serials Group, 1983.
Discussion of the objectives and initial implementation of the Birmingham and Loughborough Electronic Network Development (BLEND) project of the early 1980s.

82. Shackel, Brian. "The BLEND System: Programme for the Study of Some 'Electronic Journals.' " *Journal of the American Society for Information Science* 34 (1983): 22–30.
Describes plans for the joint 3-year experimental program by Birmingham and Loughborough Universities that has as an objective to investigate and evaluate the production of an electronic journal.

83. Singleton, Alan. *Learned Societies, Journals and Collaboration with Publishers.* Leicester: Primary Communications Research Centre, University of Leicester, 1980.
Detailed results of a study of the extent and nature of cooperation between UK societies and publishers in the production and distribution of journals.

84. Singleton, Alan. "Recent Developments in Serials." In *Resource Sharing—Its Impact on Serials,* edited by Margaret E. Graham and Brian Cox, 107–18. Stratford-upon-Avon: UK Serials Group, 1982.
Concentrates on new methods of publishing serials, particularly on the experimental electronic journal at Birmingham and Loughborough Universities. Raises several areas of potential problems in the financing and dissemination of electronically published scholarly information.

85. Singleton, Alan. *Societies and Publishers: Hints on Collaboration in Journal Publishing.* Leicester: Primary Communications Re-

search Centre, University of Leicester, 1980. (Aids to Scholarly Communication)

Following a survey of scholarly journal publishing, Singleton gives advice regarding the range of agreements in use: what to bargain for, what to beware of.

86. Stagg, Deborah Bolton. "Serials in a Small College Library." *Library Resources and Technical Services* 29 (1985): 139–44.

Discusses policies, question of staff vs. service costs, and files needed for bibliographic control of serials in the small college library.

87. Standera, O.L. "Electronic Publishing: Some Notes on Reader Response and Cost." *Scholarly Publishing* 16 (1985): 291–305.

Studies reader response and cost of a journal produced in five formats— 3 in paper, microfiche, and electronic.

88. Stine, Diane. "The Adequacy of Library School Education for Serials Librarianship: A Survey." *Illinois Libraries* 67 (1985): 448– 52.

A follow-up survey to those conducted in 1974 and 1980 indicates that library schools are making an increasing effort to add serials courses or serials topics to relevant courses, particularly the technical services aspects of serials.

89. Stine, Diane. "Centralized Serials Processing in an Automated Environment." *Serials Review* 9 (Fall 1983): 69–75.

Serials and monographs are not the same. When treated as if they are the same, serials, with problems being the norm rather than the exception, do not receive the attention they deserve.

90. Subramanyam, K. "Scientific and Technical Journals: Developments and Prospects." *Science and Technology Libraries* 4 (Fall 1983): 3–19.

After a historical overview and discussion of the importance of scientific journals, the author covers problems, current trends, and future of the communication of scientific and technical information.

91. Taylor, David C. "The Love-Hate Relationship of Librarians and Publishers of Serials." *Drexel Library Quarterly* 21 (Winter 1985): 29–36.

Airs the differing objectives of publishers and librarians. Speculates about the impact of the electronic journal.

92. Taylor, David C. *Managing the Serials Explosion: The Issues for Publishers and Libraries*. White Plains, N.Y.: Knowledge Industry Publications, Inc., 1982.

Writing in a time of unprecedented serials inflation, Taylor analyzes the serials publishing industry and the problems journals create for librarians and publishers. Taylor's objective is to make a contribution toward resolving the problems created by the serials explosion.

93. Terrant, Seldon W. *Evaluations of a Dual Journal Concept*. Washington, D.C.: National Science Foundation Division of Science Information, 1977.

Results of an American Chemical Society survey to determine the feasibility of issuing a summary journal, primarily for individual subscribers, and an archival journal, primarily for libraries.

94. Tomajko, Kathy G., and Drake, Miriam A. "The Journal, Scholarly Communication, and the Future." *Serials Librarian* 10 (Fall 1985/Winter 1985–86): 289–98.

Reviews current electronic innovation in scholarly communication and relates this to the library of the future.

95. Tuttle, Marcia. *Introduction to Serials Management*. Greenwich, Conn.: JAI Press, Inc., 1983.

A library science text and general introduction to the field for persons new to serials librarianship. Extensive bibliography.

96. Tuttle, Marcia. "Serials Files: What, Where, Why?" In *Serials and Microforms: Patron-Oriented Management*, edited by Nancy Jean Melin, 9–18. Westport, Conn.: Meckler Publishing, 1983.

Introduction to the multiple single-purpose, but interrelated, files in a research library's manual serials department—files necessary for communication within the unit and with other librarians and patrons.

97. Tuttle, Marcia. "The U.S. Serials Group: Is the British Way Right for Us?" *Serials Review* 10 (Winter 1984): 93–94.

Raises the question of whether an organization of all types of persons concerned with library serials is feasible in the United States.

98. *United Kingdom Serials Group Newsletter*. 1- 1978–   . Oxford, Eng.: UK Serials Group. semiannual. ISSN: 0140–545X.

The written communication channel for this group of librarians, publishers, vendors, binders, educators, and others concerned with serials work.

99.   Upham, Lois N. "Serials Research from a Library Faculty Point of View: A Paper Presented to the RTSD Conference Within a Conference at the Annual ALA Meeting, Philadelphia, July 11, 1982." *Serials Librarian* 8 (Winter 1983): 57–62.

Roadblocks to research and publication encountered during the author's doctoral program, and suggestions for overcoming them.

100.   Veaner, Allen B. "Into the Fourth Century." *Drexel Library Quarterly* 21 (Winter 1985): 4–28.

History of the scholarly journal and the social impact of technology on this form of communication.

101.   Vogel, J. Thomas, and Burns, Lynn W. "Serials Management by Microcomputer: The Potential of DBMS." *Online* 8 (May 1984): 68–70.

Discusses unsuccessful use of file manager software and subsequent successful use of database management software in serials management at Philadelphia College of Textiles and Science Library.

102.   Wernstedt, Irene J. "Serials' Greener Pastures." In *Serials and Microforms: Patron-Oriented Management,* edited by Nancy Jean Melin, 141–47. Westport, Conn.: Meckler Publishing, 1983.

Serials functions can be performed satisfactorily when organized by either form or function, and the preferred arrangement is likely to shift periodically from one to the other.

103.   "What is the Future for New Research Journals in the 1980s?: A Discussion." *Journal of Research Communication Studies* 2 (1979/1980): 137–47.

Six publishers from various countries discuss the impact on journal publishing of economic pressures and new technology.

104.   Winkler, Karen J. "New Company Plans 'Electronic Journals' That Can be Read on Computer Screens." *Chronicle of Higher Education* 24 (October 6, 1982): 25–26.

Describes Comtex Scientific Corporation's efforts to publish online journals, and includes reaction to the project by the scientific community.

105.   Woodward, A.M. "Methods of Information Dissemination from the Academic Viewpoint." In *Economics of Serials Management,* edited by David P. Woodworth, 32–42. Loughborough, Eng.: Serials Group, n.d.

Rising costs of scholarly communication in paper format will force the acceptance of the electronic journal.

106.   Woodworth, David P. "Education for Serials Librarianship: A British Library Research Project." In *Library Serials Standards: Development, Implementation, Impact,* edited by Nancy Jean Melin, 131–47. Westport, Conn.: Meckler Publishing, 1984.

Woodworth discusses the results of his study on the teaching of serials work in British library schools. His objectives were to determine the current status of serials education, find out whether the practitioner was getting what he or she wanted from professional library institutions, and make suggestions for future coverage.

107.   Woodworth, David P. "Literary Luddites, or, How Not to Deal with the Sorcerer's Apprentice: A State of the Art Report on Serials Education and Training." In *Serials '83: Proceedings of the UK Serials Group Conference,* edited by Rodney M. Burton, 77–95. Stratford-upon-Avon: UK Serials Group, 1984.

Analyzes results of a survey investigating the effectiveness of education for serials librarianship, primarily in the U.K.

108.   Woodworth, David P. "Serials Education: A UK Viewpoint." In *Serials and Microforms: Patron-Oriented Management,* edited by Nancy Jean Melin, 117–26. Westport, Conn.: Meckler Publishing, 1983.

The increasing significance of serial literature requires more attention to professional education in serials work. Such an effort has been developed in the United Kingdom, primarily at Loughborough Institute of Technology.

109.   Woodworth, David P. "Serials Education; Or, How to Nail Jelly to the Wall." In *The Future of Serials,* edited by Nancy Fjallbrant, 201–11. Goeteborg, Sweden: International Association of Technological University Libraries, 1984.

Reviews syllabus of Loughborough's "serials option" and gives preliminary results of a survey to determine librarians' needs for education for serials work.

II. COLLECTION DEVELOPMENT

110.   Alison, Jennifer. "Recent Australian Serial Prices." *Australian Academic and Research Libraries* 14 (1983): 55–58.

Documents rapid price increases of Australian serials between 1978 and 1981. Data show a greater rate of increase in social science and humanities journals than in the sciences.

111. Alligood, Elaine C., Russo-Martin, Elaine, and Peterson, Richard A. "Use Study of *Excerpta Medica* Abstract Journals: To Drop or Not to Drop?" *Bulletin of the Medical Library Association* 71 (1983): 251–58.
Interviews with users of the University of Virginia Health Sciences Library led to the cancellation of some parts of the expensive abstracting service.

112. Almagro, Bertha R. "Budgeting and Planning: A Tandem Approach." *Serials Librarian* 10 (Fall 1985/Winter 1985–86): 173–79.
Budgets should be planned to reflect a library's collection development priorities, preparing for cuts or windfalls.

113. Amir, Michlean J., and Newman, Wilda B. "Information: Unlimited Demands—Limited Funds (Testing the Viability of a Scientific Journal Collection in Light of Economic Realities)." *Collection Management* 3 (Spring 1979): 111–19.
In a yearly journal survey, users at Johns Hopkins University's Applied Physics Laboratory Library have an opportunity to comment for or against cancelling a title, as they use it. This advice, along with a study of interlibrary loans, citations from staff's own articles, and other factors, contributes to the decision.

114. Aspey, R. "The Average Cost of Journal Articles, 1979–1981." *Interlending & Document Supply* 11 (1983): 25–27.
A small survey was undertaken at BLLD to determine the average cost of a journal article in each of five general subject areas, based on subscription cost alone. Results indicate that articles cost more than they used to and that fewer articles are being published. The author sees the need for further research.

115. Barr, K.P. "Rational Use of Serial Resources." In *Economics of Serials Management,* edited by David P. Woodworth, 72–79. Loughborough, Eng.: Serials Group, n.d.
One must first collect accurate use statistics, then base cancellation and weeding decisions on them. Surveys various models for determining titles to be cut.

116.   Bastille, Jacqueline D., and Mankin, Carole J. "A Simple Ob-
       jective Method for Determining a Dynamic Journal Collection."
       Bulletin of the Medical Library Association 68 (1980): 357–66.
Use is related to space and cost requirements to develop criteria for maintaining a dynamic journal collection at the Library at Massachusetts General Hospital.

117.   Bennion, Bruce C., and Karschamroon, Sunee. "Multivariate
       Regression Models for Estimating Journal Usefulness in Phys-
       ics." *Journal of Documentation* 40 (1984): 217–27.
Four models are presented; all assist in the easy estimating of journal
usefulness, as judged by users.

118.   Bensman, Stephen J. "Journal Collection Management as a Cu-
       mulative Advantage Process." *College and Research Libraries*
       46 (1985): 13–29.
Academic libraries should aim not for a comprehensive journal collection,
but for a multidisciplinary core list of high-use titles. ISI's ranked lists of
highly-cited journals are valid indicators of core titles.

119.   Blake, Monica, and Meadows, A.J. "Journals at Risk." *Journal
       of Librarianship* 16 (1984): 118–28.
By means of interviews and a questionnaire, investigates the characteristics
of journals most likely to be cancelled by British university libraries.

120.   Bostic, Mary J. "Serials Deselection." *Serials Librarian* 9 (Spring
       1985): 85–101.
Advocates informed weeding as a means of improving academic library
collections. Surveys weeding techniques and illustrates each with analysis
of a published collection evaluation study.

121.   Boyce, Bert R., and Pollens, Janet Sue. "Citation-Based Impact
       Measures and the Bradfordian Selection Criteria." *Collection
       Management* 4 (Fall 1982): 29–36.
The authors compared a Bradford-ranked list of mathematics journals with
the same titles ranked by citation count and found little correlation. They
then questioned a previous study showing a high correlation.

122.   Broadus, Robert N. "The Measurement of Periodicals Use." *Se-
       rials Review* 11 (Summer 1985): 57–61.
A study of current use can predict future journal use. Evaluates the various
types of periodicals use studies.

123. Broadus, Robert N. "On Citations, Uses, and Informed Guess-work: A Response to Line." *College and Research Libraries* 46 (1985): 38–39.

Broadus reinforces his point that ISI's *Journal Citation Reports* are a place to begin the process of deselection.

124. Broadus, Robert N. "A Proposed Method for Eliminating Titles from Periodical Subscription Lists." *College and Research Libraries* 46 (1985): 30–35.

ISI's lists of most-cited titles in its *Journal Citation Reports* and other citation counts are valid indicators of candidates for periodical deselection. The library staff can then concentrate on evaluating just the seldom-cited titles.

125. Broadus, Robert N. "The Use of Serial Titles in Libraries with Special Reference to the Pittsburgh Study." *Collection Management* 5 (Spring/Summer 1983): 27–41.

Raises questions about the validity of the study's methodology and conclusions regarding serials use.

126. Bronmo, Ole A. "Backsets on Microfilm: Some Economic Considerations." *Tidskrift for Dokumentation* 38 (1982): 51–57.

Outlines a model for determining the economic feasibility of retaining journal back files on microfilm.

127. Bundy, Alan. "Periodicals: The High Cost of Convenience." In *Profiling a Periodicals Collection,* edited by Phillip Watson, 3–9. Melbourne, Aust.: Footscray Institute of Technology, 1979.

Urges an end to the wastefulness of uncritical acquisition and retention of periodicals, but urges at the same time attention to the responsibility for resource sharing.

128. Buzzard, Marion L., and Whaley, John H. Jr., "Serials and Collection Development." *Drexel Library Quarterly* 21 (Winter 1985): 37–49.

Discusses the long term implications of selecting a serial for purchase and mentions the benefits soon to be available electronically.

129. Carr, Barbara E. "Improving the Periodicals Collection Through an Index Correlation Study." *Reference Services Review* 9 (October/December 1981): 27–32.

A study of index to holdings correlation permitted St. Lawrence College Library to drop some inaccessible journals and place new subscriptions for titles accessible through indexes held in the library.

130.   Carrein, Lois H. "Periodical Review: Newcastle Upon Tyne University." In *Economics of Serials Management*, edited by David P. Woodworth, 96–102. Loughborough, Eng.: Serials Group, n.d.

The review, done by faculty members and based on data collected by librarians, proved to be labor-intensive, but it led to a 22% reduction in serials expenditures.

131.   Carter, Ruth C. "Online Services and Collection Development." *Serials Review* 9 (Summer 1983): 69–71.

Presents a relationship between online bibliographic databases and online union lists of serials in the context of collection development.

132.   Carter, Ruth C., and Bruntjen, Scott. "Pittsburgh Regional Library Center Serials Cancellation Project." *Library Resources and Technical Services* 28 (1984): 299–307.

This project showed that a large online database (OCLC in this instance) can be used as an aid in collection development by documenting cancellation decisions within a group of libraries.

133.   Cayless, Colin. "Some Quantitative Methods for Determining the Utility of Periodicals in an Academic Library." In *Profiling a Periodicals Collection*, edited by Phillip Watson, 43–60. Melbourne, Aust.: Footscray Institute of Technology, 1979.

Cayless studies the price, use, availability, and the "keeping cost" to produce a measure of relevance for periodicals.

134.   Chudamani, K.S., and Shalini, R. "Journal Acquisition—Cost Effectiveness of Models." *Information Processing and Management* 19 (1983): 307–11.

Compares three models for journal selection: the Brookes model, the precision ranking model, and the cost effectiveness model.

135.   Clack, Mary E., and Williams, Sally F. "Using Locally and Nationally Produced Periodical Price Indexes in Budget Preparation." *Library Resources and Technical Services* 27 (1983): 345–56.

An update on the reliability of the Widener Combined Index as a predictor of Harvard's journal prices.

136. Clark, Barton M., and Clark, Sharon E. "Core Journals in Anthropology: A Review of Methodologies." *Behavioral & Social Sciences Librarian* 2 (Winter 1981/Spring 1982): 95–110.
Discusses and evaluates list-checking, user studies, and citation analysis.

137. Clarke, Ann. "The Use of Serials at the British Library Lending Division in 1980." *Interlending Review* 9 (1981): 111–17.
A limited core collection of serials satisfies a high proportion of demand, although concentration of demand had dropped since a 1975 study.

138. Coplen, Ron. "Serials Bibliographic Sources: A Descriptive and Comparative Review." *Serials Review* 8 (Fall 1982): 71–75.
Compares *Ulrich's, Standard Periodical Directory, Irregular Serials and Annuals, Ayer's,* and *International Directory of Little Magazines and Small Presses,* showing the strong points of each.

139. Cornish, Rev. Graham P. "The Carrier Pigeon Breeder and The Tar Heel Nurse: Serial Cancellations at the British Library Lending Division." *United Kingdom Serials Group Newsletter* 7 (December 1985): 29–31.
Discusses criteria used to determine titles to be weeded from the BLLD collections.

140. Curl, Margo Warner. "Faxon's Infoserv: An Online Tool for Serials Collection Development." *Serials Librarian* 9 (Summer 1985): 99–105.
Description and evaluation of the online serials advertising and ordering system.

141. Delman, Bruce S. "Tailoring Periodical Collections to Meet Institutional Needs." *Bulletin of the Medical Library Association* 72 (1984): 162–67.
Core subject reference tools can be used to shape journal collections, as is demonstrated by the author's model ranked list of journals.

142. Domotor, Anna. "Periodical Acquisition in the Central Library of the Veszprem University of Chemical Engineering." In *The Future of Serials,* edited by Nancy Fjallbrant, 167–70. Goeteborg, Sweden: International Association of Technological University Libraries, 1984.
Discusses selection philosophy and the objective of providing more photocopies from within the collection than from other libraries.

143. Doreian, Patrick, and Fararo, Thomas J. "Structural Equivalence in a Journal Network." *Journal of the American Society for Information Science* 36 (1985): 28–37.

Applies concepts and techniques used in contemporary social network analyses to a citation-based network of journals.

144. Dove, H. Paul, Jr. "Subscription Costs: A Five-Year Comparison." *South Carolina Librarian* 28 (Spring 1984): 9–11.

Documents journal price increases at Francis Marion College Library between 1980 and 1984.

145. Downes, Robin N. "Journal Use Studies and the Management of Journal Collections in Research Libraries." In *Serials Collection Development*, edited by Sul H. Lee, 1–8. Ann Arbor: Pierian Press, 1981.

Access to information via support of the Center for Research Libraries' Journals Access System is the answer to the inefficiency and frustration of trying to manage the serials collection.

146. Dutton, B.G. "Economics of Periodicals Management in an Industrial Library." In *Financing Serials from the Producer to the User*, edited by David P. Woodworth, 64–70. Oxford, Eng.: Blackwell's for the UK Serials Group, n.d.

Priorities of industrial libraries differ from those of academic and public institutions, with speedy service to the user being the standard.

147. Dyl, Edward A. "A Note on Price Discrimination by Academic Journals." *Library Quarterly* 53 (1983): 161–68.

Investigates the charge of dual pricing by publishers of academic journals and finds that 59% of a sample have higher rates for institutions than for individuals.

148. Edwards, Averill M.B. "Selection of Periodicals in the National Library of Australia." In *Profiling a Periodicals Collection*, edited by Phillip Watson, 116–21. Melbourne, Aust.: Footscray Institute of Technology, 1979.

Selection is centralized and is conducted according to a written policy. The Library's role as a national resource must be kept in mind.

149. Emery, Charles D. "Forecasting Models and the Prediction of Periodical Subscription Costs." *Serials Librarian* 9 (Summer 1985): 5–22.

Results of a series of tests show that the best forecasting model, in terms of results and cost, is one based upon the geometric mean.

150. Ezzell, Joline R. "Building a Serials Collection in an Academic Library." *North Carolina Libraries* 43 (Spring 1985): 23–25.
Stresses the difficulty of selecting serials and maintaining the serials collection, and the ongoing need for adequate, knowledgeable selectors.

151. Fessenden, Ann T. "Cancellation of Serials in a Budget Crisis: The Technical Problems." *Law Library Journal* 75 (1982): 157–66.
Advocates an extensive planning period before cancellation, in order to determine disposition of volumes, records to be changed, and statistics to be kept.

152. Fex, Anna Herslow. "A Modest Evaluation of Exchange Serials; or, How Long Can We Afford Sacred Cows?" *UK Serials Group Newsletter* 5 (June 1983): 17–18.
A study at University Library of Lund, Sweden, showing that more than three-quarters of exchange serials were not consulted in five years, led to a revision of the exchange program.

153. Fjallbrant, Nancy. "Rationalization of Periodical Holdings: A Case Study at Chalmers University Library." *Journal of Academic Librarianship* 10 (1984): 77–86.
Report of a periodicals use study at a medium-sized Swedish university of technology. Among factors considered in making cancellation decisions were means of acquisition (paid, exchange, or gift) and availability elsewhere in Sweden or through BLLD.

154. Ford, Geoffrey. "The Costs of Relegation." In *Financing Serials from the Producer to the User,* edited by David P. Woodworth, 72–80. Oxford, Eng.: Blackwell's for the UK Serials Group, n.d.
Overview of the numerous costs to be considered when weeding a collection to a storage facility or discarding.

155. Goehner, Donna M. "Core Lists of Periodicals Selected by Faculty Reviewers." *Technical Services Quarterly* 1 (Summer 1984): 17–38.
Constructs six faculty-selected core lists—art, literature, history, psychology, mathematics, and physics—for libraries at institutions offering the master's degree in these subjects.

156. Goehner, Donna M. "A Lesson Learned the Hard Way; or, The Cost of Relinquishing Acquisitions Control." *Serials Librarian* 10 (Fall 1985/Winter 1985–86): 181–84.

Western Illinois University librarians, under pressure, turned over to the teaching faculty control of library materials funds. The faculty representatives' decisions often do not match those that would be made by collection development librarians.

157. Goehner, Donna M. "Periodical Coverage in Academic Collections: A Comparison Between Faculty Choices of Core Titles and Holdings of Medium-Sized Libraries." *Technical Services Quarterly* 1 (Summer 1984): 1–16.

Results from comparing 26 academic libraries and six core lists show a lack of similarity between faculty choice and library holdings, and striking similarity among libraries in funding for the subjects investigated.

158. Gordon, Martin. "Periodicals Use at a Small College Library." *Serials Librarian* 6 (Summer 1982): 63–73.

Results of a study at Franklin and Marshall College Library show high use and conformity to Bradford's Law.

159. Grefsheim, Suzanne, Bader, Shelley, and Meredith, Pamela. "User Involvement in Journal De-Selection." *Collection Management* 5 (Spring/Summer 1983): 43–52.

The library at the George Washington University Medical Center involved the faculty in determining journals to be cancelled.

160. Griscom, Richard. "Periodical Use in a University Music Library: A Citation Study of Theses and Dissertations Submitted to the Indiana University School of Music from 1975–1980." *Serials Librarian* 7 (Spring 1983): 35–52.

The study reveals that literature cited by musicologists has a low rate of obsolescence, but the rapid rate among theorists and educators makes the overall obsolescence rate for the entire field higher than that for other areas of the humanities.

161. Haarala, Arja-Riitta. "Open Access Use of Serials Collections: A Case Study at Helsinki University of Technology Library." In *The Future of Serials,* edited by Nancy Fjallbrant, 179–84. Goeteborg, Sweden: International Association of Technological University Libraries, 1984.

Analyzes results of a use study carried out in 1979, and identifies a core group of serials.

162. Hamaker, Charles A., and Astle, Deana. "Recent Pricing Patterns in British Journal Publishing." *Library Acquisitions: Practice and Theory* 8 (1984): 225–32.

Documents excessive pricing differentials between prices paid by UK and other European subscribers and North American subscribers to British scholarly journals.

163. Hanson, Roger K. "Serials Deselection: A Dreadful Dilemma." In *Serials Collection Development*, edited by Sul H. Lee, 43–59. Ann Arbor: Pierian Press, 1981.

Guidelines for deselection of serials and their application by the University of Utah Library.

164. Johnson, Steve. "Serial Deselection in University Libraries: The Next Step." *Library Acquisitions: Practice and Theory* 7 (1983): 239–46.

After three or four serials cancellation projects a library's collection has been reduced to a state that hinders student and faculty research. The next step needs to come from university administrators.

165. Joyce, Patrick, and Merz, Thomas E. "Price Discrimination in Academic Journals." *Library Quarterly* 55 (1985): 273–83.

The authors' study of top journals in six academic disciplines documents the existence of dual pricing (institutional vs. individual) and the higher increase in institutional over individual price between 1974 and 1984.

166. Kaiden, Phyllis. "From Periodicals Budget Cuts to Management Information Systems." *Serials Librarian* 9 (Winter 1984): 83–92.

Lack of knowledge of and control over the serials collection caused Union College Library to invest in a management information system giving reports that aided in collection development.

167. Kefford, Brian, and Line, Maurice B. "Core Collections of Journals for National Interlending Purposes." *Interlending Review* 10 (1982): 35–43.

The concept of core journal collections is sound, but practical problems need to be resolved before their value can be properly assessed.

168. Kent, A.K. "Economics of Information Transfer." In *Financing Serials from the Producer to the User*, edited by David P. Woodworth, 97–100. Oxford, Eng.: Blackwell's for the UK Serials Group, n.d.

There must be a better understanding of the needs of both creators and users of information, in the context of relevant technical, technological, social, and economic factors.

169.   Koenig, Michael Edward Davison. "Serials Dual Pricing: The
       Librarians' Hobgoblin." *Serials Librarian* 8 (Spring 1984): 25–28.
Dual pricing, equated here with the H. W. Wilson Company's "service
basis" and ISI's "grants," actually lowers the subscription price charged
libraries.

170.   Konopasek, Katherine, and O'Brien, Nancy Patricia. "Under-
       graduate Periodicals Usage: A Model of Measurement." *Serials
       Librarian* 9 (Winter 1984): 65–74.
This study at the University of Illinois Library fulfilled several specific
objectives useful in collection development for an undergraduate clientele.

171.   Kriz, Harry M. "Subscriptions vs. Books in a Constant Dollar
       Budget." *College and Research Libraries* 39 (1978): 105–09.
A citation analysis study in the field of engineering showed that for graduate students books are more important than journals. This result led to
shifts in the materials budget and an increase in library usefulness.

172.   Kronenfeld, Michael R., and Gable, Sarah H. "Real Inflation of
       Journal Prices: Medical Journals, U.S. Journals, and Brandon
       List Journals." *Bulletin of the Medical Library Association* 71
       (1983): 375–79.
All three categories of journals have increased in subscription rate at a
faster pace than the CPI.

173.   Lancaster, F.W., and Goldhor, Herbert. "The Impact of Online
       Services on Subscriptions to Printed Publications." *Online Review*
       5 (1981): 301–11.
Although libraries have cancelled many subscriptions to printed abstracting
and indexing services, the availability of this information online has had
a small effect on the decisionmaking.

174.   *Learned Journals Pricing and Buying Round; at Institution of
       Mechanical Engineers, Birdcage Walk, London SW1 on Friday
       22nd March 1985; Association of Learned and Professional So-
       ciety Publishers and the Publishers Association.* Letchworth,
       Eng.: Epsilon Press, 1985.
Proceedings of a seminar called to discuss: 1) the problems of differential
pricing of serials, based on subscriber status or location, and 2) the role
of the international subscription agent in distributing British journals.

175.   Leavy, Martin D. "Obliteration in the Natural and Social Sci-
       ences: Citation Data in Search of a Theory." *International Forum
       on Information and Documentation* 8 (October 1983): 27–31.

The author's calculation of a median half-life of six years for journals in both the natural and the social sciences creates questions about assumptions and the value of older social sciences materials in library collections.

176. Lenzini, Rebecca T. "Periodical Prices 1981–1983 Update." *Serials Librarian* 8 (Winter 1983): 107–18.

Lenzini takes over from Lowell, who succeeded Clasquin, in compiling this annual update, based on Faxon's files.

177. Lenzini, Rebecca T. "Periodical Prices 1982–1984 Update." *Serials Librarian* 9 (Winter 1984): 13–24.

The annual price study based on Faxon's database.

178. Lenzini, Rebecca T. "Periodical Prices, 1983–1985 Update." *Serials Librarian* 9 (Summer 1985): 119–30.

The annual study based on Faxon's files.

179. Lieberman Research, Inc. *How and Why People Buy Magazines: A National Study of the Consumer Market for Magazines.* Port Washington, N.Y.: Publishers Clearing House, 1977.

An analysis of the consumer market for magazines, based on personal interviews.

180. Line, Maurice B. "Changes in Rank Lists of Serials Over Time: Interlending vs. Citation Data." *Interlending and Document Supply* 12 (1984): 145–47; also in *College and Research Libraries* 46 (1985): 77–79.

BLLD's rank list of most-requested journals varies significantly over time, unlike ISI's *Journal Citation Reports* lists. A contributing factor may concern interlibrary loan: the impact of local finances and the population of ILL users.

181. Line, Maurice B. "Provision of Serials in Times of Stringency." In *Serials '84: Proceedings of the UK Serials Group Conference,* edited by Brian Cox, 1–22. Stratford-upon-Avon: UK Serials Group, 1985.

Reviews ways to reduce local serials expenditures, then discusses the necessary national document provision and supply systems.

182. Line, Maurice B. "Use of Citation Data for Periodicals Control in Libraries: A Response to Broadus." *College and Research Libraries* 46 (1985): 36–37.

The low stability over time of the rank order of periodicals at BLLD casts some doubt on the general validity of ISI's *Journal Citation Reports* as a means of identifying low-use titles.

183.   Lowell, Gerald R. "Periodical Prices 1980–1982 Update." *Serials Librarian* 7 (Fall 1982): 75–83.
Faxon's annual pricing study.

184.   McAllister, Paul R., Anderson, Richard C., and Narin, Francis. "Comparison of Peer and Citation Assessment of the Influence of Scientific Journals." *Journal of the American Society for Information Science* 31 (May 1980): 147–52.
A survey found a strong positive relationship between scientists' assessment of journal influence and citation influence ratings.

185.   McBride, Ruth B., and Stenstrom, Patricia. "Psychology Journal Usage." *Behavioral & Social Sciences Librarian* 2 (Fall 1980/1981): 1–12.
Profiles the relationship among a survey of psychology faculty at the University of Illinois at Urbana-Champaign, a 1963 American Psychological Association report, and data from the 1978 "Journal Citation Reports" in *Social Sciences Citation Index*.

186.   McDonough, Carol C. "Measurement of the Potential Demand for Academic and Professional Journals: A Methodology." *Journal of the American Society for Information Science* 33 (1982): 321–24.
Using economics journals, McDonough proposes a methodology to measure potential demand, then investigates the impact of potential demand on circulation.

187.   McKeehan, Nancy C. "Determining the Costs of Journals Used in Support of Federally Sponsored Research." *Bulletin of the Medical Library Association* 72 (1984): 147–49.
Describes methodology used by the Library of the Medical University of South Carolina in negotiations with the federal government.

188.   McKie, Alan, and Taylor, Colin. "Criteria for the Selection of New Periodical Subscriptions." In *Profiling a Periodicals Collection*, edited by Phillip Watson, 102–15. Melbourne, Aust.: Footscray Institute of Technology, 1979.
Recommends a standing committee on periodicals evaluation to complete a "selection criteria score sheet" for each title requested and to use it as a guide in selecting.

189.   McReynolds, Rosalee. "Limiting a Periodicals Collection in a College Library." *Serials Librarian* 9 (Winter 1984): 75–81.
Examination of several years' worth of use and citation studies to compile core lists of journals provides a basis for acquiring and weeding, based on time span of usefulness.

190.   Maher, William J., and Shearer, Benjamin F. "Undergraduate Use Patterns of Newspapers on Microfilm." *College and Research Libraries* 40 (1979): 254–60.
A study at the University of Illinois suggests criteria for purchase of microfilmed newspapers.

191.   Maricic, S. "A Fourfold Bibliometric Evaluation of Journals from Less Developed Scientific Coummunities [sic]—The Pattern of References in Medical Journals from Yugoslavia." *Annals of Library Science and Documentation* 30 (1983): 45–62.
A model for evaluation of scientific journals in less developed areas is tested against Yugoslavian medical journals.

192.   Merriman, John B. "Blackwell's Periodical Price Index: How It is Compiled and What it Aims to Achieve." In *Financing Serials from the Producer to the User,* edited by David P. Woodworth, 40–43. Oxford, Eng.: Blackwell's for the UK Serials Group, n.d.
Describes and evaluates the index published annually in *Library Association Record.* Includes comments on a library science student's evaluation of the Index. Discussion following talk refers to other indexes used to monitor prices.

193.   Merry, Karen, and Palmer, Trevor. "Use of Serials at the British Library Lending Division in 1983." *Interlending and Document Supply* 12 (1984): 56–60.
A survey shows a high level of satisfaction of serial requests and provides data toward the identification of a core serials collection.

194.   Noma, Elliot. "Co-Citation Analysis and the Invisible College." *Journal of the American Society for Information Science* 35 (1984): 29–33.
Before a co-citation matrix is constructed, the citing articles should be limited to those written by individuals in an invisible college.

195.   Osburn, Charles B. "Marketing the Collection Development Aspects of Serials Control." In *Serials Collection Development,* edited by Sul H. Lee, 9–17. Ann Arbor: Pierian Press, 1981.

Urges librarians to take the initiative in influencing academic planning, beginning with policy on serials selection.

196. Paul, Huibert. "Serials: Higher Prices vs. Shrinking Budgets." *Serials Librarian* 9 (Winter 1984): 3–12.
Librarians and publishers can both act to reduce serial prices.

197. Perk, Lawrence J., and Van Pulis, Noelle. "Periodical Usage in an Education-Psychology Library." *College and Research Libraries* 38 (1977): 304–08.
A study at Ohio State University analyzed circulation data from a closed reserve to measure use.

198. Peters, Andrew. "Evaluating Periodicals." *College and Research Libraries* 43 (1982): 149–51.
Central State University (Oklahoma) Library evaluates journals according to a formula based on relevance to the collection, use, and availability.

199. Pieters, Don L. "Perennial Problems with Periodicals." *Catholic Library World* 54 (1983): 280–82.
The author cites problems for the small college library with rising costs of periodicals, then five other librarians comment.

200. Pinzelik, Barbara P. "Serials De-Acquisition." In *Projects and Procedures for Serials Administration,* edited by Diane Stine, 61–73. Ann Arbor: Pierian Press, 1985.
Describes in detail the procedures and criteria used at Purdue University Libraries to evaluate and weed the serials collection.

201. Pond, Kurt, and Burlingame, Dwight F. "Library Cooperation: A Serials Model Based on Philosophical Principles." *College and Research Libraries* 45 (1984): 299–305.
Librarians and faculty members at Bowling Green State University and the University of Toledo began a cooperative serials project in which co-ordination of beliefs, attitudes, and actions was a central factor.

202. Pope, Michael J. "Use of Periodical Backfiles in a Community College Library." *Community/Junior College Research Quarterly* 2 (1978): 163–77.
A use study of 140 journals in a community college library shows consultation of nonscholarly titles and periodicals included in standard indexes.

203. *Profiling a Periodicals Collection: A Seminar for College of Advanced Education Libraries on Collection Evaluation and Rationalisation*, conducted by Footscray Institute of Technology Library, 23 November 1978. Editor: Phillip Watson. Melbourne, Aust.: Footscray Institute of Technology, 1979.

Papers in this work are listed separately in the Annotated Bibliography.

204. Rice, Barbara A. "Selection and Evaluation of Chemistry Periodicals." *Science and Technology Libraries* 4 (Fall 1983): 43–59.

No one method of selection and evaluation is best, for this is a complex process which must be recognized as subjective.

205. Rowse, Dorothea E. "The Storage of Science Journals at the University of South Africa." *South African Journal of Library and Information Science* 52 (1984): 105–08.

A use study helped determine which journals should be placed in compact storage and which comprise a core collection.

206. Ruschin, Siegfried. "Why Are Foreign Subscription Rates Higher for American Libraries Than They Are for Subscribers Elsewhere?" *Serials Librarian* 9 (Spring 1985): 7–17.

Documents the practice of discriminatory pricing and calls for further discussion among librarians and publishers.

207. *Serials Collection Development: Choices and Strategies*, ed. Sul H. Lee. Ann Arbor: Pierian Press, 1981.

Proceedings of a conference held in Oklahoma City. Articles are listed separately in the Annotated Bibliography.

208. Singleton, Alan. "Financing Serials—An Overview." In *Financing Serials from the Producer to the User*, edited by David P. Woodworth, 101–10. Oxford, Eng.: Blackwell's for the UK Serials Group, n.d.

Singleton pulls together the issues raised during the UK Serials Group Conference.

209. Stankus, Tony, and Rice, Barbara. "Handle with Care: Use and Citation Data for Science Journal Management." *Collection Management* 4 (Spring/Summer 1982): 95–110.

Guidance in using citation data to obtain valid results.

210. Stankus, Tony. "Negotiating Journal Demands With Young Scientists Using Lists Derived from Thesis Advisor Records." *Collection Management* 5 (Fall/Winter 1983): 185–98.

Advocates the use of journal lists based on the interests of the thesis advisor to ease the first conference with a newly-graduated science faculty member.

211. Stankus, Tony, and Diodato, Virgil P. "Selecting Multispecialty Mathematics Research Journals via Their Underlying Subject Emphases." *Science and Technology Libraries* 4 (Fall 1983): 61–78.

Because few sci-tech selection guidelines seem to apply to mathematics, the authors have devised a method emphasizing best matching of multi-specialty mathematics journals with given mathematical specialties.

212. Taylor, Colin. "Practical Solutions to Weeding Periodicals Collections." In *Profiling a Periodicals Collection*, edited by Phillip Watson, 61–72. Melbourne, Aust.: Footscray Institute of Technology, 1979.

Asks if weeding is necessary in college libraries, considers ways of identifying candidates for weeding, and lists a number of things to do with withdrawn volumes.

213. Trubkin, Leone. "Building a Core Collection of Business & Management Periodicals: How Databases Can Help." *Online* 6 (July 1982): 43–49.

Databases can serve as well as a sample issue in journal evaluation, both by giving a picture of the journal's contents and by the fact of inclusion or exclusion.

214. Tuttle, Marcia. "Serials." In *Selection of Library Materials in the Humanities, Social Sciences, and Sciences*, edited by Patricia A. McClung, 34–48. Chicago: American Library Association, 1985.

Selection sources used in collection development of serials, featuring nontraditional products issued by vendors, as well as heavily-used printed sources.

215. Urquhart, D.J. "The Present Economic Crisis and Its Effects on Publishers and Libraries." In *Economics of Serials Management*, edited by David P. Woodworth, 1–8. Loughborough, Eng.: Serials Group, n.d.

Libraries will come to depend more on synoptic journals than on comprehensive collections. Extensive discussion follows.

216. Urquhart, John A. "Coping with the Cuts." *UK Serials Group Newsletter* no. 7 (December 1981): 2–5.

Reveals the impact on British libraries of the fall in the pound sterling and gives ways in which libraries can minimize the reduction in materials (especially serials) acquired.

217. Urquhart, John A. "Has Poisson Been Kicked to Death?—A Rebuttal of the British Library Lending Division's Views on the Inconsistency of Rank Lists of Serials." *Interlending Review* 10 (1982): 97–99.

Urquhart presents data refuting the BLLD's conclusions based on 1975 and 1980 studies.

218. Usdin, B. Tommie. "Core Lists of Medical Journals: A Comparison." *Bulletin of the Medical Library Association* 67 (1979): 212–17.

A comparison of five core lists shows significant agreement, but there is no clear relationship with SCI's *Journal Citation Reports*.

219. Varma, D.K. "Increasing Subscription Costs and Problems of Resource Allocation." *Special Libraries* 74 (1983): 61–66.

Discusses, in the context of an academic business library, the implications of documented rapid increase in subscription rates.

220. Wainwright, Eric. "Is There an Over-Emphasis on Periodicals Provision in Colleges of Advanced Education Libraries?" In *Profiling a Periodicals Collection*, edited by Phillip Watson, 10–42. Melbourne, Aust.: Footscray Institute of Technology, 1979.

States the need for a balance between periodicals and monographs that is appropriate for each college library.

221. Wall, Raymond Alwyn. "Publisher Pricing Policies and the Reprographic Copyright Controversy." *ASLIB Proceedings* 36 (1984): 325–32.

A survey at Loughborough University of Technology supports earlier findings that the difference between institutional and individual subscription prices is increasing.

222. Wall, Raymond Alwyn. "What Price Copyright? Discriminatory Serials Subscriptions and the Photocopying Controversy." *United Kingdom Serials Group Newsletter* 6 (December 1984): 8–11.

Wall believes that many publishers justify high institutional subscription rates by claiming that they include payment for library photocopying. He feels that with fair use copying exempt, the library is paying an excessive royalty to the publisher.

223. Watson, Phillip, "The Development and Implementation of the Periodicals Evaluation and Rationalisation Programme at Footscray Institute of Technology Library." In *Profiling a Periodicals Collection,* edited by Phillip Watson, 73–101. Melbourne, Aust.: Footscray Institute of Technology, 1979.

A use study model, featuring "unit cost per activity," is presented as a guide to other librarians in evaluating and weeding their collections.

224. Weisheit, Ralph A., and Regoli, Robert M. "Ranking Journals." *Scholarly Publishing* 15 (1984): 313–25.

Discusses general issues in ranking, then considers reputational approach and citation analysis.

225. Wender, Ruth W. "Counting Journal Title Usage in the Health Sciences." *Special Libraries* 70 (1979): 219–26.

A study of hospital users of the Extension Division of the University of Oklahoma Health Sciences Center Library suggests that such a project should include number of requesters, as well as number of requests.

226. White, Herbert S. "Strategies and Alternatives in Dealing with the Serials Management Budget." In *Serials Collection Development,* edited by Sul H. Lee, 27–42. Ann Arbor: Pierian Press, 1981.

Overview of the findings of the author's National Science Foundation sponsored studies of the economic interaction between libraries and the publishers of scholarly serials.

227. Wiberley, Stephen E., Jr. "Journal Rankings from Citation Studies: A Comparison of National and Local Data from Social Work." *Library Quarterly* 52 (1982): 348–59.

Tests Maurice Line's argument that citation rankings from one study are not transferrable to another situation, and finds that in this study the argument does not hold true.

228.   Williamson, Marilyn L. "Seven Years of Cancellations at Georgia Tech." *Serials Librarian* 9 (Spring 1985): 103–14.

Discusses planning, criteria, implementation, and implications of a series of serial cancellation projects.

229.   Woodward, Hazel M., and Evans, Anthony J. "Serials Cuts (and the Use of a Blunt Knife)." In *The Future of Serials,* edited by Nancy Fjallbrant, 171–78. Goeteborg, Sweden: International Association of Technological University Libraries, 1984.

Expresses the frustration of attempting to cut serials budgets equitably.

230.   Woodward, Hazel M., and Evans, Anthony J. "Serials Cuts (and the Use of a Blunt Knife)." In *Serials '83: Proceedings of the UK Serials Group Conference,* edited by Rodney M. Burton, 111–22. Stratford-upon-Avon: UK Serials Group, 1984.

Reviews common ways of responding to serials budget problems, then recommends a comprehensive review of the collection as a means of identifying core journals and journals that can be cancelled.

231.   Yu, Priscilla C. "Cost Analysis: Domestic Serials Exchanges." *Serials Review* 8 (Fall 1982): 79–82.

The University of Illinois Library's domestic exchange program appears to be cost beneficial, based on subscription price and value to the library collection.

III. ACQUISITIONS

232.   Allardyce, Alan. "Gift and Exchange Schemes: National Schemes." In *Resource Sharing—Its Impact on Serials,* edited by Margaret E. Graham and Brian Cox, 45–60. Stratford-upon-Avon: UK Serials Group, 1982.

Reviews the history of international exchange of materials, then centers on exchange programs of the British Library Lending Division, National Library of Canada, and Universal Serials and Book Exchange.

233.   Allcock, David. "Serials Control Services Available from Subscription Agents: LIDAS." In *Serials '83: Proceedings of the UK Serials Group Conference,* edited by Rodney M. Burton, 49–51. Stratford-upon-Avon: UK Serials Group, 1984.

Brief, general description of a serials control and distribution system de-

veloped by a computer services company for England's Management and
Personnel Office Library.

234. Banks, P.J. "The Role of the Agent: The British Viewpoint." In
      The Information Chain, edited by John A. Urquhart, 48–58.
      Stratford-upon-Avon: UK Serials Group, 1983.
Twenty-five attributes of a subscription agent are followed by four areas
of current interest that need further attention.

235. Basch, N. Bernard. "Library Subscription Agencies: Past, Pres-
      ent, and Future." In *Bridging the Gaps: Proceedings of the Third
      Annual Meeting of the Society for Scholarly Publishing,* edited
      by Dave Dobson, 137–38. Washington, D.C.: Society for Schol-
      arly Publishing, 1981.
Describes Faxon's services and plans for the future, with emphasis on
the benefits for the publisher.

236. Basch, N. Bernard, and Kochoff, Stephen T. "Serials Fulfillment:
      An Overview of the Publisher, Library, and Agent Interface."
      Public Library Quarterly 4 (Fall 1983): 37–45.
The three-way relationship is discussed in the context of claiming missing
issues.

237. Blackwell, Julian. "Serials Distribution Problems and Costs." In
      Economics of Serials Management, edited by David P. Wood-
      worth, 17–25. Loughborough, Eng.: Serials Group, n.d.
The talk centers around postage costs and negotiations with the Post Office. Subsequent discussion brings out creative distribution schemes.

238. Bostic, Mary J. "Serials Claiming." *Serials Librarian* 10 (Fall
      1985/Winter 1985–86): 185–94.
Reviews the claiming capabilities of several automated systems, including
OCLC, LINX, EBSCONET, NOTIS, PHILSOM, BASIS, Brigham
Young University, University of California Berkeley, and UCLA
Biomedical Library.

239. Cheda, Sherrill. "Help for the Serials Librarian: The Canadian
      Periodical Publishers' Association's Work as a Periodicals Dis-
      tributor." *Serials Librarian* 7 (Fall 1982): 43–49.
This group provides, among other things, subscription information on its
members' journals, one of the few sources of data on Canadian magazines.

240. Clasquin, Frank F. "Automation and the Subscription Agency." In *Management of Serials Automation,* edited by Peter Gellatly, 257–71. New York: Haworth Press, 1982.

History of electronic data processing in U.S. subscription agencies, with particular attention to Faxon.

241. Clasquin, Frank F. "Library and Subscription Agent Electronics." *Serials Librarian* 7 (Spring 1983): 7–15.

New technology is changing the relationship between the library and the subscription agency.

242. Courtney, Keith R. "Publishers' Distribution Methods and Problems: The UK." In *Serials '84: Proceedings of the UK Serials Group Conference,* edited by Brian Cox, 79–87. Stratford-upon-Avon: UK Serials Group, 1985.

Subscription fulfillment as practiced by Taylor & Francis, Ltd., including payment, transportation, claims, renewals, and dealing with subscription agents.

243. Daughtree, Sheilah. "A Dilemma in Serials Control: The Effect of Amalgamation on Mt. Gravitt CAE, Brisbane." *United Kingdom Serials Group Newsletter* 6 (June 1984): 16–19.

The merger of four Australian Colleges of Advanced Education forced decentralized serials receipt to avoid separating users from records. The planning for this change is discussed.

244. Davis, Susan. "Checking It In the OCLC Way." In *Projects and Procedures for Serials Administration,* edited by Diane Stine, 251–75. Ann Arbor: Pierian Press, 1985.

Describes planning, implementation, and procedures for using the OCLC Serials Control Subsystem at the Illinois Institute of Technology Library.

245. De Bardeleben, Marian Z., Wilson, Martha M., and Rosenberg, Murray D. "Off-Site Journal Check-In: An Alternative to Internal Control of Serials." *Serials Review* 9 (Winter 1983): 56–62.

Richmond's Philip Morris Research Center Library uses EBSCO's off-site check-in service as an economical alternative to adding a staff member.

246. Edgar, Neal L. "Missing Issues: One Technique for Replacement." *Library Acquisitions: Practice and Theory* 6 (1982): 295–304.

An unusual procedure is designed to keep back issues dealers from
"pushing [the librarian] around." Followed by comment from David Lup-
ton and Margaret Landesman.

247.   Facente, Gary. "Publishers' Distribution Methods and Problems:
       The USA." In *Serials '84: Proceedings of the UK Serials Group
       Conference,* edited by Brian Cox, 73–78. Stratford-upon-Avon:
       UK Serials Group, 1985.
Distribution practices and marketing strategies at the American Library
Association's Publishing Services Division.

248.   Fletcher, Marilyn P. "Serials Reconciliation at the University of
       New Mexico General Library." In *Projects and Procedures for
       Serials Administration,* edited by Diane Stine, 23–38. Ann Arbor:
       Pierian Press, 1985.
Describes the exhaustive review, analysis, and record reconciliation project undertaken by this library.

249.   Frumkin, Jerry. "Government Publications to the Library Com-
       munity." *Serials Review* 9 (Winter 1983): 52–53.
Describes the standing order and new title alerting services of Bernan
Associates, for U.S. Government publications (and now also for foreign
and international documents).

250.   Garg, K. C., and Gupta, S. P. "Serials Librarianship in India."
       Serials Librarian 10 (Fall 1985/Winter 1985-86): 263–67.
Reviews the problems and practices related to the acquisition of periodicals
in India.

251.   Goehner, Donna M. "Financial Management in Acquisitions:
       Things They Never Told Me in Library School." *Illinois Libraries*
       67 (1985): 435–37.
Presents weaknesses in formal preparation for acquisitions work and gives
suggestions for areas in which one needs background, particularly accounting and publishing.

252.   Green, Paul Robert. "The Performance of Subscription Agents:
       A Detailed Survey." *Serials Librarian* 8 (Winter 1983): 7–22.
Data showing number of claims per issue and percentage of first, second,
and third claims, are used to monitor performance of agents over a period
of time.

253. Green, Paul Robert. "Recent Research in Serials: Subscription Agents' Services." In *Serials '84: Proceedings of the UK Serials Group Conference,* edited by Brian Cox, 113–27. Stratford-upon-Avon: UK Serials Group, 1985.

Reports the results of a study made by the University of Leeds Library on the necessity for and effectiveness of claims through agents. Also discusses binding economies.

254. Greene, Philip E. N., III. "Beyond Online Ordering: Future Trends in Subscription Agency Services." *Technical Services Quarterly* 1 (Fall/Winter 1983): 249–52.

Speculates about the future role of the agency and emphasizes the need for a partnership between the librarian and the vendor.

255. Hall, W. "Serials Control Services Available from Subscription Agents: Dawson International Subscription Service." In *Serials '83: Proceedings of the UK Serials Group Conference,* edited by Rodney M. Burton, 32–34. Stratford-upon-Avon: UK Serials Group, 1984.

Presents objectives and advantages of Dawson's SMS online serials management system, then under development.

256. Hickey, Tom. "The Role of the Back Issue/Reprint Dealer." In *Information Chain,* edited by John A. Urquhart, 23–27. Stratford-upon-Avon: UK Serials Group, 1983.

Describes the operation of the dealer who buys, stocks, and sells old journals. Followed by transcription of extensive question and answer session.

257. Holmes, Phil L. "Serials Control Services Available from Subscription Agents: Blackwell's PERLINE." In *Serials '83: Proceedings of the UK Serials Group Conference,* edited by Rodney M. Burton, 26–31. Stratford-upon-Avon: UK Serials Group, 1984.

The developer of PERLINE/BOOKLINE promotes his distributed-network system.

258. Intner, Sheila S. "Choosing and Using Subscription Agents in Sci-Tech Libraries: Theory and Practice." *Science and Technology Libraries* 4 (Fall 1983): 31–42.

Reviews pros and cons of using agents, then discusses results of a survey of 10 science and technology libraries regarding their use of agents and their criteria for selecting those agents.

259. Ireland, Jeanetta M. "Faxon LINX at Brandeis University Libraries: A User's Appraisal." *Library Hi-Tech* no. 5 (1984): 29–35.

Evaluates the system after one year of use and finds it a good investment, with excellent support from the vendor.

260. Jones, Herbert, and McKinley, Margaret M. "Automated Exchanges Control: An Interim Report." In *Projects and Procedures for Serials Automation,* edited by Diane Stine, 51–59. Ann Arbor: Pierian Press, 1985.

UCLA is used as a case study to show that the library participating in exchange programs acts as vendor as well as customer. Increased costs of the programs forced UCLA to reduce its exchange activity, based on reports from the computer-assisted processing system.

261. Kemp, Arnoud de, and Waller, T. "Swets Subscription Service Facing the 1980s." In *Current Trends in Serials Automation,* edited by Ahmed H. Helal and Joachim W. Weiss, 177–96. Essen: Gesamthochschulbibliothek Essen, 1981.

Describes the agency's services to libraries, with emphasis on the internal automated system.

262. Koenig, Michael Edward Davison, and Morse, Elizabeth A. "Sci-Tech Libraries and Serials Agents: The Unused Leverage." *Science & Technology Libraries* 5 (Winter 1984): 33–43.

Explains the agents' ways of calculating the library service charge and speculates that sci-tech libraries are paying a higher rate than is necessary.

263. Landenberger, Sally A. "Systematizing Serials Operations: Eliminating Crisis Claiming." *Serials Review* 9 (Spring 1983): 87–90.

Implementation of claiming guidelines, after a thorough examination of the CSR, brought order and better service at Michigan State University Library.

264. Lenzini, Rebecca T., and Horn, Judith. "1975–1985: Formulative Years for the Subscription Agency." *Serials Librarian* 10 (Fall 1985/Winter 1985–86): 225–38.

The subscription agency—Faxon is used as an example—has responded to a changing marketplace by expanding services provided through the evolution of electronic technology.

265. Lungu, Charles B. M. "Serials Acquisition Problems in Developing Countries: the Zambian Experience." *International Library Review* 17 (1985): 189–202.

The necessity for austerity is the primary problem in developing country libraries. All other problems stem from it. Based on his experience at the University of Zambia, Lungu makes suggestions for resolving the problems.

266. Marshall, Mary. "Serials Control Services Available from Subscription Agents: EBSCONET Online Services." In *Serials '83: Proceedings of the UK Serials Group Conference,* edited by Rodney M. Burton, 40–45. Stratford-upon-Avon: UK Serials Group, 1984.

Discussion of EBSCO's online system, emphasizing claiming and access to title and publisher information.

267. Norton, T. H. "Gift and Exchange Schemes: A Medical Exchange Scheme." In *Resource Sharing–Its Impact on Serials,* edited by Margaret E. Graham and Brian Cox, 61–63. Stratford-upon-Avon: UK Serials Group, 1982.

In 1975 the Wellcome Institute ended its distribution of excess periodicals to medical libraries, and those libraries set up their own exchange program, which is efficient and a valuable means of acquisition.

268. O'Connor, Margaret. "Factors Influencing the Choice of an Agent." In *Profiling a Periodicals Collection,* edited by Phillip Watson, 129–35. Melbourne, Aust.: Footscray Institute of Technology, 1979.

The specific library's requirements are matched to the capabilities of the agent.

269. Paul, Huibert. "Are Subscription Agents Worth Their Keep?" *Serials Librarian* 7 (Fall 1982): 31–41.

Paul feels serials can be acquired more economically without agents.

270. Paul, Huibert. "Automation of Serials Check-In: Like Growing Bananas In Greenland?" *Serials Librarian* 6 (Winter 1981/Spring 1982): 3–16, and (Summer 1982): 39–62.

Until automated check-in systems outperform manual systems, it is better to restrict automation to other library functions. Simpler can be better, while avoiding "computer overkill."

271.   Paul, Huibert. "Streamlining Claiming Processes: Manual Serials
       Check-In Systems." *Serials Review* 9 (Spring 1983): 91–93.
Notations on check-in records and a moving tab system replaced awkward
files and laborious filing and unfiling at the University of Oregon.

272.   Postlethwaite, Bonnie. "Kardex to Keyboard: Creating a Serials
       Check-In File in Faxon's LINX System." In *Projects and Pro-
       cedures for Serials Administration,* edited by Diane Stine, 227–
       43. Ann Arbor: Pierian Press, 1985.
Explains how Faxon's database can be used to expedite conversion of
serial check-in records to the vendor's automated system.

273.   Prior, Albert. "How Serials Agents Can Help Libraries Cut
       Costs." In *Financing Serials from the Producer to the User,* ed-
       ited by David P. Woodworth, 44–55. Oxford, Eng.: Blackwell's
       for the UK Serials Group, n.d.
Besides discussing agents' direct services to libraries, Prior looks at ways
agents help publishers cut costs, also beneficial to the library.

274.   Quinn, Joan M. "Serials Services and Records Unit: Genealogy
       and General Information." *Serials Review* 11 (Spring 1985): 67–68.
Ten commandments for serials acquisitions assistants.

275.   Rangra, V. K., and Mathur, J. B. "A Study on the Loss in Transit
       of Journals Subscribed Through a Vendor." *Annals of Library
       Science and Documentation* 29 (1982): 16–18.
Suggests measures for minimizing the loss of journal issues before the
library receives them.

276.   Riddick, John. "OCLC's Claims Component: Implementation at
       CMU." *Serials Review* 9 (Winter 1983): 75–79.
An early assessment of the long-awaited claiming component of OCLC's
Serials Control Subsystem, based on the experience at Central Michigan
University Library.

277.   Rovelstad, Howard. "The Economics of the Universal Serials
       and Book Exchange (USBE)." *Interlending Review* 7 (1979): 98–
       101.
Describes USBE and its objectives.

278.   Rowe, Richard R. "The Role of the Agent: The American View-
       point." In *Information Chain,* edited by John A. Urquhart, 40–
       45. Stratford-upon-Avon: UK Serials Group, 1983.

The president of Faxon speculates about the vendor's role in the future distribution of information. He also describes the agency's LINX system.

279. Rowe, Richard R. "Serials Control Services Available from Subscription Agents: Faxon's LINX." In *Serials '83: Proceedings of the UK Serials Group Conference,* edited by Rodney M. Burton, 35–39. Stratford-upon-Avon: UK Serials Group, 1984.

Emphasizes LINX's speed, publisher information, and information sharing among library customers. It also discusses SISAC's work toward developing an issue- and article-specific standard information code.

280. Schmidt, Karen A. "Distributed Check-In of Serials: A Case Study of the University of Illinois—Urbana Library." In *Projects and Procedures for Serials Administration,* edited by Diane Stine, 219–26. Ann Arbor: Pierian Press, 1985.

In order to get most-needed journals to departmental libraries as quickly as possible, the Library now has selected domestic periodicals shipped directly to the libraries.

281. Singleton, Alan. *The Role of Subscription Agents; With a Supplementary Report on U.K. Libraries' Trade with Agents, by Alan Cooper.* Leicester: University of Leicester, Primary Communications Research Centre, 1981. (Occasional Papers)

This report, based on interviews with agents, publishers, and librarians, investigates the relationships among the three and the perceptions each has of the other.

282. Smith, Alan. "Serials Automation and the Subscription Agent Facing the 1980s." In *Current Trends in Serials Automation,* edited by Ahmed H. Helal and Joachim W. Weiss, 197–201. Essen: Gesamthochschulbibliothek Essen, 1981.

Blackwells' new Mark II database management system will permit enhanced service to library customers. Speculation about the future role of the subscription agent.

283. Stevens, Rosemary. "Acquisition of Serials from Asia and Africa at the School of Oriental and African Studies (SOAS) Library." *Library Acquisitions: Practice and Theory* 7 (1983): 59–70.

Notes special problems relating to serial publication and access in these geographical areas and lists a number of published aids and procedures that help identify and acquire them.

284. Thyden, Wayne. "Subscription Agency Size: Threat or Benefit?" *Serials Librarian* 7 (Spring 1983): 29–34.
A response to Nancy Melin's charge that the purchase of smaller agencies by large ones would be detrimental to libraries.

285. Tuttle, Marcia. "Can Subscription Agents Survive?" *Canadian Library Journal* 42 (1985): 259–64.
Subscription agents' survival depends on their ability to adapt services to the needs of their library customers, through technology.

286. Tuttle, Marcia. "Magazine Fulfillment Centers: What They Are, How They Operate, and What We Can Do About Them." *Library Acquisitions: Practice and Theory* 9 (1985): 41–49.
Investigates the fulfillment center and its impact on libraries; gives guidelines for libraries in their acquisition of mass-circulation magazines.

287. Waller, T. "Serials Control Services Available from Subscription Agents: Swets Subscription Service." In *Serials '83: Proceedings of the UK Serials Group Conference,* edited by Rodney M. Burton, 46–48. Stratford-upon-Avon: UK Serials Group, 1984.
Introduces SAILS, Swets Automated Independent Library System, then being tested.

288. Wernstedt, Irene J. "The Effectiveness of Serials Claiming." *Serials Review* 8 (Spring 1982): 43–47.
A study at Pennsylvania State University Library indicates that claiming is effective and is worth the effort by staff members. Wernstedt identified factors that have enabled her library to begin claiming selectively.

289. Wernstedt, Irene J. "Serial Supplier Controversy Revisited." *Science & Technology Libraries* 5 (Spring 1985): 113–22.
Clarifies points regarding vendor service charge attributed to Wernstedt in Intner's article about the use of subscription agents in sci-tech libraries. Explains services libraries receive from vendors. Includes Intner's response.

290. Willmering, William J. "Check-In for Indexing: NLM Serial Control System." In *Projects and Procedures for Serials Administration,* edited by Diane Stine, 277–86. Ann Arbor: Pierian Press, 1985.
The National Library of Medicine's check-in system, designed to be an online indexing system, uses machine validation to ensure consistent data entry.

291.   Wisneski, Martin E. "Manual Serials Management Systems: The Claiming Function." *Serials Review* 9 (Spring 1983): 97–102.
Prediction of date of receipt and "claiming tape" make a workable system for the University of Kansas Law Library.

292.   Wright, Jean Acker. "Monographic Series: OCLC's Local Data Record." *Serials Review* 9 (Spring 1983): 103–04.
Describes Vanderbilt University Library's use of the OCLC Serials Control Subsystem for recording receipt and treatment of monographic series.

293.   Yu, Priscilla C. "Berkeley's Exchange Program: A Case Study." *Journal of Library History, Philosophy and Comparative Librarianship* 17 (1982): 241–67.
Examines the program in a historical context and identifies three essentials for a successful exchange program: commitment, funding, and available publications.

IV. CATALOGING

294.   Allen, Kimberly G. "Serials Conversion: One Supervisor's Account." *Technicalities* 3 (December 1983): 12–15.
Details difficulties encountered by the supervisor of a joint conversion project in Michigan, as a guide to persons directing such projects in the future.

295.   Barwick, Margaret. "A Basic Guide to Serials Cataloguing and Practice." *United Kingdom Serials Group Newsletter* 7 (December 1985): 46–48.
Brief descriptions of standards for cataloging serials and of online serials databases.

296.   Beatty, Alison, and Humphreys, Betsy L. "Serial Cataloging Under AACR2: Differences and Difficulties at the National Library of Medicine." *Cataloging and Classification Quarterly* 3 (Winter 1982/Spring 1983): 77–85.
NLM welcomed the opportunity provided by AACR2 to conform to LC cataloging practice. However, the new code and LC's rule interpretations create problems for NLM serials catalogers, particularly in the areas of earliest-issue description, uniform titles, and linking notes.

297.   Bloss, Alexander. "AACR2 North and South: Serials Cataloging from the Library of Congress and the National Library of Canada." *Serials Review* 9 (Winter 1983): 84–90.

Rule interpretations by the National Library of Canada do not necessarily agree with those by the Library of Congress, a situation that could lead to different codes for different countries.

298.   Bloss, Marjorie E. "Commas, Colons, and Parentheses: The International Standardization of Serials Holdings Statements." *Technical Services Quarterly* 3 (Fall 1985/Winter 1986): 59–71.
A discussion of international efforts to standardize the rules for serials holdings statements.

299.   Bross, Rex. "Serials Departments and AACR2." *Cataloging and Classification Quarterly* 3 (Winter 1982/Spring 1983): 121–24.
AACR2 means more training for all serials department staff members, more complex problemsolving, and more time spent changing records.

300.   Callahan, Patrick F. "Retrospective Conversion of Serials Using OCLC." In *Projects and Procedures for Serials Administration,* edited by Diane Stine, 115–44. Ann Arbor: Pierian Press, 1985.
Procedures for conversion of manual serials records to machine readable records, based on the experience at Center for Research Libraries.

301.   Cannan, Judith Proctor. *Serial Cataloging: A Comparison of AACR1 and 2.* New York: New York Metropolitan Reference and Research Library Agency, 1980. (METRO Miscellaneous Publications. 28)
An instructional tool prepared by the Head of the English Language Serials Cataloging Section at the Library of Congress. Examples included.

302.   Cipolla, Wilma Reid. "Serials Management and AACR2 in Large Academic Libraries." *Cataloging and Classification Quarterly* 3 (Winter 1982/Spring 1983): 125–30.
The impact of full implementation of AACR2 on the work load of serials catalogers is such that the new code must be used selectively, with priorities documented. Serials that do not change can be left in AACR1 until there is time to deal with them.

303.   Clack, Doris Hargrett. "AACR2 and the Small Academic Library." *Cataloging and Classification Quarterly* 3 (Winter 1982/Spring 1983): 131–40.
Identifies areas in which catalogers in small academic libraries should make policy decisions in using AACR2.

304. Clarke, Andrew. "Borge's Rules for Series, Serials and Supplements: The New Uniform Titles Reconsidered." *Catalogue and Index* no. 66 (Winter 1982): 2–3.
Practical suggestions for clarifying the cataloging of generic titled serials.

305. Cole, Jim E. "AACR2 and ISBD(S): Correspondence or Divergence?" *Serials Review* 8 (Fall 1982): 67–69.
AACR2 will not truly be the international code it claims to be until its differences with ISBD(S) have been reconciled.

306. Cole, Jim E., and Madison, Olivia M. A. "A Decade of Serials Cataloging." *Serials Librarian* 10 (Fall 1985/Winter 1985–86): 103–16.
With special attention to CONSER, discusses the evolution of serials cataloging and the impact of ISDS, ISBD(S), and AACR2.

307. Cole, Jim E., and Griffin, David E. *Notes Worth Noting: Notes Used in AACR2 Serials Cataloging.* Ann Arbor: Pierian Press, 1984.
The AACR2 counterpart to an earlier work by Ruth Schley and Jane B. Davies, this is arranged by rule number and is a compilation of notes drawn from NST, *Monthly Catalog,* and CONSER records found in the Washington Library Network database.

308. Collver, Mitsuko. "AACR2 and Serials Management." *Cataloging and Classification Quarterly* 3 (Winter 1982/Spring 1983): 141–44.
The adaptation of the many serials records and files proceeds smoothly in a unified serials department where staff members are familiar with the complexities of serials.

309. Collver, Mitsuko. "Periodicals Inventory as a Library Event." In *Projects and Procedures for Serials Administration,* edited by Diane Stine, 75–85. Ann Arbor: Pierian Press, 1985.
Describes planning, organization, implementation, and results of an inventory of serials conducted at SUNY Stony Brook Library, involving the entire library staff.

310. Comaromi, John P. "Cataloging Theory and Serials." *Cataloging and Classification Quarterly* 3 (Winter 1982/Spring 1983): 9–17.
From a devotee of the ALA Cataloging Rules, an introduction to serials cataloging and the differences among ALA, AACR, and AACR2.

311.   Cooper, Byron. "Cataloging Loose-Leaf Publications." *Library Resources and Technical Services* 26 (1982): 370–75.
While AACR2 and earlier cataloging codes treat looseleaf publications as monographs, patrons and librarians would be best served by serial treatment.

312.   Craig, James D. "Series Authority Files: The Glasgow University Experience." *Journal of Librarianship* 14 (1982): 289–96.
The history of an attempt to maintain traditional cataloging standards, featuring the impact of extra-library policy decisions. States lessons learned and suggestions for applying them.

313.   Cummins, Lynn Mealer. "Serials Cataloging in Transition." *Serials Librarian* 10 (Fall 1985/Winter 1985–86): 129–31.
In the last decade serials cataloging has become standardized through automation. The next need is flexibility in online catalogs to recover lost benefits and to develop new services.

314.   Decker, Jean S. "AACR2 and Series." *Cataloging and Classification Quarterly* 3 (Winter 1982/Spring 1983): 59–63.
AACR2 has lessened problems of corporate entry and created problems of series entry and authority work.

315.   Decker, Jean S. "Series Control and Procedures." In *Projects and Procedures for Serials Administration,* edited by Diane Stine, 207–17. Ann Arbor: Pierian Press, 1985.
Describes the means used at SUNY Buffalo to control series authority.

316.   Edgar, Neal L., ed. *AACR2 and Serials: The American View.* New York: Haworth Press, 1983. (*Cataloging & Classification Quarterly,* vol. 3, nos. 2/3)
Serials librarians discuss the impact of AACR2. Each article in this collection is listed separately in the Annotated Bibliography.

317.   Edgar, Neal L. "Computer Cataloguing for Serials: Ramblings of a Curmudgeon." In *Management of Serials Automation,* edited by Peter Gellatly, 119–34. New York: Haworth Press, 1982.
An evaluation of the changes brought about by AACR2.

318.   Edgar, Neal L. "Serials Cataloging Up To and Including AACR2." *Serials Librarian* 7 (Summer 1983): 25–46.
Serials cataloging under AACR2 requires understanding of the history of and changes in this code.

319.	Flaspeter, Marjorie, and Lomker, Linda. "Earliest Online . . ."
	Serials Review 11 (Summer 1985): 63–70.
A cataloger and an acquisitions librarian from the University of Minnesota
Library propose entry of serials under earliest title in an online system.

320.	Fleeman, Mary Grace. "The Availability and Acceptability of
	Serial Records in the OCLC Data Base." In *Management of Se-
	rials Automation,* edited by Peter Gellatly, 151–61. New York:
	Haworth Press, 1982.
The University of Oklahoma Library catalogers found nearly a 90% hit
rate, but less than 10% of the records were accepted without modification.

321.	Franzmeier, Gunther. "Authority File for Corporate Authors in
	the German Serials Data Base." In *Current Trends in Serials Au-
	tomation,* edited by Ahmed H. Helal and Joachim W. Weiss, 59–
	67. Essen: Gesamthochschulbibliothek Essen, 1981.
The benefits and the problems created by this longstanding online authority
file.

322.	Franzmeier, Gunther. "The Miraculous Multiplication of Serial
	Titles." *International Cataloguing* 11 (January/March 1982): 9.
Asks for a solution to the problem of multiple titles for a single serial:
uniform title, title proper, key title, and abbreviated key title, all differing
slightly.

323.	Franzmeier, Gunther. "Serials Cataloging in the Federal Republic
	of Germany: Main Features and Main Differences from AACR2."
	Serials Review 11 (Summer 1985): 71–72.
The German cataloging rules handle corporate main entries differently
(and better?) than AACR2.

324.	Frost, Carolyn O. "A Comparison of Cataloging Codes for Serials:
	AACR2 and Its Predecessors." *Cataloging and Classification
	Quarterly* 3 (Winter 1982/Spring 1983): 27–37.
An overview of the treatment of serials by four major twentieth-century
cataloging codes. Topics studied are title change, title differentiation, rules
for entry and heading, and rules for description.

325.	Garner, Diane. "International Documents Collections: An Ap-
	proach to Record Keeping." *Serials Review* 8 (Fall 1982): 97–
	102.
With a small staff and a primary obligation to public service, Pennsylvania
State University Library's International Documents unit has adopted a

policy of minimal processing that makes materials available quickly, at the expense of detailed subject access.

326. Graham, Crystal. "Serials Cataloging on RLIN: A User's Viewpoint." *Serials Review* 9 (Fall 1983): 87–91.
Describes and evaluates RLIN from the perspective of a serials cataloger.

327. Griffin, David E. "Serials Cataloging and the MARC Format: Time for Reassessment." *Technical Services Quarterly* 1 (Fall/ Winter 1983): 143–47.
MARC-S fields that seemed important in the beginning may no longer be so, and the format may need to be adjusted to meet today's serials cataloging needs.

328. Griffin, David E. "Serials Review in the Washington Library Network." *Serials Review* 10 (Spring 1984): 61–73.
Describes and justifies the unique WLN policy of reviewing serial records before they enter the database. Speculates about future direction of the process.

329. Heroux, Marlene Sue. "Automated Serials Cataloging." *Serials Librarian* 9 (Spring 1985): 69–83.
Defines and places in context the acronyms and rules employed in automated cataloging of serials.

330. Kovacic, Ellen Siegel. "Serials Cataloging: What It Is, How It's Done, Why It's Done That Way." *Serials Review* 11 (Spring 1985): 77–86.
Overview of serials cataloging philosophy and issues, intended for nonserials librarians.

331. Landesman, Betty. "Standing-Order Series: Serials or Monographs?" In *Projects and Procedures for Serials Administration,* edited by Diane Stine, 199–206. Ann Arbor: Pierian Press, 1985.
At Wellesley College Library the Serials Department handles the serials aspects of monographic series received on standing order, the Catalog Department the monographic aspects.

332. McBride, Ruth B. "Copy Cataloguing of Serials According to AACR2 Using OCLC: The University of Illinois Experience." In *Management of Serials Automation,* edited by Peter Gellatly, 135–49. New York: Haworth Press, 1982.
Analyzes the effectiveness of using OCLC copy and determines the effect of AACR2 on such cataloging.

333. McBride, Ruth B. "Copy Cataloging of Serials: Proceedings of the ALA/RTSD/CCS Copy Cataloging Discussion Group Meeting, July 10, 1982 in Philadelphia." *Serials Librarian* 8 (Winter 1983): 23–47.

Serials catalogers are beginning to trust non-librarians and online records from other libraries in their work. Sometimes this trust is planned, sometimes not.

334. McIver, Carole R. "The AACRs and Serials Cataloging." *Serials Librarian* 10 (Fall 1985/Winter 1985-86): 117–27.

Covers the planning and implementation of AACR2 and its advantages and disadvantages. Speculates about the next code revision.

335. McKinley, Margaret. "AACR2 Serials Cataloging and Management: Concerns in Academic Libraries." *Cataloging and Classification Quarterly* 3 (Winter 1982/Spring 1983): 145–49.

The integration of AACR2 records into existing serials files requires changed operating procedures, retraining of staff, and an extended period of transition.

336. Matson, Susan. "Series Authority Control." In *Projects and Procedures for Serials Administration,* edited by Diane Stine, 145–79. Ann Arbor: Pierian Press, 1985.

At Southern Illinois University Library series authority decisions are made in the Serials Department. Matson explains and illustrates the procedures followed.

337. Monson, Mary H. "Serials Catalogers: Isolation or Integration?" *Serials Review* 9 (Fall 1983): 65–67.

Automated cataloging presents the opportunity to unite all cataloging administratively for higher quality cataloging.

338. Nichols Randall, Barbara L. "AACR2 and the New York State Library's CONSER Project." *Serials Review* 8 (Spring 1982): 75–77.

The transition to AACR2 by a CONSER participant was made more difficult by the lateness of documentation and direction from CONSER and the Library of Congress.

339. Petersen, Karla D. "Planning for Serials Retrospective Conversion." *Serials Review* 10 (Fall 1984): 73–78.

Covers the Center for Research Libraries' conversion of serial records to machine-readable form using OCLC. Stresses the planning process.

340. Postlethwaite, Bonnie. "Art Sales and Exhibitions: The New Era of Bibliographic Control." *Cataloging and Classification Quarterly* 3 (Winter 1982/Spring 1983): 87–93.
AACR2 requires changes in the cataloging of these two types of materials. While its use for exhibition catalogs is acceptable, it is not adequate for auction catalogs.

341. Prichard, R. J. "Access Points for Serials." *Library Review* 30 (1981): 74–76.
Urges the adoption of Eva Verona's definition of corporate authorship in cataloging serials.

342. Reuland, Beth. "Successive Entry: Another Look." *Serials Review* 9 (Fall 1983): 92–93.
Discusses the benefits of the current method of choosing serial entry.

343. Robertson, Howard W. "Andrew Osborn and Serials Cataloging." *Serials Librarian* 6 (Winter 1981/Spring 1982): 133–38.
Evaluates Osborn's treatment of serials cataloging in the 1973 edition of *Serial Publications*.

344. Romero, Nancy. "AACR2 and Serial Cataloging: Is There Any Need for Alarm?" *Cataloging and Classification Quarterly* 3 (Winter 1982/Spring 1983): 65–71.
A positive assessment of the changes in serials cataloging caused by the implementation of AACR2.

345. Romero, Nancy. "Copy Cataloging of Serials." In *Projects and Procedures for Serials Administration*, edited by Diane Stine, 109–14. Ann Arbor: Pierian Press, 1985.
Describes University of Illinois-Urbana/Champaign Library's procedure for cataloging serials for which OCLC copy is found.

346. Roughton, Karen, and Duke, John K. "Analytical Access: Old Problems, New Frontiers. In *Projects and Procedures for Serials Administration*, edited by Diane Stine, 181–97. Ann Arbor: Pierian Press, 1985.
Presents the philosophy of and procedures for cataloging serial analytics in the Serials Department at Iowa State University Library.

347. Sadowski, Frank E., Jr. "Serials Cataloging Developments, 1975–1985: A Personal View of Some Highlights." *Serials Librarian* 10 (Fall 1985/Winter 1985–86): 133–40.

Emphasizes change and discusses uniform titles, microform problems, and CONSER.

348. Smith, Sharon, Watkins, Robert, and Richardson, Shirley. "Retrospective Conversion of Serials at the University of Houston: Midterm Report." *Serials Librarian* 9 (Spring 1985): 63–68.
Describes the project to consolidate files and have all current serials titles cataloged in machine-readable form. Suggestions for planning a conversion project.

349. Soper, Mary Ellen. "Cataloguing in a Time of Change." In *Management of Serials Automation,* edited by Peter Gellatly, 107–17. New York: Haworth Press, 1982.
Cataloging, especially of serials, in the context of a new code and increasing automation.

350. Stine, Diane. "The Effect of AACR2 and Serials Cataloging on Medium-Sized Research Libraries." *Cataloging and Classification Quarterly* 3 (Winter 1982/Spring 1983): 73–76.
AACR2's effect was neither as great nor as negative as expected. Staff training and authority work slowed production, but the end result was better access to library serials for the patron.

351. Unsworth, Michael E. "Treating IEEE Conference Publications as Serials." *Library Resources and Technical Services* 27 (1983): 221–24.
Because of the cooperation of IEEE, the practical reasons for serial cataloging of its conference publications outweigh the theoretical reasons for monographic cataloging.

352. Williams, James W. "Pre-1950 Serials in OCLC: A Second Look at Database Records and a Comparison with *Union List of Serials* and *National Union Catalog, Pre-1956 Imprints*." *Serials Librarian* 8 (Summer 1984): 69–77.
OCLC appears to be a developing source for information about pre-1950 serials, with ULS and NUC Pre-1956 as valuable backups.

353. Williams, James W., and Romero, Nancy. "A Comparison of the OCLC Database and *New Serial Titles* as an Information Resource for Serials." *Library Resources and Technical Services* 27 (1983): 188–98.
A sample of 200 titles from each source gave 217 journals included in both. A comparison of data indicated that OCLC is the better source of information for current materials, NST for older.

V. PRESERVATION AND BINDING

354.   Barker, N. "Economics of Conservation." In *Financing Serials from the Producer to the User,* edited by David P. Woodworth, 81–88. Oxford, Eng.: Blackwell's for the UK Serials Group, n.d.
The head of conservation at the British Library advises on storage, environment, binding, and photoreproduction.

355.   Dean, John F. "Serials Binding: Options and Problems." In *Serials '84: Proceedings of the UK Serials Group Conference,* edited by Brian Cox, 101–09. Stratford-upon-Avon: UK Serials Group, 1985.
Reviews binding methods and discusses Johns Hopkins University Library's quarter buckram binding for low-use periodicals.

356.   Farrington, Jean Walter. "The Use of Microforms in Libraries: Concerns of the Last Ten Years." *Serials Librarian* 10 (Fall 1985/Winter 1985–86): 195–99.
Despite the emergence of the new disc technologies, microforms will continue to be the appropriate medium for retention of some types of library materials. Reviews advances in bibliographic control of microforms and in quality of readers and printers.

357.   Feinman, Valerie Jackson. "Store It, But Don't Ignore It." *Serials Librarian* 10 (Fall 1985/Winter 1985–86): 201–10.
Storage is necessary in libraries today, but this means of retention should be made easily accessible and publicized. Adelphi University Library's storage annex is given as an example.

358.   Gleaves, Edwin S., and Carterette, Robert T. "Microform Serials Acquisition: A Suggested Planning Model." *Journal of Academic Librarianship* 8 (1982): 292–95.
Proposes retention of journals in microform as a means of combatting soaring costs of binding, storage, and replacement.

359.   Green, Paul Robert. "The Binding of Periodicals: An Overview." *Serials Librarian* 9 (Winter 1984): 25–33.
In response to funding cuts in budgets of British libraries, Green presents an assessment of the stages of the binding procedure and emphasizes the decisions to be made.

360. Gyeszly, Suzanne, and Donahue, Mary Kaye. "Circulating Serials at Texas A. & M.: A Preservation and Collection Development Project." *Serials Review* 9 (Winter 1983): 91–96.
The circulating nonperiodical serials were first identified and then evaluated for appropriateness of preservation treatment, including a number of types of commercial and in-house binding.

361. Haigh, P. A. "Binding at Boston Spa." *Interlending Review* 7 (1979): 139–40.
Covers BLLD's binding policy and specific concerns.

362. Hoskins, Mildred B., and Reid, Marion T. "Online Communication with Binders: The Hertzberg Connection." *Serials Librarian* 9 (Summer 1985): 83–87.
Description and evaluation of a pilot project undertaken at Louisiana State University Library.

363. Kim, David U. "Computer-Assisted Binding Preparation at a University Library." *Serials Librarian* 9 (Winter 1984): 35–43.
Introduces the system developed and used successfully at Sam Houston State University Library.

364. Kuney, J. H. "The Role of Microforms in Journal Publication." *Journal of Chemical Documentation* 12 (May 1972): 78–80.
Promotes the American Chemical Society's microfilm supplements to printed "communications" journals.

365. Marx, Patricia C., and Marx, John N. "Automating the Production of Bindery Slips." *Technicalities* 5 (March 1985): 15–16.
Texas Tech University uses microcomputers to produce bindery slips and record printouts. The change from manual production has increased employee morale and permitted reduction in staff handling this procedure.

366. Mottice, Robert. "Quality Standards for Microfilmed Serials." *International Journal of Micrographics & Video Technology* 2 (1983): 203–05.
Description of University Microfilms International's procedures to ensure quality control in filming serials commercially.

367. Okerson, Ann. "Microform Conversion—A Case Study." *Microform Review* 14 (1985): 157–63.
Simon Fraser University Library established an operating policy and procedures in its conversion of serials to microform.

368. Pourciau, Lester J., Jr. "Development and Management of Microform Serial Collections." In *Serials Collection Development,* edited by Sul H. Lee, 19–26. Ann Arbor: Pierian Press, 1981.

Concentrates on the development of a retrospective serials collection in microform at Memphis State University Library.

369. Rebsamen, Werner. "Performance Comparison of Oversewn, Double Fanned and Cleat-Laced Bindings." *Library Scene* 11 (July/August 1982): 18–22.

The results of the comparison contribute toward the construction of an "Optimum Binding Index."

370. Starr, Mary Jane. "Canadian Newspapers: Collection, Preservation and Access." *Technical Services Quarterly* 1 (Spring 1984): 83–91.

Overview, based on nationwide surveys, of the present situation; discusses options for a decentralized program of newspaper conservation.

371. Tiwari, P. C. "Binding of Periodicals Publications." *Herald of Library Science* 21 (1982): 260–61.

A "technical note," giving procedures to follow in preparing volumes for binding.

372. Turner, Stephen J., and O'Brien, Gregory. "A Fuzzy Set Theory Approach to Periodical Binding Decisions." *Journal of the American Society for Information Science* 34 (1984): 228–34.

The results of the authors' study are mixed, and they admit that their method may be more labor intensive than a normal decision process.

373. Walker, Dorothy. "Accessioning and Storage of Serials in Microform in Libraries." *International Journal of Micrographics & Video Technology* 3 (1984): 9–14.

Results of a survey assist Britain's India Office Library in making decisions regarding a feasible and cost-effective method of treating microform serials. The procedure is applicable to other library situations.

374. Watson, Phillip. "Microforms in Libraries: A Viable Alternative?" In *Profiling a Periodicals Collection,* edited by Phillip Watson, 122–28. Melbourne, Aust.: Footscray Institute of Technology, 1979.

Pro-microforms article reviews the various uses of this format in the library and predicts better service in the future because of materials available by this means.

VI. PUBLIC SERVICE

375. Adalian, Paul T., Jr., Rockman, Ilene F., and Rodie, Ernest. "Student Success in Using Microfiche to Find Periodicals." *College and Research Libraries* 46 (1985): 48–54.
Interviews with students at Cal-Poly, San Luis Obispo showed that over 80 percent were able to locate journals using a COM catalog.

376. Adams, Marjorie E. "On-Line Public Access to Serial Holdings: Ohio State University." In *Serials and Microforms: Patron-Oriented Management,* edited by Nancy Jean Melin, 63–77. Westport, Conn.: Meckler Publishing, 1983.
Patrons have access to serial bibliographic records and volume-specific holdings records online through LCS, the Library Control System.

377. Alldredge, Noreen S. "The Non-Use of Periodicals: A Study." *Serials Librarian* 7 (Summer 1983): 61–64.
At Texas A & M University Library, journals identified as not used during a 2-year study were analyzed for possible cancellation, faculty review, or further study.

378. Baron, Catherine. "Open Versus Closed Periodicals Stacks in a Research Library: How to Study the Question." *North Carolina Libraries* 40 (1982): 134–40.
Presents a methodology for determining whether closing journal stacks would be more economical than replacement costs of lost and mutilated periodicals.

379. Benedict, Betty Z. "Changing Patterns of Access to Periodical Literature." *Serials Librarian* 6 (Winter 1981/Spring 1982): 27–38.
Covers access to materials outside one's library. Describes OCLC, a national periodicals center, and online bibliographic searching.

380. Bourke, D. O'D. "Abstracting and Indexing Services—A Practical Example." In *Information Chain,* edited by John A. Urquhart, 77–87. Stratford-upon-Avon: UK Serials Group, 1983.
An account of the editorial production of *Horticultural Abstracts.*

381. Boyle, F. T. "Are Serials and Serial Librarians Meeting User Needs? The Industrial User's View." In *Information Chain,* edited by John A. Urquhart, 138–59. Stratford-upon-Avon: UK Serials Group, 1983.

Analysis of a survey of chemists and bioscientists shows: 1) a high use of online databases as the preferred method for retrieval of current reporting in their specialties, and 2) satisfaction with the number and quality of journals available in their field.

382. Boyle, L. L. "Are Serials and Serial Librarians Meeting User Needs? The Academic User's View." In *Information Chain,* edited by John A. Urquhart, 125–33. Stratford-upon-Avon: UK Serials Group, 1983.

Most of the academic user's problems and criticisms relate to access. Boyle uses the British Library (Reference Division) for most examples.

383. Brahmi, Frances A. "Reference Use of *Science Citation Index.*" *Medical Reference Services Quarterly* 4 (Spring 1985): 31–38.

The author documents her thesis that *SCI*'s "value is limited only by one's imagination."

384. Brett, H. "Copyright and Serials: Document Supply—A Legal View." In *Serials '83: Proceedings of the UK Serials Group Conference,* edited by Rodney M. Burton, 54–59. Stratford-upon-Avon: UK Serials Group, 1984.

Discusses UK copyright law, with special attention to applications affecting libraries.

385. Cameron, James. "Market Research and User Needs in Journal Publishing." In *Financing Serials from the Producer to the User,* edited by David P. Woodworth, 10–16. Oxford, Eng.: Blackwell's for the UK Serials Group, n.d.

The success of a new scientific journal may depend upon the publisher's ability to gain reader support and participation during the planning process.

386. Carey, Kevin. "Problems and Patterns of Periodical Literature Searching at an Urban University Research Library." *RQ* 23 (1983): 211–18.

Analysis of user patterns in consulting periodical and newspaper indexes can lead to more successful use of these resources.

387. Cornog, Martha. "Out of the Shoebox and Into the Computer: Serials Indexing 1975–1985." *Serials Librarian* 10 (Fall 1985/ Winter 1985–86): 161–68.

Automation and the proliferation of journals have caused changes in the production, scope, and complexity of indexes, as well as a growth in number of users of indexes.

388.   Diodato, Virgil P. "Author and Source Indexing and Abstracting of Journal Articles." *Indexer* 14 (1984): 91–94.
Discusses author preparation of abstracts and index terms and the ease with which this desirable practice can be done electronically.

389.   Duke, John K. "AACR2 Serial Records and the User." *Cataloging and Classification Quarterly* 3 (Winter 1982/Spring 1983): 111–17.
While AACR2 has brought much that is good to cataloging and the catalog, much unnecessary repetition clutters the serial bibliographic records. More access points exist for the user, but form of heading can be confusing. Finally, use of records cataloged according to the new code along with older records creates problems for users.

390.   Florance, Valerie. "Access to U.S. Government Periodicals in Health Sciences Libraries: An Overview." *Serials Librarian* 10 (Fall 1985/Winter 1985-86): 215–23.
The *Monthly Catalog,* rather than periodical indexes, provides best access to government documents for health sciences libraries. However, access to these materials is still a problem.

391.   Gannett, E. K. "An Experiment in Selective Dissemination of Journal Articles." *Scholarly Publishing* 15 (1983): 73–81.
Discussion and evaluation of the failure of the *Annals of the IEEE,* an experimental SDI system in the mid-1970s.

392.   Golden, Susan U., and Golden, Gary A. "Access to Periodicals: Search Key versus Keyword." *Information Technology and Libraries* 2 (1983): 26–32.
A study shows that keyword is not more effective than search key; both means of access would be improved by the ability to limit search by type of material and to specify that the title is one word.

393.   Golden, Susan. "Online Serials Circulation in a Library Network." *Wilson Library Bulletin* 56 (1982): 511–15.
Describes and evaluates the Library Computer System (LCS) in use in the State of Illinois.

394.   Goodemote, Rita L. "A Computer-Based Routing System for Serials." *Science and Technology Libraries* 4 (Fall 1983): 21–29.
Automation solves the problems of changes in routing lists and a logical flow of material, in a pharmaceutical library.

395. Gordon, Martin. "Article Access—Too Easy?" *Serials Librarian* 10 (Fall 1985/Winter 1985–86): 169–71.
Gordon worries about the detrimental effects on undergraduates of depending on online searches to collect citations for their class papers.

396. Hallman, Clark N., and McGruer, Jean. "Local Periodical Indexes Provide Access to Regional Publications." *Reference Services Review* 13 (Summer 1985): 35–40.
Advocates the compilation of indexes to the contents of local periodicals and uses South Dakota State University Library's experience as a case study.

397. Johnson, E. Diane. "OCTANET: Interlibrary Loan of Journal Articles in the Health Sciences." *Show-Me Libraries* 35 (April 1984): 23–26.
Describes this regional automated ILL system and explains its advantages over other such systems.

398. Keenan, Stella. "The Changing Role of Secondary Information Services." In *The Future of Serials,* edited by Nancy Fjallbrant, 213–18. Goeteborg, Sweden: International Association of Technological University Libraries, 1984.
With technological developments such services are becoming problem oriented instead of discipline oriented. Focuses on Arthur D. Little report regarding the development of these services.

399. Keenan, Stella. "The Impact of On-Line Services on Traditional Abstracting and Indexing Services." In *Serials '84: Proceedings of the UK Serials Group Conference,* edited by Brian Cox, 34–40. Stratford-upon-Avon: UK Serials Group, 1985.
Automation has changed these secondary serials into components of the "online information supermarket."

400. Kleinmuntz, Dalia S. "TACOS: TAble of COntents Service in the Hospital Library." *Medical Reference Services Quarterly* 4 (Fall 1985): 17–26.
Describes and evaluates this service offered to physicians, faculty members, and administrators. The system is simple, inexpensive, and effective.

401. Lea, Peter W. "Electronic Document Delivery: Current European Developments." *Technical Services Quarterly* 1 (Fall/Winter 1983): 233–39.
Describes and evaluates ADONIS, HERMES, and ARTEMIS.

402. Line, Maurice B. "Document Delivery, Now and in the Future." *ASLIB Proceedings* 35 (1983): 167–76.

Concentrates on the future and speculates about method of delivery, broker, and cost.

403. Line, Maurice B. "The National Supply of Serials—Centralization versus Decentralization." *Serials Review* 8 (Spring 1982): 63–65.

Line advocates a centralized system of interlibrary lending/photocopy of serials, such as the British Library Lending Division, as a means of effecting the rapid supply of materials outside one's library as economically as possible.

404. Lurie, Howard R. "The Ownership of Copyright in Journal Articles." *Technical Services Quarterly* 1 (Spring 1984): 31–36.

Discusses the topic in light of provisions of the Copyright Act of 1976.

405. McBride, Ruth B. "Accessibility of Serials." *Serials Librarian* 10 (Fall 1985/Winter 1985–86): 149–60.

Librarians often process serials for best accessibility to themselves, forgetting the needs of the patron and even adding to the user's difficulty in locating the needed article. The University of Illinois Urbana-Champaign has changed procedures to ease the patron's search. This plan is described.

406. Payne, June. "Serials Routing, Lending, and SDI in Australian Academic Libraries." *Australasian College Libraries* 3 (1985): 21–26.

The results of a survey give these libraries' practices in promoting access to their serials. There are differences among the various types of libraries.

407. Pichuraman, S., and Gopalakrishnan, S. "Increasing the Utilisation of Periodicals in College Libraries: A Case Study." *Annals of Library Science and Documentation* 30 (1983): 1–5.

Introduces the "Quick Glance Service," one-day routing of new journals to faculty members, in use at Madras Institute of Technology.

408. Pinzelik, Barbara P. "The Periodical, the Patron, and AACR2." *Cataloging and Classification Quarterly* 3 (Winter 1982/Spring 1983): 41–45.

AACR2 provides an opportunity for the library to offer a more patron-oriented catalog than before. It is up to the library to ensure that this happens.

409.   Pinzelik, Barbara P. "The Serials Maze: Providing Public Service for a Large Serials Collection." *Journal of Academic Librarianship* 8 (1982): 89–94.

Charts obstacles to a library patron's locating desired journals and analyzes factors contributing to the failure to locate material.

410.   Pitkin, Gary. "Automated Serials Systems: Putting the Patron First." In *Serials and Microforms: Patron-Oriented Management*, edited by Nancy Jean Melin, 27–43. Westport, Conn.: Meckler Publishing, 1983.

Appalachian State University Library successfully introduced its patrons to Faxon's LINX, through a "display only" terminal.

411.   Poyer, Robert K. "Journal Article Overlap Among Index Medicus, Science Citation Index, Biological Abstracts, and Chemical Abstracts." *Bulletin of the Medical Library Association* 72 (1984): 353–57.

Poyer found that 92% of the articles in his survey were indexed in at least two services. He discusses the implications of the overlap.

412.   Regan, Lee, and Olivetti, L. James. "Access to Periodical Indexes and Abstracts in Academic Libraries: A Survey." *Serials Librarian* 6 (Winter 1981/Spring 1982): 39–45.

Documents housing of and access to printed indexes and abstract journals in medium-sized academic libraries.

413.   Reynolds, Thomas H. "Indexing of Legal Journal Literature and the History and Development of the *Index to Foreign Legal Periodicals*." *Law Librarian* 15 (1984): 38–46.

Describes planning for and compilation of the index. Lists other sources for citations to legal periodical literature.

414.   Rowley, Jennifer E. "A Future for Printed Indexes?" *ASLIB Proceedings* 35 (1983): 234–38.

There is a future for printed indexes, but it will be restricted by the availability of machine readable indexes, and the quality of indexing may suffer.

415.   *Serials and Microforms: Patron-Oriented Management. Proceedings of the Second Annual Serials Conference and Eighth Annual Microforms Conference*, edited by Nancy Jean Melin. Westport, Conn.: Meckler Publishing, 1983.

Conference papers are listed separately in the Annotated Bibliography.

416. Shapiro, Beth J. "Serials Resource Sharing and Public Services." *Serials Review* 11 (Summer 1985): 51–56.
Reviews and critiques current resource sharing projects and looks toward future ventures in the area of document delivery.

417. Simpson, Donald B. "The Expanded Journals Access Service at the Center for Research Libraries: Its Impact on North American Libraries." In *Serials Collection Development,* edited by Sul H. Lee, 61–77. Ann Arbor: Pierian Press, 1981.
Gives the history, philosophy, and future direction of CRL, concentrating on the JAS program.

418. Somerfield, G. A. "Copyright and Serials: Document Supply— The ADONIS Project." In *Serials '83: Proceedings of the UK Serials Group Conference,* edited by Rodney M. Burton, 60–72. Stratford-upon-Avon: UK Serials Group, 1984.
A representative of Elsevier Science Publishers, speaking before the project was abandoned, discusses the objectives of ADONIS.

419. Stankus, Tony. "The Serials Librarian As a Shaper of Scholars and Scholarship." *Drexel Library Quarterly* 21 (Winter 1985): 112–19.
The serials librarian can ease the student's introduction to serials by promoting journals' significance to scholarship, often relating specific titles to persons or concerns in the local community.

420. Toney, Stephen. "Telefacsimile Experiment at the Smithsonian Institution Libraries." *Serials Librarian* 7 (Winter 1982): 17–26.
As an alternate means of delivery for rush journal articles, this experiment succeeded and will be developed.

421. Vaughn, Susan. "Making it With the Public." In *Serials and Microforms: Patron-Oriented Management,* edited by Nancy Jean Melin, 1–8. Westport, Conn.: Meckler Publishing, 1983.
Public service librarians, who interpret serials records, need serials librarians to remember the user of the materials they process.

422. Walker, Dorothy. "Recent Research in Serials: Accessioning, Storing and Recording Serials in Microform." In *Serials '84: Proceedings of the UK Serials Group Conference,* edited by Brian Cox, 128–34. Stratford-upon-Avon: UK Serials Group, 1985.
Results of a survey documented that the India Office Library's decision

to treat microform serials in the identical manner as hard copy formats
was a sound one.

423.   Watson, William. "A Periodicals Access Survey in a University
       Library." *College and Research Libraries* 45 (1984): 496–501.
University of British Columbia Library staff conducted surveys to determine whether the policy of circulating periodicals was responsible for patrons' complaints that journals were not available. A high percentage was
located on the shelves, with binding more responsible for the problem
than circulation.

424.   Wesley, Threasa L., and Werrell, Emily. "Making the Most of
       a Limited Opportunity: Instruction for Periodical Assignments."
       Research Strategies 3 (1985): 108–15.
Ways to enhance periodical use assignments by giving meaning and direction to undergraduate projects.

425.   Woo, Linda. "University of Washington 'Online' Serials Cata-
       log." In *Projects and Procedures for Serials Administration,* ed-
       ited by Diane Stine, 87–98. Ann Arbor: Pierian Press, 1985.
Describes the production and use of a COM catalog of serials in libraries
on the University of Washington campus. The project uses the WLN database and provides multiple access points.

426.   Wood, David N. "Reprography and Copyright with Particular
       Reference to Inter-Library Lending Activities—A View from the
       BLLD." *ASLIB Proceedings* 35 (1983): 457–67.
Defends library borrowing and copying practices and urges cooperation
between publishers and librarians to resolve the copyright dilemma.

VII. RESOURCE SHARING AND UNION LISTS OF SERIALS

427.   Anand, A. K., and Malhan, I. V. "Some Investigations on Re-
       source Sharing on Chemistry Journals for the University Libraries
       of Punjab, Haryana, Himachal Pradesh and Chandigarh." *Annals
       of Library Science and Documentation* 29 (1982): 76–89.
Cites duplication among the libraries and urges sharing subscriptions of
all except ten core journals.

428.   Barnholdt, B. "Scandiaplan Union Catalogue of Conference Pro-
       ceedings Accessioned in the Scandinavian Techn. Univ. Libr."

In *Current Trends in Serials Automation,* edited by Ahmed H. Helal and Joachim W. Weiss, 69–83. Essen: Gesamthochschul-bibliothek Essen, 1981.
The catalog is a multiple-access, multiple-format record and is available online throughout Europe.

429. Bloss, Marjorie E. "And in Hindsight . . . The Past Ten Years of Union Listing." *Serials Librarian* 10 (Fall 1985/Winter 1985–86): 141–48.
The impact of the economy, technology, and library standards on union lists of serials. The changes characteristic of the last decade will continue.

430. Bloss, Marjorie E. "The Dregs in the Union List Bottle: Titles Not in the Database." *Serials Review* 10 (Summer 1984): 49–53.
The unique titles held by libraries contributing to the Rochester (N.Y.) Regional Research Library Council's Union List of Serials were cataloged centrally from surrogates and entered into the OCLC database.

431. Bloss, Marjorie E. "The Impact of AACR2 on Union Lists of Serials." *Cataloging and Classification Quarterly* 3 (Winter 1982/ Spring 1983): 97–109.
AACR2, created for automated cataloging, works well enough for online union lists; there may be access problems for card, book, and COM union lists. The concept of title entry, with LC rule interpretations, has created separate rules for entry of serials.

432. Bloss, Marjorie E. "In Order to Form a More Perfect Union . . . List of Serials." In *Management of Serials Automation,* edited by Peter Gellatly, 191–97. New York: Haworth Press, 1982.
Describes the history, the work, and the future of the ALA/RTSD Serials Section's Ad Hoc Committee on Union Lists of Serials.

433. Bloss, Marjorie E. "In Order to Form a More Perfect Union . . . List of Serials: A Report of the Workshop." *Serials Review* 8 (Spring 1982): 67–68.
Includes summaries of talks related to union listing developments and standards, plus four reports on regional union listing projects.

434. Bloss, Marjorie E. "Quality Control: Centralized and Decentralized Union Lists." *Serials Review* 8 (Fall 1982): 89–95.
Reviews the history of the Rochester (N.Y.) Regional Research Library Council's Union List of Serials and advocates centralized operation of union lists to ensure adherence to standards, consistency in record selection, and adequate time given to the project.

435. Bloss, Marjorie E. "The Serials Pastiche: Union Lists of Serials."
      Drexel Library Quarterly 21 (Winter 1985): 101–11.
A general article concentrating on union list planning and politics, quality
control, and maintenance.

436. Bloss, Marjorie E. "Uniformity in Union Lists of Serials: Meas-
      uring Up to Standards." In *Library Serials Standards: Devel-
      opment, Implementation, Impact,* edited by Nancy Jean Melin,
      61–70. Westport, Conn.: Meckler Publishing, 1984.
Union list editors need guidance in the areas of bibliographic data and
holdings statements, if their work is to have meaning. Bloss reviews current
work toward these ends.

437. Bloss, Marjorie E. "Union Lists of Serials' Futures: Buy? Sell?
      or Keep What You've Got?" *Technical Services Quarterly* 1 (Fall/
      Winter 1983): 159–70.
Examines variables influencing the compilation of a union list of serials,
in light of anticipated technological changes.

438. Boadi, B. Y. "International Developments in Resource Sharing:
      West Africa." In *Resource Sharing—Its Impact on Serials,* edited
      by Margaret E. Graham and Brian Cox, 94–106. Stratford-upon-
      Avon: UK Serials Group, 1982.
Discusses existing cooperative programs and resources, plus the need for
coordination at the national level for development of further means of
resource sharing.

439. Bowen, Johanna E. "The Management of Quality Control in a
      Decentralized Union Listing Project." *Serials Review* 8 (Fall
      1982): 87–88.
Careful planning, training, documentation, and communication ensured
that quality standards would be met in the South Central Research Library
Council (N.Y.) decentralized union list of serials.

440. Carter, Ruth C., and Bruntjen, Scott. "The Pennsylvania Union
      List of Serials: Continuing Development." *Serials Librarian* 6
      (Winter 1981/Spring 1982): 47–55.
Early accomplishments of the state-funded union list, and plans for continued development and maintenance.

441. Carter, Ruth C., and Bruntjen, Scott. "The Pennsylvania Union
      List of Serials: From Development to Maintenance." *Serials Li-
      brarian* 8 (Summer 1984): 55–67.

In the fourth year of its existence PaULS faces long-term maintenance questions.

442.   Clarke, A.S.M. "Failed Serial Requests: Report of a Survey to Identify Weaknesses in Serial Provision." *Interlending Review* 7 (1979): 137–39.
The purpose of the study was to identify gaps to be filled at BLLD and libraries to be included in the British Library union catalog.

443.   Clews, John. "Overlap of Major Lists of Serials: A Survey of Lists Used by the British Library Lending Division." *Interlending Review* 9 (1981): 26–29.
The survey's objective was to make best use of serial location lists. Results showed a surprisingly large number of unique titles in each list.

444.   Conochie, Jean A. "Has Serials Union Listing Come of Age? A Review of Four Recent Works on Union Listing." *Serials Librarian* 9 (Summer 1985): 67–72.
The four sets of guidelines stress the need for careful planning, adequate funding, and a clearly-defined scope.

445.   Drubba, Helmut. "The University Library Hannover and Technische Informationsbibliothek as a Library of Last Resort—Or as a Library of First Resort: Some Aspects of the Operation of the Largest Technical Library in the Federal Republic of Germany." In *The Future of Serials,* edited by Nancy Fjallbrant, 13–25. Goteborg, Sweden: International Association of Technological University Libraries, 1984.
This central library may be used as a last resort for interlibrary loan or be accessed directly by users having prepaid request forms. The evolution of the electronic transmission of data is being watched.

446.   Dugall, B. "Development, Use, and Future of the Periodicals Union Catalogue of Hesse." In *Current Trends in Serials Automation,* edited by Ahmed H. Helal and Joachim W. Weiss, 95–107. Essen: Gesamthochschulbibliothek Essen, 1981.
Discusses one of West Germany's regional union catalogs, its operation and its plans for the future.

447.   Ellsworth, Dianne J., and Newman, Edward. "The California Union List of Periodicals." In *Management of Serials Automation,* edited by Peter Gellatly, 199–217. New York: Haworth Press, 1982.
Description of this regional union list, with its history and its future plans.

448. Fagerli, H. M. "Norwegian Union Catalogue Within the NOSP Project." In *Current Trends in Serials Automation,* edited by Ahmed H. Helal and Joachim W. Weiss, 89–94. Essen: Gesamthochschulbibliothek Essen, 1981, 89–94.
Data from an offline, non-MARC union catalog is incorporated into an online system in Norway.

449. Fayad, Susan, and Wecker, Charlene D. "The OCLC Union List Product: Michigan's Recommendations on Design Options." *Serials Review* 10 (Winter 1984): 69–87.
Primarily descriptive, although problems are mentioned. Well illustrated.

450. Gadzikowski, Claire. "Octanet/PHILSOM: Using a Serials Control System for Interlibrary Loan." *Technical Services Quarterly* 1 (Spring 1984): 45–53.
Development and implementation of the Midcontinental Regional Medical Library Program's online interlibrary loan network, with attention to its link with PHILSOM.

451. Glasby, Dorothy J. "International Developments in Resource Sharing: The United States." In *Resource Sharing—Its Impact on Serials,* edited by Margaret E. Graham and Brian Cox, 77–85. Stratford-upon-Avon: UK Serials Group, 1984.
Discusses CONSER, NSDP, the cooperative name authority project, union listing, and serials standards.

452. Harris, K. G. E. "Aspects of Resource Sharing: Local Co-Operation in Serials." In *Resource Sharing—Its Impact on Serials,* edited by Margaret E. Graham and Brian Cox, 39–44. Stratford-upon-Avon: UK Serials Group, 1984.
Views local serials resource sharing in the UK in the context of the services of the British Library Lending Division, and recommends local enhancements to the program.

453. Hartman, Anne-Marie. "Quality Control in a Decentralized Union List Using OCLC." *Serials Review* 8 (Fall 1982): 88–89.
Describes training and follow-up procedures used by libraries of the City University of New York in creating their union list of serials.

454. Helal, Ahmed H. "International Developments in Resource Sharing: West Germany." In *Resource Sharing—Its Impact on Serials,* edited by Margaret E. Graham and Brian Cox, 86–93. Stratford-upon-Avon: UK Serials Group, 1984.

Covers cooperative collection development, regional union catalogs, and planning for a national library network in West Germany.

455.   Hirst, Frank C. "Aspects of Resource Sharing: Government Departments." In *Resource Sharing—Its Impact on Serials,* edited by Margaret E. Graham and Brian Cox, 26–33. Stratford-upon-Avon: UK Serials Group, 1984.
UK government libraries share their resources actively at the national and international levels, by means of cooperative acquisition, indexing, and document delivery.

456.   Hooks, James D. "Union Listing—A Tool for Reference Service." *West Virginia Libraries* 38 (Fall 1985): 8–14.
The OCLC-based Pennsylvania Union List of Serials is a valuable reference/interlibrary loan tool at the Indiana University of Pennsylvania.

457.   Jeffreys, A. E. "Current Trends in Serials Automation in British Academic Libraries." In *Current Trends in Serials Automation,* edited by Margaret E. Graham and Brian Cox, 25–40. Essen: Gesamthochschulbibliothek Essen, 1981.
Concentrates on automated union listing activities.

458.   Landwehrmeyer, Richard. "Periodicals Collections in Academic Libraries of the Federal Republic of Germany: Development and Managerial Aspects." In *The Future of Serials,* edited by Nancy Fjallbrant, 55–68. Goteborg, Sweden: International Association of Technological University Libraries, 1984.
Postwar economic prosperity fostered the growth of German library collections, but the decline of prosperity led to cancellation of periodicals and dependence on decentralized special collections.

459.   McKinley, Margaret M. "A Cooperative Serials Data Conversion Project in California." In *Management of Serials Automation,* edited by Peter Gellatly, 95–106. New York: Haworth Press, 1982.
An account of this project conducted among UCLA, Berkeley, and Stanford, to assist other libraries engaging in similar efforts.

460.   Moules, Mary L. "Producing a Local Union List of Serials with Word Processing Equipment." *Serials Librarian* 7 (Winter 1982): 27–34.
For the Illinois Valley Library System, the best union list was one that did not meet all national standards.

461. O'Malley, Terrence J. "Union Listing via OCLC's Serials Control Subsystem." *Special Libraries* 75 (1984): 131–50.

An OCLC union listing user describes the service and examines its advantages and shortcomings. Extensive illustrations.

462. Palmer, Doris. "Aspects of Resource Sharing: The Old Boy Network." In *Resource Sharing—Its Impact on Serials,* edited by Margaret E. Graham and Brian Cox, 34–38. Stratford-upon-Avon: UK Serials Group, 1984.

Gives several specific ways for special libraries to economize by sharing journals of marginal importance to their collections.

463. Peacock, P. G. "The Need for Resource Sharing in the 1980's." In *Resource Sharing—Its Impact on Serials,* edited by Margaret E. Graham and Brian Cox, 1–11. Stratford-upon-Avon: UK Serials Group, 1984.

Factors within and outside research libraries influence the willingness to share resources and the success of such projects.

464. Rast, Elaine K. "Serials in Illinois Libraries On-Line (SILO)." *Illinois Libraries* 65 (1983): 348–50.

Describes new online union list of serials, managed through OCLC.

465. Rast, Elaine, and Tieberg-Bailie, John. "SILO: Serials of Illinois Libraries Online—Union List Agency Management." *Serials Review* 9 (Summer 1983): 73–76.

Uses the experience of creating this prototype union list to advise others planning union listing projects.

466. *Resource Sharing—Its Impact on Serials; Proceedings of the UK Serials Group Conference held at University of Manchester, 30 March—2 April 1981.* Edited by Margaret E. Graham and Brian Cox. Stratford-upon-Avon: UK Serials Group, 1982. (Serials Monograph No. 4)

Articles in this collection are listed separately in the Annotated Bibliography.

467. Rodgers, Linda. "The University of London's Union List of Serials." In *Automation and Serials,* edited by Margaret E. Graham, 59–74. Stratford-upon-Avon: UK Serials Group, 1981.

A discussion of the planning, implementation and maintenance of this online union list, including justification for its adherence to international standards.

468. Schaffner, Ann C. "Implementation of the Faxon Union List System by the Boston Library Consortium." *Serials Librarian* 9 (Spring 1985): 45–62.
Serving as a test site for the Faxon system benefits the consortium, as well as creating feedback for the use of the vendor.

469. Shaw, Debora. "A Review of Developments Leading to On-Line Union Listing of Serials." In *Management of Serials Automation,* edited by Peter Gellatly, 185–90. New York: Haworth Press, 1982.
Describes developments in union listing, in a historical context. Emphasizes importance of standards.

470. Thomas, Suzanne L. "OCLC Union Lists On-Line, Using the Local Data Record." *West Virginia Libraries* 37 (Fall 1984): 11–13.
Describes the construction of union list data through OCLC. Union list users can maintain the currency of their lists by ordering offline products from OCLC.

471. Tieberg-Bailie, John, and Rast, Elaine. "Union Listing on the OCLC Serials Control Subsystem." In *Projects and Procedures for Serials Administration,* edited by Diane Stine, 287–322. Ann Arbor: Pierian Press, 1985.
Describes and evaluates this means of union listing, covering record selection and creation, holdings, and management considerations.

472. Tracy, Joan I. "The Spokane Area Combined List of Periodicals: History of a Regional Resource." *Serials Review* 11 (Summer 1985): 43–46.
The history of this regional union list, maintained on computer at Eastern Washington University.

473. Whiffen, Jean. "Union Catalogues of Serials: Guidelines for Creation and Maintenance, with Recommended Standards for Bibliographic and Holdings Control." *Serials Librarian* 8 (Fall 1983): 1–138.
The text of the first draft of a proposed new international standard. A report to IFLA.

474. Woodward, Hazel M., and Vickery, Barbara. "EMALIST: East Midlands Academic Libraries Union List of Serials: An Interim Report." *United Kingdom Serials Group Newsletter* 5 (December 1983): 3–7.

Planning for and development of a union list of the serials of Leicester, Loughborough, and Nottingham university libraries. Points out compromises made in the interest of standardization.

475. Zandvliet, Hans. "A National Serials Collection in the Netherlands." In *The Future of Serials,* edited by Nancy Fjallbrant, 99–108. Goteborg, Sweden: International Association of Technological University Libraries, 1984.

Designated libraries safeguard the quality and diversity of Dutch serials holdings by taking responsibility for acquiring specific titles.

VIII. AUTOMATION

476. Allcock, David. "The Development of LIDAS (Library Information on the Distribution of All Serials)." *UK Serials Group Newsletter* No. 7 (December 1981): 7–10.

Discusses the need for and creation of an online serials control system for a British special library subscribing to a large number of "difficult" serials (e.g., looseleaf services, government publications).

477. Allison, Anne Marie. "Automated Serials Control: A Bibliographic Survey." In *Management of Serials Automation,* edited by Peter Gellatly, 5–15. New York: Haworth Press, 1982.

Overview of the topic introducing selective bibliography that follows.

478. Allison, Anne Marie, and Donahue, Janice E. "Automated Serials Control: A Selected Bibliography." In *Management of Serials Automation,* edited by Peter Gellatly, 17–26. New York: Haworth Press, 1982.

Cites works published in 1970s (especially the latter years of the decade) on all aspects of automation of serials work, except those issued by bibliographic utilities, and those dealing with cataloging codes and a few other matters.

479. Allman, Linda K., and Freeman, Gretchen L. "Automated Standing Order List Using ListHandler." *South Carolina Librarian* 28 (Fall 1984): 12–15.

The automated file at Richland County Public Library supplements the online acquisitions system with holdings and management data.

480. *Automation and Serials: Proceedings of the UK Serials Group Conference held at South Glamorgan Institute of Higher Edu-*

cation, Cardiff 31 March–3 April 1980. Edited by Margaret E. Graham. Stratford-upon-Avon: UK Serials Group, 1981. (Serials Monograph No. 3)

Recent developments in serials automation from a variety of perspectives. Conference papers are listed separately in the Annotated Bibliography.

481. Bailey, Dorothy C., and Citron, Helen R. "Automated Serials Control: One Library's Perspective." *Serials Librarian* 8 (Spring 1984): 43–53.

The experience of Georgia Tech in changing from a manual system to Faxon's LINX. Includes evaluation of LINX.

482. Baker, Anne. "Computerisation of Periodical Holdings Lists at the University of East Anglia." *United Kingdom Serials Group Newsletter* 7 (June 1985): 8–10.

The library changes from a manually-produced strip index to a locally-developed computer list of serials.

483. Begg, Karin E., and Miller, Linda D. "Faxon's LINX: Test Library Reports." *Serials Review* 8 (Summer 1982): 57–62.

A survey of test libraries shows the positive effects of LINX and the creative uses the libraries have made of the features of the system.

484. Behles, Richard J. "Evolution and Efficiency in Serials Systems: Choices." *Serials Review* 10 (Summer 1984): 54–56.

Answers the question, "What makes a system good?" by examining what a system provides versus what it demands.

485. Bernstein, Barry, and Buell, Vivian. "Ballen Booksellers International: Automated Serials System." *Serials Review* 9 (Summer 1983): 61–64.

Describes the conversion to, and operation and benefits of, Ballen's internal system for series.

486. Bloss, Alexander. "Coping with the Evolving Serial Record." *Serials Review* 8 (Winter 1982): 91–94.

Advice for handling serial changes in an online environment.

487. Bracken, Jim, and Calhoun, John. "Use of the OCLC Serials Subsystem at the Knox College Library." *Illinois Libraries* 64 (1982): 81–83.

The reviews are mixed for this system at Knox College; it is better as a serials management tool than as a public record of serial holdings.

488. Brown, David J. "Automating the Links between Scholarly Publisher and Subscription Agency in the International Information Business." *International Journal of Micrographics & Video Technology* 3 (1984): 115–19.

Agents are extending their services to publishers, as illustrated by Faxon's INFOSERV.

489. Brown, David J. "The Use of INFOSERV: An Online Interactive Buying System to Enhance Collection Development Within the Library." *Library Hi-Tech* no. 6 (1984): 33–35.

Describes the service in terms of its benefit to library bibliographers having access to a personal computer or ASCII terminal. INFOSERV provides timely, standardized information about new serials.

490. Bueren, Martin. "A Model for Storage of Different Volumes of a Journal in Electronic Data Processing: The Dortmund Online Library System DOBIS." In *The Future of Serials*, edited by Nancy Fjallbrant, 195–200. Goteborg, Sweden: International Association of Technological University Libraries, 1984.

Describes the "Cataloguing of Periodicals" function of DOBIS, with its feature of displaying latest volumes first.

491. Campbell, Neil A. "On Paperless-ness." *Canadian Library Journal* 41 (1984): 181–86.

Scholarly publishing is moving toward electronic communication—Lancaster's paperless information systems. The electronic editorial processing center may be an interim phenomenon.

492. Card, Sandra E. "Serials Automation at UCLA: Planning, Conversion, Impact." *Serials Review* 10 (Summer 1984): 83–96.

A detailed discussion, with illustrations, of UCLA's experience in implementing its own system, using OCLC as a means of retrospective conversion of serials.

493. Cargill, Jennifer. "The Vendor Services Supermarket: The New Consumerism." In *Serials and Microforms: Development, Implementation, Impact*, edited by Nancy Jean Melin, 97–109. Westport, Conn.: Meckler Publishing, 1984.

Serials vendors differ, not in the materials they can provide, but in the services they offer. Librarians need to be aware of the services that can best meet their needs.

494.   Case, Donald. "The Personal Computer: Missing Link to the Electronic Journal?" *Journal of the American Society for Information Science* 36 (1985): 309–13.
The widespread use of personal computers will accelerate the development of electronic publishing.

495.   Chatterton, Leigh A. "The Boston College Libraries: A Case Study in Serials Automation." *Serials Review* 10 (Summer 1984): 65–71.
The experience of Boston College Library in selecting a turnkey system for serials control, and the implementation of the chosen system, Faxon's LINX.

496.   Clark, Cynthia D., and Feick, Christina L. "Monographic Series and the RLIN Acquisitions System." *Serials Review* 10 (Fall 1984): 68–72.
Princeton University Library considered several automated acquisitions systems and decided to use the RLIN system for monographic series.

497.   Corbin, Roberta A. "The University of California, San Diego, Automated Serials System, 1980." In *Management of Serials Automation,* edited by Peter Gellatly, 27–42. New York: Haworth Press, 1982.
Describes the development and future plans of this system from its beginning in 1961.

498.   Corrigan, Pauline. "Testing 'SAILS' at UCD." *United Kingdom Serials Group Newsletter* 6 (June 1984): 8–11.
University College Dublin Library is the first site for Swets Automated Independent Library System (SAILS). This report was prepared midway through the testing period.

499.   Cox, Brian. "The Elimination of Paper: Electronic Communication between Publishers and Subscription Agents." *United Kingdom Serials Group Newsletter* 7 (December 1985): 49–52.
Covers progress made by Pergamon and several large subscription agencies in moving from exchange of paper to exchange of magnetic tapes, to electronic exchange of data.

500.   *Current Trends in Serials Automation: Essen Symposium 6 October–8 October 1980,* edited by Ahmed H. Helal and Joachim W. Weiss. Essen: Gesamthochschulbibliothek Essen, 1981. (Publications of Essen University Library. 1)

Proceedings of the Symposium. Each presentation is listed separately in the Annotated Bibliography.

501. D'Andraia, Frank. "The Effects of Automation on Serial Record Staffing." In *Projects and Procedures for Serials Administration,* edited by Diane Stine, 245–50. Ann Arbor: Pierian Press, 1985.

Automation has less effect on serial record personnel than on those in cataloging, but it does enhance the position of the clerical worker.

502. Ede, Stuart, and Mullis, Albert. "British Library Serials Databases." In *Serials '84: Proceedings of the UK Serials Group Conference,* edited by Brian Cox, 23–32. Stratford-upon-Avon: UK Serials Group, 1985.

Reviews progress in enhancing the databases, particularly those supporting two publications, *Serials in the British Library* and *Keyword Index to Serial Titles.*

503. Fallon, Marcia. "Planning and Implementing an On-Line Periodicals System." *Serials Librarian* 9 (Fall 1984): 87–98.

The system provides individual and group benefits for four Miami-Dade Community College libraries.

504. Farrington, Jean Walter. "Automated Serials Control: Preparation and Planning." *Drexel Library Quarterly* 21 (Winter 1985): 77–86.

Using the University of Pennsylvania Library as a case study, Farrington recommends that libraries begin to produce online bibliographic records in MARC format, even before the decision is made to automate serials control.

505. Feick, Christina L., and Clark, Cynthia D. "Converting Monographic Series Check-In Records to the RLIN Acquisitions System." *Serials Review* 11 (Spring 1985): 69–75.

Describes the conversion process used at Princeton University Library and lists benefits of the use of RLIN in this way.

506. Fleischmann, Janis D., and Houghton, Jean. "Serials Automation: An Annotated Bibliography and Review, 1976–1984. *Serials Librarian* 10 (Fall 1985/Winter 1985-86): 29–63.

Lists 150 works, arranged by topic. Suggests subjects for further research.

507. Forsman, Rick B. "EBSCONET Serials Control System: A Case History and Analysis." *Serials Review* 8 (Winter 1982): 83–85.

Alabama's Lister Hill Library uses EBSCO's Serials Control System. Describes the system's features.

508. Forsman, Rick B. "A Vendor-Supported Experiment in Union Listing." *Serials Librarian* 9 (Summer 1985): 73–82.
Five Birmingham, Alabama, libraries of varying types experimented with an online union list, using EBSCO's database.

509. Foster, A. J. "Automated Serials Control: An Overview." In *Serials '83: Proceedings of the UK Serials Group Conference,* edited by Rodney M. Burton, 1–18. Stratford-upon-Avon: UK Serials Group, 1984.
Reviews the state of serials automation, concentrating on U.K. opportunities and experiences.

510. Franzmeier, Gunther. " 'Zeitschriftendatenbank (ZDB)': The German National Serials Database—A Short Overview." *United Kingdom Serials Group Newsletter* 7 (June 1985): 11–12.
Describes this database, its products, and its plans.

511. Giachetti, Katherine, and Pettenati, Corrado. "On-Line Serials Control with GEAC at the European University Institute Library in Florence, Italy." *United Kingdom Serials Group Newsletter* 7 (December 1985): 7–10.
A small library finds that the GEAC system is more powerful than, but not as tailored to its needs as, its original in-house system.

512. Ginneken, Jos van. "Serials Automation at the Central Library of the University of Agriculture at Wageningen, The Netherlands." *United Kingdom Serials Group Newsletter* 7 (December 1985): 24–27.
By use of a Canadian database management system, MINISIS, this library has online control of acquisition of materials and of serials processing.

513. Graffin, Brigette, and Pettenati, Corrado. "Automated Serials Check-In System in the European University Institute of Florence." *INSPEL* 18 (1984): 122–34.
Concentrates on check-in and claiming, with other processes described more briefly.

514. Graham, Frank A. "Automated Serials Control: A Librarian's Viewpoint." *Serials '83: Proceedings of the UK Serials Group Conference,* edited by Rodney M. Burton, 19–25. Stratford-upon-Avon: UK Serials Group, 1984.

PERLINE's first customer advises librarians preparing to plan for serials automation.

515. Graham, Frank A., and Holt, Eric. "PERLINE at Risley: Black-well's Serials System." *Serials Review* 9 (Fall 1983): 77–85.
Describes the selection, implementation, and use of PERLINE at this British special library. Evaluates the system positively.

516. Greenberg, Esther. "OCLC's Serials Subsystem: Success at CWRU." *Serials Review* 8 (Winter 1982): 77–81.
An original test library, Case Western Reserve University Library continues to make full use of the OCLC Serials Subsystem.

517. Griffin, David E., and Ziegman, Bruce. "Automated Serials Acquisitions in the Washington Library Network." *Management of Serials Automation,* edited by Peter Gellatly, 237–43. New York: Haworth Press, 1982.
Discusses WLN's acquisition subsystem with special attention to serials.

518. Hamilton, G. "Serials Automation in the British Library Reference Division." In *Automation and Serials,* edited by Margaret E. Graham, 40–48. Stratford-upon-Avon: UK Serials Group, 1981.
Discussion of planning for automation and problems being considered by various departments of the British Library.

519. Harley, A. J. "The British Library Lending Division Automated Serials System." In *Automation and Serials,* edited by Margaret E. Graham, 49–58. Stratford-upon-Avon: UK Serials Group, 1981.
A case study of the early 1960s-developed automated serials control system and its evolution from punched cards to online status.

520. Heitshu, Sara C., and Quinn, Joan M. "Serials Conversion at the University of Michigan." *Drexel Library Quarterly* 21 (Winter 1985): 62–76.
Emphasizes policies and standards related to bibliographic records for serials entered into RLIN under a Title II-C grant.

521. Helal, Ahmed H. "Serials Automation in the GHB-Essen." In *Current Trends in Serials Automation,* edited by Ahmed H. Helal and Joachim W. Weiss, 157–75. Essen: Gesamthochschulbibliothek Essen, 1981.

Concentrates on journal check-in subsystem and its management reports from the minicomputer-based and locally developed system.

522. Helal, Ahmed H. "Serials Handling in Essen University Library." In *The Future of Serials,* edited by Nancy Fjallbrant, 139–53. Goteborg, Sweden: International Association of Technological University Libraries, 1984.
Describes the journal module of EASY, Essen Automated System, a comprehensive means of serials control.

523. Hepfer, William. "Serials and the OCLC Acquisitions Subsystem." *Serials Review* 10 (Summer 1984): 72–76.
While ACQS is perfectly acceptable for ordering serials, other processes are not handled so well.

524. Holmquist, Lennart Johan. "Periodical Management at the Apple Computer Library." *Database* 7 (December 1984): 31–36.
Advocates the use of a microcomputer for periodicals management, specifically using PFS: File.

525. Jacob, M. E. L. "OCLC's CONSER Activities." In *Current Trends in Serials Automation,* edited by Ahmed H. Helal and Joachim W. Weiss, 85–88. Essen: Gesamthochschulbibliothek Essen, 1981.
History and goals of CONSER; description of OCLC.

526. James, Peter V. "Low Cost Serials Budgetary Control." *United Kingdom Serials Group Newsletter* 7 (December 1985): 32–34.
The library at University College of Wales, Aberystwyth, uses an 8-bit program, Masterfile, by Cambell Systems, for serials control. James discusses its advantages for a small library and its disadvantages.

527. James E. Rush Associates, Inc. *Serials Control.* Powell, Ohio: James E. Rush Associates, Inc., 1983. (Library Systems Evaluation Guide. 1)
Presents detailed methodology for evaluating online serials control systems. Includes checklist and directory of available systems.

528. Johnson, Millard F., Jr., Stucki, Loretta, and Igielnik, Simon. "Medical Periodicals Control—Evolution into Networking." *Technical Services Quarterly* 1 (Spring 1984): 37–43.
Tracks evolution of PHILSOM from a batch program into a national online network, and discusses the system's future.

529. Kadota, Katsuhiro. "Several Experimental Trials at the Kana-zawa Institute of Technology Library Center Using its Online System." In *The Future of Serials*, edited by Nancy Fjallbrant, 129–37. Goteborg, Sweden: International Association of Technological University Libraries, 1984.

The library was established in 1982 and uses innovative means of staffing, controlling the collection, and serving patrons.

530. Kelley, Gloria A. "Networking and Serials Control, 1975–1985." *Serials Librarian* 10 (Fall 1985/Winter 1985–86): 97–101.

Serials networking has developed from a dream to increasingly successful control of bibliographic description, acquisitions, and inventory.

531. Kelley, Gloria A. "Serials Management: A Microcomputer Application." *South Carolina Librarian* 28 (Fall 1984): 6–9.

Winthrop College Library uses a locally-developed serials management system for financial and statistical control.

532. Kemp, Arnoud de. "Automated Serials Handling: The Perfect Future? The Swets Concept for Serials Control at an Affordable Price." In *The Future of Serials*, edited by Nancy Fjallbrant, 155–66. Goteborg, Sweden: International Association of Technological University Libraries, 1984.

Discusses the Swets philosophy that led to the development of its SAILS automated library system.

533. Kemp, Arnoud de. "Technical Cooperation Between Libraries and the Advanced Subscription Agents." In International Association of Technological University Libraries. Conference, Lausanne, Sw., 1981. *Libraries and the Communication Process.* Goteborg: The Association, 1981, 193–96.

Increasingly necessary, the cooperation extends beyond acquisition and uses the automated facilities of the agent for additional serials functions.

534. Kershner, Lois M. "The Research Libraries Group, Inc. Programs for Serials." In *Management of Serials Automation*, edited by Peter Gellatly, 229–35. New York: Haworth Press, 1982.

Covers the serials aspects of RLG programs: RLIN, Collection Management and Development, Shared Resources, and Preservation.

535. Kilgour, Frederick G. "Serials Processing in the OCLC System." In *Resource Sharing—Its Impact on Serials*, edited by Margaret E. Graham and Brian Cox, 64–74. Stratford-upon-Avon: UK Serials Group, 1982.

An overview of OCLC in early 1981, followed by detailed examination of the serials control system, union listing, and interlibrary loan.

536. Kilton, Tom D. "Serials Automation at the University of Illinois at Urbana: Present Benefits from Inventory Control; Future Plans for Acquisition Control." In *Management of Serials Automation,* edited by Peter Gellatly, 53–59. New York: Haworth Press, 1982.
With most of its serials holdings data available online, Illinois is planning for online ordering, check-in, and fund accounting.

537. Krumm, Carol R. "Conversion of Serial Holdings to On-Line Automated Library Control System at the Ohio State University Libraries." In *Management of Serials Automation,* edited by Peter Gellatly, 83–94. New York: Haworth Press, 1982.
The conversion merged 12 files into one and provided better access to serials.

538. Lastrapes, Edwin P. "Implementation Decision: Consideration of the Inadequacies of the OCLC Serials Control Subsystem." *Serials Review* 8 (Spring 1982): 69–73.
A survey of the evaluations of OCLC's system by six user libraries emphasizes the shortcomings. Contrast is provided by a brief description of the UCLA Biomedical Library serials system.

539. Leatherbury, Maurice C. "Serials Control Systems on Microcomputers." *Drexel Library Quarterly* 20 (Fall 1984): 4–24.
Describes seven microcomputer-based serials systems available commercially. Includes a checklist of system features.

540. Lenzini, Rebecca T., and Koff, Eileen. "Converting Serial Holdings to Machine-Readable Format: An Account of the University of Illinois-Urbana Experience." In *Management of Serials Automation,* edited by Peter Gellatly, 71–81. New York: Haworth Press, 1982.
Describes the conversion process and offers suggestions for other libraries planning a similar project.

541. Lenzini, Rebecca T. "Vendor Services in the Information Age." *Technical Services Quarterly* 1 (Fall/Winter 1983): 253–56.
The future role of the vendor will be as a provider of operational support to the library's technical services team in an interactive relationship.

542. Leonard, James. "OCLC's Serials Control Subsystem: Its Suitability to Legal Serials and Continuations." *Law Library Journal* 75 (1982): 403–19.

A detailed description and evaluation of the system as implemented at
Wake Forest University Law Library.

543.   Line, Maurice B. "Redesigning Journal Articles for On-Line
       Viewing." In *Trends in Information Transfer,* edited by Philip
       J. Hills, 31–46. Westport, Conn.: Greenwood Press, 1982.
Online articles require a different structure from printed articles. Papers
reporting research findings are easily adaptable.

544.   Line, Maurice B. "Resource Sharing: The Present Situation and
       the Likely Effect of Electronic Technology." In *The Future of
       Serials,* edited by Nancy Fjallbrant, 1–11. Goteborg, Sweden:
       International Association of Technological University Libraries,
       1984.
Technology does not remove the obstacles to resource sharing, but it may
ease them and promises more help for the future.

545.   Line, Maurice B. "Some Implications for Publishing of Electronic
       Document Storage and Supply." In *The Future of Serials,* edited
       by Nancy Fjallbrant, 219–30. Goteborg, Sweden: International
       Association of Technological University Libraries, 1984.
The implications Line finds will be considered extreme by some, since
they include a user-driven system and the takeover of publishers by large
commercial corporations.

546.   Lowell, Gerald R. "LINX: The Integrator." *Serials Librarian* 7
       (Spring 1983): 17–27.
Description and history of Faxon's online serials management system.

547.   Mackenzie, A. Graham. "Why Automate Anything?" In *Auto-
       mation and Serials,* edited by Margaret E. Graham, 1–15. Strat-
       ford-upon-Avon: UK Serials Group, 1981.
Sensible advice to librarians eager to automate, advice based on good and
bad reasons to change to computerized systems.

548.   McKinley, Margaret M. "Management of Serials Automation:
       Two Libraries in Transition." *Drexel Library Quarterly* 21 (Winter
       1985): 50–61.
Discusses the implementation of ORION at the serials departments of
UCLA and University of California, Irvine libraries. The project was
managed differently at each library, and the account of problems faced
will be useful to libraries planning serials data conversion.

549. McKinley, Margaret. "Victims, Villains or Victors: The Impact
      of Serials Automation on a Library Organization." *Serials Review*
      10 (Summer 1984): 43–48.
Identifies and discusses issues critical to the success of serials automation:
the nature of organizational change, influencing change, communication,
planning for optimum impact of automation and for flexibility during development and implementation.

550. McQueen, Judy, and Boss, Richard W. "Serials Control in Li-
      braries: Automated Options." *Library Technology Reports* 20
      (1984): 89–282.
Discusses considerations in automating serials control and describes
available systems.

551. *The Management of Serials Automation: Current Technology &
      Strategies for Future Planning.* Edited with an Introduction by
      Peter Gellatly. New York: Haworth Press, 1982. (Supplement to
      Serials Librarian 6 (1981/82).
Articles are listed separately in the Annotated Bibliography.

552. Marks, Taube. "PERLINE at Risley." *Information Technology
      and Libraries* 2 (1983): 56–57.
Description of installation and implementation of the first PERLINE system and the first UK automated serials control system.

553. Martin, Dohn H., and Rutledge, Ruth M. "The Evolution of a
      Serials Control System." *Mississippi Libraries* 47 (Spring 1983):
      12–13.
Describes the 10-year history of the system designed by and for the University of Mississippi's Medical Library.

554. Maruyama, Lenore S. "What Has Technology Done for Us
      Lately?" *Serials Librarian* 10 (Fall 1985/Winter 1985–86): 65–89.
Covers progress or change since 1976 in "CONSER, bibliographic networks, union lists of serials, stand-alone systems, electronic mail, full text
services, copyright, and organizations providing services involving serials."

555. Memmott, H. Kirk, Jordan, K. Paul, and Taylor, John R. "On-
      Line Serials at Brigham Young University." In *Management of
      Serials Automation,* edited by Peter Gellatly, 61–70. New York:
      Haworth Press, 1982.
Describes and justifies this system based on that of the UCLA Biomedical
Library.

556. Metcalfe, Nigel, "OCLC and Serials." *United Kingdom Serials Group Newsletter* 7 (June 1985): 37–41.
Reviews OCLC's serials control activities and projects, emphasizing SC350.

557. Micciche, Pauline F. "The OCLC Serials Control Subsystem." In *Management of Serials Automation,* edited by Peter Gellatly, 219–27. New York: Haworth Press, 1982.
Description and future plans.

558. Millican, Rita. "Serials Conversion: LSU's Experience." *Serials Librarian* 9 (Summer 1985): 45–51.
Describes the use of Title II-C grant funding at Louisiana State University Library to convert records for current serials to machine-readable form.

559. Millson, Dave. "Serials Automation at the British Library Lending Division." *United Kingdom Serials Group Newsletter* 7 (June 1985): 19–20.
A status report on automation of serials processing and access at BLLD. Microfiche keyword access is being replaced by POLKA, an online system, but check-in, claiming, and accounting are still manual.

560. Morton, Larry, and Youmans, Mary. "HUSH, An Automated Multi-purpose Periodical System; or, From Rotary File to Computer." *Serials Librarian* 9 (Summer 1985): 53–62.
The locally-developed system at Western Carolina University Library benefits library patrons as well as staff members.

561. Noethiger, Rudolph. "Online Serials Control at the ETH Library." In *The Future of Serials,* edited by Nancy Fjallbrant, 109–27. Goteborg, Sweden: International Association of Technological University Libraries, 1984.
Describes the locally-developed PEKOS (PEriodica-KOntroll-System) and covers future plans.

562. Noethiger, Rudolph. "PEKOS: Periodicals Control System at the ETH Library, Swiss Federal Institute of Technology, Zurich." *United Kingdom Serials Group Newsletter* 7 (December 1985): 19–21.
Describes the serials control unit of a projected integrated online system to be used in several Swiss libraries.

563. Noethiger, Rudolph. "Serials Automation in the ETH-Zuerich." In *Current Trends in Serials Automation,* edited by Ahmed H.

Helal and Joachim W. Weiss, 135–56. Essen: Gesamthochschulbibliothek Essen, 1981.

The main library of the Swiss Federal Institute of Technology developed its own automation systems. Noethiger concentrates on journal checking.

564. Paul, Huibert. "Serials and Automation: Yesterday, Today and Tomorrow." *Serials Librarian* 10 (Fall 1985/Winter 1985–86): 91–95.

Automation of serials processing and access has come of age during the first decade of *Serials Librarian*. Computer technology has eliminated many of the serials specialist's frustrating problems.

565. Pitkin, Gary. "State of the Art of Serials Automation and Networking in the United States." In *Automation and Serials,* edited by Margaret E. Graham, 17–39. Stratford-upon-Avon: UK Serials Group, 1981.

Spotlights CONSER, Summary Holdings Standard, Faxon's serials control system, and various regional projects in the United States.

566. Pletzke, Chet. "PHILSOM and the Uniformed Services University of the Health Sciences Learning Resource Center." *Serials Review* 10 (Summer 1984): 77–82.

Discusses the experience of implementing and using first PHILSOM II, then PHILSOM III.

567. Pullinger, David J. "Attitudes to Traditional Journal Procedure." *Electronic Publishing Review* 3 (1983): 213–22.

Analyzes present reading habits of a group of scientists and their attitudes toward traditional refereeing procedure, as considerations in the preparation for an electronic journal.

568. Pullinger, David J., and Howey, Kate. "Development of the *Reference, Abstract and Annotations Journal* (RAAJ) on the BLEND System." *Journal of Librarianship* 16 (1984): 19–33.

Description and evaluation of the creation of an online abstract journal, with suggested enhancements.

569. Pullinger, David J. "Facilities in an Electronic Journal System: Towards the Cost Evaluation of the BLEND Experiment." *Electronic Publishing Review* 4 (1984): 275–87.

Considers the services provided to authors and readers and the relationship between some of these.

570. Reeve, Phyllis, and Dobbin, Geraldine F. "An Automated Processing System for Government Serials: Its Merger with the Gen-

eral Serials System in an Academic Library." *Serials Librarian*
7 (Winter 1982): 41–49.
This project, conducted at the University of British Columbia, has made
government publications accessible on a COM catalog and provided an
online check-in system for document serials.

571. Regenstreif, Herbert. "Automated Serials Management Systems
      in Law Libraries: The Acquisitions Component." *Serials Li-
      brarian* 9 (Winter 1984): 133–41.
Review of available systems and pointers for law librarians contemplating
automation.

572. Roughton, Karen. "Thinking of OCLC Serials Control? Read
      This." *Serials Librarian* 7 (Fall 1982): 23–30.
Iowa State University Library tested OCLC's check-in system in 1980
and encountered a number of problems. Only 111 of 284 sample titles
could be checked in automatically.

573. Roughton, Michael. "OCLC Serial Records: An Update." In
      Management of Serials Automation, edited by Peter Gellatly,
      163–70. New York: Haworth Press, 1982.
The OCLC database is not yet updated adequately for cessations and other
information.

574. Rowe, Richard R. "Subscription Fulfillment and Technology."
      In *Scholarly Publishing in an Era of Change: Proceedings of the
      Second Annual Meeting, Society for Scholarly Publishing*, edited
      by Ethel G. Langlois, 18–20. Washington, D.C.: Society for
      Scholarly Publishing, 1981.
An overview of the changes expected through computerization in the dissemination of scholarly information.

575. Rush, James E., and Tannehill, Robert S. "A Methodology for
      the Evaluation of Serials Control Systems." In American Society
      for Information Science. Conference, Columbus, Ohio, 1982.
      Proceedings. vol. 19: *Information Interaction*, 254–58. White
      Plains, N.Y.: Published for the American Society for Information
      Science by Knowledge Industries Publications, Inc., 1982.
The five-phase methodology is "thorough, systematic, objective, and
simple to use." Preview of Rush's book on the topic.

576. Rush, James E., and Tannehill, Robert S. "A Methodology for
      the Evaluation of Serials Control Systems." *INSPEL* 18 (1984):
      27–40.

An 8-phase methodology is described and illustrated. Abridged version of Rush's book *Serials Control*.

577.   Schmidt, Nancy P. "Choosing an Automated Serials Control System." *Serials Librarian* 9 (Fall 1984): 65–86.
Offers criteria by which systems can be evaluated and compared. Studies CHECKMATE, EBSCONET, LINX SC–10, OCLC, and NOTIS.

578.   Schrader, David, and Houlne, Dan. "Serials Automation at 3M— An Unusual Telecommunications Implementation." *Information Technology and Libraries* 3 (1984): 398–400 + .
3M selected Faxon's LINX for its network of nine libraries. This article discusses the 3M LINX telecommunications link, from both 3M and Faxon perspectives.

579.   Schriefer, Kent. "INNOVACQ: Serials Control at Boalt Hall." *Serials Review* 10 (Winter 1984): 51–68.
The Law School Library at the University of California selected IN- NOVACQ as its serials check-in and invoice processing system. Positive discussion of start-up procedures. Fully illustrated.

580.   Schriefer, Kent. "Serials Control at Boalt Hall." *Law Library Journal* 77 (1985): 58–75.
Describes selection and implementation of the INNOVACQ online serials control system and discusses its impact on the University of California at Berkeley Law School Library.

581.   Senders, John W. "I Have Seen the Future, and It Doesn't Work: The Electronic Journal Experiment." In *Scholarly Publishing in an Era of Change: Proceedings of the Second Annual Meeting, Society for Scholarly Publishing,* edited by Ethel G. Langlois, 8– 9. Washington, D.C.: Society for Scholarly Publishing, 1981.
A participant in the experimental electronic journal on the Electronic In- formation Exchange System analyzes the failure of the project.

582.   *Serials '83: Proceedings of the UK Serials Group Conference Held at University of Durham, 21–24 March 1983.* Edited by Rodney M. Burton. Stratford-upon-Avon: UK Serials Group, 1984. (Serials monograph no. 6)
The conference theme was automation. Each presentation is listed sep- arately in the Annotated Bibliography.

583.   Shackel, Brian, Pullinger, D. J., Maud, T. I., and Dodd, W. P. "The BLEND-LINC Project on 'Electronic Journals' after Two Years." *ASLIB Proceedings* 35 (1982): 77–91.

Describes progress in this joint project of Birmingham and Loughborough universities, emphasizing hardware problems and their resolution.

584.   Shackel, Brian. "Progress of the BLEND-LINC 'Electronic Journal' Project." In *The Future of Serials*, edited by Nancy Fjallbrant, 69–82. Goteborg, Sweden: International Association of Technological University Libraries, 1984.

The status of the BLEND Project after 3 years.

585.   Shaw, Dennis. "Investigation of the Costs and Benefits of On-Line Serials Handling." In *Current Trends in Serials Automation*, edited by Ahmed H. Helal and Joachim W. Weiss, 109–21. Essen: Gesamthochschulbibliothek Essen, 1981.

Compares the costs and benefits of an optimized online system with those of an existing manual system, and shows evidence of significant cost recovery.

586.   Shaw, Dennis, and Sly, Niel. "A Survey of IATUL for Serials Automation: Future Prospects." In *The Future of Serials*, edited by Nancy Fjallbrant, 27–45. Goteborg, Sweden: International Association of Technological University Libraries, 1984.

The survey results show the extent of automation among members and analyze their plans for future uses of automation through microprocessing.

587.   Singleton, Alan, and Pullinger, David J. "Ways of Viewing Costs of Journals: Cost Evaluation of the BLEND Experiment." *Electronic Publishing Review* 4 (1984): 59–71.

Describes ways of viewing costs of journals and illustrates some problems of costs facing an electronic journal in a traditional environment.

588.   Skerratt, Peter W. "Implementing Blackwell's PEARL at the Ministry of Agriculture, Fisheries and Food Library." *United Kingdom Serials Group Newsletter* 7 (December 1985): 12–16.

The automated serials system gets mixed reviews from this library system, and the author suggests enhancements.

589.   Somerfield, G. A. "Selective Article Delivery." In *The Future of Serials*, edited by Nancy Fjallbrant, 83–97. Goteborg, Sweden: International Association of Technological University Libraries, 1984.

The ability to identify articles more easily leads to the need for efficient physical transport of documents, such as the ADONIS Project.

590. Steele, Peggy. "Automated Serials Control Using NOTIS." *Serials Review* 9 (Winter 1983): 64–73.

An enthusiastic description of automated serials processing at Northwestern University Library.

591. Steiner, Phyllis A. "On-Line Journal Subscription Records." *Serials Librarian* 6 (Summer 1982): 25–38.

Detailed description of an online serials receipt and accounting system developed by a small special library.

592. Teagle, Josephine A. "Planning for an On-Line System." In *Automation and Serials,* edited by Margaret E. Graham, 76–90. Stratford-upon-Avon: UK Serials Group, 1981.

Detailed discussion of automation planning process for a small industrial library that must show savings in staffing costs.

593. Thomas, Sarah E. "Collection Development at the Center for Research Libraries: Policy and Practice." *College and Research Libraries* 46 (1985): 230–35.

A study of CRL's current subscriptions revealed that about one-third are held by more than 20 libraries. Thomas discusses the implications of this finding in light of the Center's policy of collecting journals that are "rarely-held" in North America.

594. Tonkery, Dan. "The Necessity of Serials Automation." *Serials Librarian* 7 (Summer 1982): 57–60.

An automation specialist replies to Huibert Paul's "Growing Bananas in Greenland."

595. Tonkery, Dan, and Lenzini, Rebecca T. "Serials Automation: Fact or Phobia—A Progress Report." In *The Future of Serials,* edited by Nancy Fjallbrant, 47–54. Goteborg, Sweden: International Association of Technological University Libraries, 1984.

Compares features and design philosophies between UCLA's ORION system and Faxon's LINX system.

596. Trivedi, Harish, and Newcombe, Barbara. "The Story of a Neglected Resource: Information Storage and Retrieval in Newspaper Libraries." *United Kingdom Serials Group Newsletter* 5 (December 1983): 7–15.

Surveys newspaper libraries in developed and in less developed countries and finds that problems ranging from lack of communication and concern about national security to lack of electricity hinder progress in this area.

597. Turoff, Murray, and Hiltz, Starr Roxanne. "The Electronic Journal: A Progress Report." *Journal of the American Society for Information Science* 33 (1982): 195–207.

Examines four forms of experimental journal on the Electronic Information Exchange System (EIES): informal newsletter, unreferreed "Paper Fair," duplication of the traditional journal, and highly structured inquiry-response system.

598. Wernstedt, Irene. "Destination: Automated Serials Check-In." *Serials Review* 10 (Summer 1984): 57–64.

Wernstedt, from Pennsylvania State University Library, leads serials librarians through the automation planning process.

599. Willmering, William J. "Automated Serial Records in the On-Line Catalog: The Northwestern LUIS System." In *Management of Serials Automation,* edited by Peter Gellatly, 43–52. New York: Haworth Press, 1982.

Discusses enhancement of bibliographic, holdings, and location functions of the catalog, by means of automation.

600. Wright, Jean Acker. " 'Serials As a Project' at Vanderbilt: An Early Library Computer Utilization." In *Projects and Procedures for Serials Administration,* edited by Diane Stine, 99–108. Ann Arbor: Pierian Press, 1985.

Case history of the COM union list of serials, covering planning, implementation, enhancement, use, and plans for the future.

601. Wright, Jean Acker. "Serials Automation in the Vanderbilt University Library." In *Current Trends in Serials Automation,* edited by Ahmed H. Helal and Joachim W. Weiss, 123–34. Essen: Gesamthochschulbibliothek Essen, 1981.

Vanderbilt's experience as an OCLC member represents the efforts of North American libraries to resolve problems cooperatively through automation.

IX. NATIONAL PROGRAMS

602. Bartley, Linda K. "ISSN and NSDP: A Guide for the Initiated." In *Management of Serials Automation,* edited by Peter Gellatly, 171–77. New York: Haworth Press, 1982.

Orientation for all—librarians, publishers, anyone—who use the ISSN.

603. Bartley, Linda K. "Standards and Serials: Meaningful Relationships." In *Library Serials Standards: Development, Implementation, Impact,* edited by Nancy Jean Melin, 71–75. Westport, Conn.: Meckler Publishing, 1984.

The interrelatedness of serials standards is documented in a discussion of several aspects of the CONSER Project.

604. Baskin, Judith. "Serials and ABN." *Australian Academic & Research Libraries* 16 (1985): 51–54.

Describes serials component of the Australian Bibliographic Network and its uses, then mentions possible future enhancements.

605. Biggs, Mary. "The Proposed National Periodicals Center, 1973–1980: Study, Dissension, and Retreat." *Resource Sharing and Information Networks* 1 (Spring/Summer 1984): 1–22.

Traces the development of the concept and evaluates the effort.

606. Bloss, Marjorie E. "The Standard Unfurled: ANSI Z39 SC42: Holdings Statements at the Summary Level." *Serials Review* 9 (Spring 1983): 79–83.

Acquaints us with the standard, emphasizing areas needing additional interpretation.

607. Crisswell, Lela Beth. "Serials on Optical Disks: A Library of Congress Pilot Program." *Library Hi-Tech* 1 (Winter 1983): 17–21.

Describes the program and the technology employed.

608. Fawcett, Georgene E., Johnson, Judy, and Tseng, Sally C. "Standards and Bibliographic and Serials Control in a Multicampus/Multibranch University Library System." In *Library Serials Standards: Development, Implementation, Impact,* edited by Nancy Jean Melin, 109–16. Westport, Conn.: Meckler Publishing, 1984.

Nebraska libraries experiment with a union list of serials by means of a commercial vendor's online circulation system.

609. Hensley, Charlotta C. "Serials Standards: A Bibliography." In *Library Serials Standards: Development, Implementation, Impact,* edited by Nancy Jean Melin, 149–61. Westport, Conn.: Meckler Publishing, 1984.

Annotated and classified list of references on specific official and other standards related to serials.

610. Hensley, Charlotta C. "Serials Standards (and Guidelines): Who
      Cares?" In *Library Serials Standards: Development, Implemen-
      tation, Impact*, edited by Nancy Jean Melin, 85–97. Westport,
      Conn.: Meckler Publishing, 1984.
Hensley reviews national and international standards making bodies and
some of their products. She then reviews the professional literature and
concludes that librarians' interest in standards is primarily practical.

611. Huff, William H. "The National Periodicals Center." *Catholic
      Library World* 52 (1981): 276–79.
Reviews and comments on various studies concerning the establishment
of a National Periodicals Center.

612. *Library Serials Standards: Development, Implementation,
      Impact. Proceedings of the Third Annual Serials Conference.* Ed-
      ited by Nancy Jean Melin. Westport, Conn.: Meckler Publishing,
      1984.
Conference papers are listed separately in the Annotated Bibliography.

613. Maruyama, Lenore S. "Nationwide Networking and the Network
      Advisory Committee." In *Management of Serials Automa-
      tion*, edited by Peter Gellatly, 245–55. New York: Haworth Press,
      1982.
Activities of the NAC from its beginning in 1976, showing progress toward
a nationwide library network.

614. Mullis, Albert A. "The International Serials Data System
      (ISDS)." *United Kingdom Serials Group Newsletter* 6 (June
      1984): 12–14.
History, objectives, and products of ISDS, with particular attention to
the assigning and use of the ISSN.

615. Mullis, Albert A. "The International Standard Serial Number in
      the Organization and Retrieval of Bibliographic Information."
      International Cataloguing 12 (January/March 1983): 7–9.
The origins, history, use, and benefit of the ISSN.

616. Neubauer, K. W. "National Serials Data System in the Federal
      Republic of Germany." In *Current Trends in Serials Automation*,
      edited by Ahmed H. Helal and Joachim W. Weiss, 41–57. Essen:
      Gesamthochschulbibliothek Essen, 1981.
The evolution of a West German national serials database from a series
of regional union catalogs, its governance, and future enhancements.

617. Radke, Barbara, and Montgomery, Teresa. "CALLS ISSN Project." *Serials Review* 8 (Summer 1982): 65–67.
Since records in the California Academic List of Serials did not contain the ISSN and key title, this means of matching records with variant entries was not considered useful. However, the unique identifier should be added, for it may be a valuable online access point.

618. Rice, Patricia Ohl, and Mitlin, Laurance R. "The ISSN as Retriever of OCLC Records." In *Management of Serials Automation,* edited by Peter Gellatly, 179–84. New York: Haworth Press, 1982.
A study at Winthrop College Library found the ISSN useful in retrieving OCLC local data records, but the authors urge OCLC to make greater efforts in the area of quality control.

619. Sabosik, Patricia E. "SISAC: Industry Group Develops Standardized Formats for the Processing of Serials Information." In *Serials '84: Proceedings of the UK Serials Group Conference,* edited by Margaret E. Graham, 41–51. Stratford-upon-Avon: UK Serials Group, 1985.
Gives history, goals, and current work of the subcommittees of the Serials Industry Systems Advisory Committee, and explores the group's relation to other standards organizations.

620. Sapp, Linda H. "The USMARC Format for Holdings and Locations." *Drexel Library Quarterly* 21 (Winter 1985): 87–100.
Discusses the need for and the purposes of this format, from the perspective of a member of the Holdings Committee.

621. Szilvassy, Judith. "ISDS: World-Wide Serials Control." *INSPEL* 17 (1983): 145–54.
Covers ISDS birth and objectives, and suggests ideas on potential of unexploited advantages of ISDS.

622. Szilvassy, Judith. "ISDS: Worldwide Serials Control." *IFLA Journal* 8 (1982): 371–78.
A 10th anniversary look back at the development and influence of ISDS, with a look at the new effort to make the system more user-oriented.

623. Williams, Martha E., and Lannom, Laurence. "Lack of Standardization of the Journal Title Element in Databases." *Journal of the American Society for Information Science* 32 (1981): 229–33.

There is little standardization within or across databases, hindering exhaustive searches on a specific data element. A study using the journal title data element demonstrates the extent of this problem.

624. Wolf, D. "Impact of ISDS on the Registration of Serials in the Deutsche Bibliothek." In *Current Trends in Serials Automation,* edited by Ahmed H. Helal and Joachim W. Weiss, 13–24. Essen: Gesamthochschulbibliothek Essen, 1981.

Exposes the duplication of effort required to meet both ISDS and German standards and considers ways of decreasing the workload.

625. Zajanc, Jackie. "Adherence to National Standards: The WSUL Experience." *Serials Review* 11 (Spring 1985): 63–66.

At Washington State University Libraries the use of national standards has helped make materials accessible in a timely and consistent manner.

INDEX TO BIBLIOGRAPHY